Fundamentals of Airport Planning

Airport planning, especially the airside, is based on strict compliance with regulatory requirements. In heavily urbanized, industrialized countries, where suitable sites for new airport developments are increasingly hard to find – and subjected to unprecedented public scrutiny – the role of the airport planner is more crucial than ever.

Fundamentals of Airport Planning aims to explain airport planning from the ground up. Utilizing a basic framework and step-by-step approach, the author introduces the critical parameters for selecting a suitable and 'best' location from among multiple sites. International and country-specific regulations are described and accounted for. The master planning process is described with suitable illustrations and examples, and the benefits and best practices of master planning are discussed. The location of visual aids (lighting and marking) and non-visual aids Communication, Navigation and Surveillance systems (CNS) is considered, and readers will also learn how to prepare technically feasible plans with various infrastructures and how to assess a project's financial viability. This book includes a chapter on land use planning to maximize the utilization of the asset, with appropriate control within and outside the airport.

This book is aimed at postgraduate students who are specializing in aviation or air transport management, as well as professionals studying or working in airport planning and design and related aviation topics.

Ravi Lakshmanan is an Advisor to GMR Airports and is based in India. He has worked in the aviation industry for over 30 years, and since retiring in 2016 he has worked as an airport planning advisor for GMR. His areas of expertise are delivering cost-effective infrastructure planning that meets regulatory criteria; revenue and cost analyses for airport operations; and techno-economic feasibility of airport planning operations. He is also a guest lecturer at the Indian Aviation Academy.

Aviation Fundamentals
Series Editor: Suzanne K. Kearns

Aviation Fundamentals is a series of air transport textbooks that incorporate instructional design principles to present content in a manner that is engaging to the learner, at an accessible level for young adults, allowing for practical application of the content to real-world problems via cases, reflection questions and examples. Each textbook will be supported by a companion website of supplementary materials and a test bank. The series is designed to help facilitate the recruitment and education of the next generation of aviation professionals (NGAP), a task which has been named a 'Global Priority' by the ICAO Assembly. It will also support education for new air transport sectors that are expected to rapidly evolve in future years, such as commercial space and the civil use of remotely piloted aircraft. The objective of *Aviation Fundamentals* is to become the leading source of textbooks for the variety of subject areas that make up aviation college/university degree programmes, evolving in parallel with these curricula.

Fundamentals of International Aviation Law and Policy
Benjamyn I. Scott and Andrea Trimarchi

Fundamentals of Airline Operations
Gert Meijer

Fundamentals of International Aviation
Suzanne K. Kearns

Fundamentals of Airline Marketing
Scott Ambrose and Blaise Waguespack

Fundamentals of Statistics for Aviation Research
Michael A. Gallo, Brooke E. Wheeler and Isaac M. Silver

Fundamentals of Airport Planning
Theory and Practice
Ravi Lakshmanan

For more information about this series, please visit: www.routledge.com/Aviation-Fundamentals/book-series/AVFUND

Fundamentals of Airport Planning

Theory and Practice

Ravi Lakshmanan

Routledge
Taylor & Francis Group

LONDON AND NEW YORK

Designed cover image: Photograph by Lakshmanan Ravi

First published 2024
by Routledge
4 Park Square, Milton Park, Abingdon, Oxon OX14 4RN

and by Routledge
605 Third Avenue, New York, NY 10158

Routledge is an imprint of the Taylor & Francis Group, an informa business

© 2024 Ravi Lakshmanan

British Library Cataloguing-in-Publication Data
A catalogue record for this book is available from the British Library

Library of Congress Cataloging-in-Publication Data
Names: Ravi, Lakshmanan, author.
Title: Fundamentals of airport planning : theory and practice / Lakshmanan Ravi.
Description: 1 Edition. | New York : Routledge, 2024. | Series: Aviation fundamentals | Includes bibliographical references and index.
Identifiers: LCCN 2023014430 (print) | LCCN 2023014431 (ebook) | ISBN 9781032335148 (hardback) | ISBN 9781032335131 (paperback) | ISBN 9781003319948 (ebook)
Subjects: LCSH: Airports—Planning. | Airports—Management.
Classification: LCC TL725.3.P5 R38 2024 (print) | LCC TL725.3.P5 (ebook)
DDC 629.136—dc23/eng/20230506
LC record available at https://lccn.loc.gov/2023014430
LC ebook record available at https://lccn.loc.gov/2023014431

ISBN: 978-1-032-33514-8 (hbk)
ISBN: 978-1-032-33513-1 (pbk)
ISBN: 978-1-003-31994-8 (ebk)

DOI: 10.4324/9781003319948

Typeset in Times New Roman
by codeMantra

Access the Support Material: www.routledge.com/9781032335131

Contents

Preface

The aim of this book is for the readers to comprehend both the theory and the application of the planning concepts and thus describe the fundamentals of airport planning with a basic framework and step-by-step approach. This book describes the critical parameters to be considered for selecting a suitable and best location among multiple sites identified for a greenfield airport. For brownfield airport development, this book explains the process for capacity addition.

This book explains the guiding principles of airport planning through ICAO SARPs, especially the airside, in order to meet the compliance with regulatory requirements. Master planning process is described with suitable illustrations and examples. The readers will learn about the basics of visual aids (airfield lighting and marking) and non-visual aids and most importantly, the criteria to be adopted to locate the Communication, Navigation, and Surveillance (CNS) systems.

Environmental impact of the airport is briefed with mitigating measures including the land use planning.

The description includes the best practices of airport planning for operational flexibility and enhanced capacity and few design concepts of the airport facilities with visuals.

It is essential to prepare technically feasible planning with various infrastructures and assess the project's financial viability. Thus, a chapter is included with the assessment in the form of pre-feasibility study of the project. With this assessment, the business model and scope of the development can be revisited to make the project more viable.

This book will provide a good foundation for aviation students and entry-level professionals to understand airport planning.

I owe a lot to my colleagues for their support and encouragement. I would like to express my special thanks to Charulatha and Srilakshmi for their contributions to this book. I was able to complete this book with the support of conversations I had with Charulatha about the practices, as well as illustrations drawn by Srilakshmi. I would like to convey my gratitude to my parents, who encouraged me to teach people from my experiences and the knowledge I've gained.

1   Introduction to airport planning

Introduction

Airport planning is a vast subject, continually evolving with learnings from operations and feedback from aviation stakeholders. To understand the subject, one must be aware of the fundamentals starting with the aviation industry's economic contribution and employment opportunities. The passenger traffic growth in the last ten years is phenomenal, especially in developing countries, and is projected to grow in future. Thus, airport planning is an important subject to learn and apply for airport development. In addition, the aviation industry is regulatory driven to minimize accidents/incidents, which affect traffic growth and cause massive losses to the operators. Thus, it is essential to be aware of the organizations contributing to the aviation safety and planned development of airports.

First, one should know which documents to refer to while planning. Planning for a new airport or expansion of an existing airport is based on expected passenger traffic growth. The infrastructure at the airports is to match the operational requirements specific to the airport. Thus, knowing these requirements with some of the common facilities established at the airports is required. The following are the sections that describe these aspects:

- Economic benefits, employment opportunities, and projected traffic growth.
- Roles, functions, and contributions of the International Civil Aviation Organization (ICAO), Airports Council International (ACI), International Air Transport Association (IATA), and a few States' Civil Aviation Authorities (CAAs) and the reference documents for planning.
- Various infrastructures/facilities at airports and some brief about those specific to the airports.
- Aeroplane dimensions for airport planning, type of operations based on visibility and their importance in planning.

The description in this book does not include the detailed design, for example, the structural design of the infrastructures. Instead, the narrative helps the readers understand the airport planning requirement and study the proposed airport development, whether for an existing or new airport.

Economic contribution and employment potential

The aviation industry accounts for around eighty-eight million jobs.

Out of eighty eight million jobs, the direct employment is about twelve million personnel engaged in airport operations, immigration, and customs, as well as renting, concessionaires, freight forwarders, and catering, directly associated with the operations of airlines, aircraft manufacturing industry, and Air Navigation Services. Indirect employment such as employees of fuel suppliers, construction firms, suppliers of aeroplane components, producers of goods sold

DOI: 10.4324/9781003319948-1

in airports, and a range of responsibilities in business support, such as those held in call centres, information technology, and accountancy, constitute around eighteen million jobs.

Around fourteen million employees of an induced kind are created by individuals spending their income on products and services. In addition, the tourism business accounts for 44.8 million jobs worldwide (Aviation Benefits 2020).

Direct employment in Indian aviation is around 250,000.

The industry supports $3.5 trillion in economic activity (4.1% of the global gross domestic product). The global air transport industry is larger than both the automobile manufacturing sector and the pharmaceutical manufacturing industry by GDP. If air transport were a country, its GDP would rank 17th in the world, like Indonesia or the Netherlands.

Given the speed and reliability of air transport across long distances, business aviation in delivering air cargo facilitates effective trade between cities and countries. Costs associated with air freight are naturally higher than those associated with other shipping options. As a result, it is the conveyance of choice for time-sensitive and delicate packages, such as those containing valuables, perishables, or precision instruments. Thirty-five percent of the value of global trade and 1% of the trade volume are carried by air cargo (IATA). For airports and airlines alike, a rise in cargo traffic – especially from passenger planes carrying belly cargo – means better utilization of resources, economies of scale, and revenue growth with just a slight increase in expense. In 2019, air cargo was worth $6.5 trillion.

World air passenger traffic growth for the 20 years from 1980 to 2020 is shown in Figure 1.1.

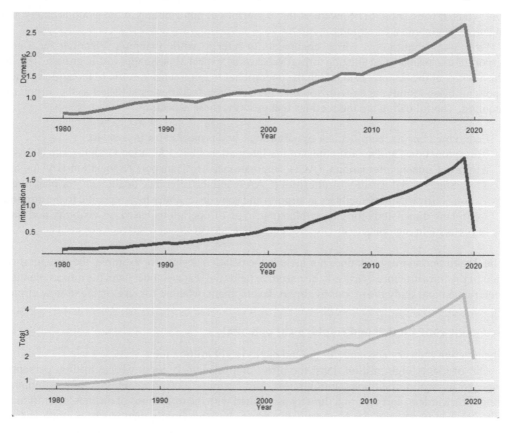

Figure 1.1 World air passenger traffic growth from 1980 to 2020

Source: World air passenger traffic evolution, 1980–2020 – IEA

Air passengers handled in 2019 globally was 4.56 billion. Demand for air transport is expected to increase by an average of 3% per annum over the next 20 years. If this growth is achieved, by 2038, the air transport industry will contribute:

- Around 13.7 million direct jobs and $1.7 trillion in GDP to the world economy.
- Seventy-six million jobs, including indirect and induced contributions, and $4.3 trillion in GDP.
- Once the impact of global tourism is taken into account, the air transport industry will contribute 143 million jobs and $6.3 trillion in GDP.

Infrastructure requirement

To handle the long-term trend in passenger demand until 2040, the world's airports will need to invest about $2.4 trillion in total capital. According to the 'Global Outlook of Airport Capital Expenditure – Meeting Sustainable Development Goals and Future Air Travel Demand' study published on June 2021, significant investment in greenfield airports and a substantial investment to expand and maintain existing airport infrastructure are necessary. The research project was funded by Hamad International Airport and conducted in collaboration with Oxford Economics. Between 2019 (the baseline year before COVID-19) and 2020 (the year of maximum global COVID-19 lockdown), it was predicted that investment will drop by 33%, or about $28 billion. ACI World estimated that by 2021, capital investment will partially recover at about 14% (approximately $12 billion) below the 2019 baseline. However, as air transport demand recovers to pre-pandemic levels, passenger demand will put increased pressure on airports' infrastructure. Failure to invest in addressing capacity needs will have socioeconomic consequences. According to ACI World, the number of travellers might drop by as much as 5.1 billion people worldwide by 2040 if longer-term capacity restrictions are not addressed through capital investment. Since airport infrastructure is vital to the growth of air travel, the loss of a million passengers in 2040 owing to airport capacity constraints would mean the loss of about 10,500 jobs and $346 million in GDP.

Aviation organizations

International Civil Aviation Organization (ICAO)

The Chicago Convention was a treaty on international civil aviation signed on 7 December 1944 in Chicago. One hundred ninety-three nations are signatories to the Chicago Convention fund and oversee ICAO to assist their air transport diplomacy and cooperation.

The signing States to the Convention have agreed on several principles and structures for international civil aviation to expand safely and orderly and for international air transport services to be established on an equal basis and run soundly and economically. Governments could prevent abuse of the expansion of international civil aviation by agreeing to the abovementioned principles. This can also lessen conflict and encourage international collaboration.

One example of the principle is regarding Sovereignty.

"The contracting States recognize that every State has complete and exclusive sovereignty over the airspace above its territory".

The primary function of the ICAO is to maintain an administrative and expert bureaucracy. For example, the ICAO Secretariat supports diplomatic interactions. Furthermore, it researches innovations in air transport policy and standardization as directed and approved by the ICAO assembly or the ICAO council, which is chosen by the ICAO assembly. In addition, invited organizations, the industry, public society, and other relevant regional and global organizations participate in developing new standards.

The ICAO secretariat organizes panels, task groups, conferences, and seminars to examine many new priorities' technical, political, socioeconomic, and other aspects as these stakeholders identify them. It then offers governments the best outcomes and recommendations for setting new global Standards and Recommended Practices (SARPs) for civil aviation.

Through its seven Regional Offices, the ICAO not only possesses these essential diplomatic and research skills but also plays a crucial coordination role in the civil aviation industry. In addition, in accordance with the needs and priorities that governments define and formally establish, it also carries out educational outreach, creates alliances, and conducts audits, training, and capacity development activities across the globe.

The States' CAAs are the regulators for the respective State. However, ICAO is not an aviation regulator as it works with the following principles:

- The requirements contained in ICAO standards are never more stringent than those mandated by individual countries. Air operators using applicable airspace and airports must comply with the local and national regulations implemented by sovereign governments.
- ICAO have no power over national governments in the worldwide priority areas for which they are responsible.
- Airports and airlines cannot be singled out for criticism based on their safety record or their treatment of customers, and national airspace cannot be closed or restricted arbitrarily.
- It facilitates discussions, condemnations, and sanctions that governments may desire to pursue if another country violates a particular international norm established in accordance with the Chicago Convention and the Articles and Annexes it contains under international law.

ICAO SARPs

The formulation and maintenance of international SARPs and Procedures for Air Navigation Services (PANS) are key elements of the Convention on International Civil Aviation (Chicago Convention) and a central aspect of ICAO's Mission and role. SARPs and PANS are crucial to ICAO Member States and other stakeholders as they provide the fundamental basis for harmonized global aviation safety and efficiency in the air and on the ground. It also provides the international standardization of functional and performance requirements of air navigation facilities and services and the orderly development of air transportation.

ICAO manages over 12,000 SARPs across the Convention's 19 Annexes and 6 PANS, many continually changing to reflect the most recent advancements and breakthroughs. Various technical and non-technical groups that are either in-house experts or directly linked to ICAO participate in the development of SARPs and PANS in an organized, open, and multi-staged procedure known as the ICAO 'amendment process' or 'standards-making process'. An initial proposal for a new or enhanced SARPs, or procedure typically takes around two years to be fully adopted or approved for inclusion in an Annex or a PANS.

In addition to the above, ICAO publications like manuals and documents are popular and valuable. These documents provide guidelines for the implementation of SARPs. These do have the same stature as that of the Annex and PANS. In addition, ICAO undertakes consultancy assignments through its Technical Cooperation Bureau (TCB). Annex 14 and Design Manuals (Doc 9157) are the most essential documents for airport planning.

ICAO's publications can be seen on its website. ICAO e-library is also very popular and helpful as the e-library has ICAO Annex, which can be viewed, not for downloading.

Brief of the few other aviation organizations

ACI is a global organization that promotes the interest of 1950 airports and 717 members from 185 nations to advance aviation excellence. This is accomplished by developing policies, initiatives, and best practices that promote airport standards globally in collaboration with governments, regional ACI members, specialists, and international organizations like ICAO. Safety, security, economics, statistics, customer experience, facilitation, I.T., environment, and ACI world corporate are areas of interest for ACI. Both the Airport Health Accreditation programme and its Airport Service Quality (ASQ) programme, which rates and measures the service quality performance of airports, are highly regarded. It also organizes webinars, offers consulting services, and offers training on various airport-related topics. (Visit the ACI website to view the list of publications.)

International Air Transport Association (IATA)

IATA was founded in Havana, Cuba, in April 1945. IATA has 290 airlines in 120 countries as its members, representing 83% of total scheduled traffic.

IATA's vision is 'Working together to shape the future growth of a safe, secure and sustainable air transport industry that connects and enriches our world', and their Mission is to represent, lead, and serve the airline industry. As stated on IATA's website, these three visions show their role and importance to aviation.

Vision 1 Representing the airline industry

To improve understanding of the air transport industry among decision-makers and increase awareness of aviation's benefits to national and global economies, it advocates for airlines' interests across the globe, challenging unreasonable rules and charges, holding regulators and governments to account, and striving for sensible regulation.

Vision 2 Leading the airline industry

For over 70 years, IATA has developed global commercial standards upon which the air transport industry is built. They aim to assist airlines by simplifying processes and increasing passenger convenience while reducing costs and improving efficiency.

Vision 3 Serving the airline industry

IATA helps airlines to operate safely, securely, efficiently, and economically under clearly defined rules. Professional support is provided to all industry stakeholders with a wide range of products and expert services.

IATA has many publications and monthly newsletters on all aspects of airline operations. For example, its Airport Development Reference Manual (ADRM) (currently 12th Edition) is a preferred guideline for airport planners. IATA also provides training on all aspects of airline and airport operations, including safety, security, and handling dangerous goods. IATA also provides consultancy services (for example, traffic forecast). In addition, it conducts safety audits of the airlines through its IATA Operational Safety Audit (IOSA). IATA's monthly publications can be seen on its website.

Federal Aviation Administration (FAA)

The FAA's Mission is to offer the world's safest, most efficient aerospace system. FAA ensures that the nation's airport network satisfies the requirements of the travelling public while also being efficient, effective, safe, and ecologically responsible. FAA is the biggest transportation organization in the United States that oversees all facets of domestic civil aviation and airspace over adjacent international waterways. In addition to regulating rules for airports and managing air traffic, it has the authority to safeguard U.S. assets during the launch or re-entry of commercial spacecraft. Furthermore, the ICAO granted the FAA sovereignty over neighbouring international waters.

Created in August 1958, the FAA replaced the former Civil Aeronautics Administration (CAA) and later became an agency within the U.S. Department of Transportation.

The FAA's roles include (As stated on the website):

- Regulating U.S. commercial space transportation.
- Regulating air navigation facilities' geometric and flight inspection standards.
- Encouraging and developing civil aeronautics, including new aviation technology.
- Issuing, suspending, or revoking pilot certificates.
- Regulating civil aviation to promote transportation safety in the United States, primarily through local offices called Flight Standards District Offices.
- Developing and operating a system of air traffic control and navigation for both civil and military aircraft.
- Researching and developing the National Airspace System and civil aeronautics.
- Developing and carrying out programs to control aircraft noise and other environmental effects of civil aviation.

FAA's publications include Advisory Circulars (ACs) covering many areas of aviation. Its ACs (Series 150) on airport planning and development provide valuable guidance, and these circulars are based on lessons/feedback on implementation. A few are listed below:

- AC No: AC 150/5300-13A Airport Design.
- AC: 150/5060-5 – Airport Capacity and delay.
- AC: 150/5070-6B – Airport Master Plan.

Civil Aviation Authority (UK)

The CAA is the statutory authority that oversees and regulates civil aviation in the United Kingdom and is the UK's aviation regulator.

As the UK's aviation regulator, it works to ensure.

- The aviation industry meets the highest safety standards.
- Consumers have a choice, value for money, and are protected and treated fairly when they fly.
- The environmental impact of aviation on local communities is effectively managed, and CO_2 emissions are reduced through efficient use of airspace.
- The aviation industry manages security risks effectively.

CAA (UK) is a public corporation established by Parliament in 1972 as an independent specialist aviation regulator. Its costs are met entirely from charges they levy to provide a service to or regulate. Its regulation and policy are harmonized worldwide to ensure consistent levels of safety and consumer protection.

It also economically regulates some airports (Gatwick and Heathrow) and specific aspects of air traffic control. CAA undertakes economic regulation of these airports by assessing whether airport operators have substantial market power and, where appropriate, licence those that do. Airport economic licences include conditions on price controls, specifying the quality of the services the airport operator must deliver and how much it can charge from them.

Its responsibilities spread across the aviation spectrum – airlines, airports, aviation safety, and airspace.

CAA (UK) has many publications related to airports and airlines. CAP-168 is a relevant document for airport planning and CAA uses CAP 168 in support of granting an aerodrome licence.

CASA (Australia)

The Civil Aviation Safety Authority (CASA) is a government body that regulates aviation safety in Australia. It licenses pilots, registers aircraft, oversees aviation safety, and promotes safety awareness. Also, ensure that the aviation community and the public use and administer Australian airspace safely. Its vision is safe skies for all. And its Mission is to promote a positive and collaborative safety culture through a fair, effective, and efficient aviation safety regulatory system, supporting our aviation community.

In July 1995, it was established as an independent statutory authority. It operates within a legislative framework of acts, regulations, associated legislative instruments and guidance material. The Civil Aviation Act 1988 describes CASA roles. The Act also forms the basis of the Civil Aviation Safety Regulations. These regulations are broken into parts, which may have an associated Manual of Standards and supporting guidance materials.

CASA work across these areas:

- Regulatory Oversight.
- National Operations and Standards.
- Stakeholder Engagement.
- Legal International and Regulatory Affairs.
- Corporate Services.
- Transformation and Safety Systems.
- Finance.

CASA has many publications, and Part 139 (Aerodromes) Manual of Standards is a relevant document for airport planning.

European Union Aviation Safety Agency (EASA)

EASA's Mission states, 'Your safety is our mission'. EASA is the centrepiece of the European Union's strategy for aviation safety.

Its objectives are:

- To promote and achieve the highest common safety and environmental protection standards in civil aviation.

- To ensure you have the safest possible flight.
- To ensure that flight is safe in all phases: beginning with the rules, the airlines and crew need to follow through to the aircraft certification.

EASA regularly revises the risks and improves the common regulations applied among EU countries and airlines, so they are always of the highest standard. It works hand in hand with the National Aviation Authorities and aviation manufacturers across Europe to achieve these goals. In addition, the Agency's experts apply strict certification and inspection standards to provide European citizens with the world's safest and most environmentally friendly aviation system.

EASA was founded in 2002 and was initially known as the European Aviation Safety Agency. The name was changed to European Union Aviation Safety Agency in 2018 when its responsibilities were also widened. EASA has 27 members of EU, Switzerland, Norway, Iceland, and Liechtenstein.

EASA is responsible for setting the rules, guidelines, and standards for all safety and environmental aspects of civil aviation, offering the safety that you, your family, and all business partners need.

EASA monitors all players in the field of aviation to follow a standard set of rules and report any safety concerns they may uncover. In addition, EASA continuously analyses the safety data received from airlines, maintenance organizations, manufacturers, and other aviation-related entities and takes the necessary actions to ensure the highest safety standards.

EASA constantly adapts to the demands of new technologies and the latest trends. Innovations and developments such as cyber-security, green technologies, or sustainable fuels often need to be aligned with existing rules, so we need to update these and adapt them. Environmental regulations compiled by EASA make a vital contribution to minimizing the impact of aviation on the environment. The Agency sets the minimum environmental standards an aircraft needs to comply with and supports efforts to reduce environmental impact in our skies with initiatives such as CO_2 emissions offsetting, sustainable aviation fuel, and noise reduction.

All accidents in civil aviation are registered, analysed, and taken into consideration to improve rules, work with Member States, industry and, where relevant, with the public.

EASA publication titled 'Certification Specifications and Guidance Material for Aerodromes Design' is relevant for airport planning.

The list of CAAs continues, but the idea is to brief a few CAAs as an example, and the readers/ planners use the appropriate guidelines of the States in their work

This book's planning parameters and specifications are primarily based on ICAO SARPs, Manuals, and Documents, supplemented with IATA/FAA/ACI guidelines, where required. In addition, best practices and some additional information on ICAO publications are included.

Airport development and planning

Airport planning can be categorized into two types of development, viz. greenfield airport, i.e., an airport at a new site and for an existing airport in operation, is required to expand to increase its capacity. The capacity addition for an airport in operations could be for a passenger terminal building by extension to the existing building or a new building along with its necessary components. If capacity addition is required in the airfield, it could be like an additional runway, taxiway system, or apron.

The development of an airport may not always be for a commercial purpose; it could be for social benefits like the place is inaccessible or difficult to access through other modes of transport, to improve the quality of life at the location and improve connectivity to another city will be of great help for trade, medical reasons. Let us assume that an airport necessity has been examined, and it was found that there is a requirement. A wide range of criteria could be identified for identifying a site/location for a greenfield airport. After reviewing these criteria for each site, various location options can be examined to shortlist a few preferred sites or rank the locations. One of the first and foremost criteria is to decide the required land area, including its minimum length and width.

Airport components

One way to classify the airport facilities and understand the planning requirement is based on their location. Under this, the airport could be divided into three broad areas based on its functions: (1) Landside – where passengers and bags are processed (pre-security) and access to the Passenger Terminal Building (PTB) is established; (2) airside – where aircraft movement happens and a sterile area for passengers and their bags; and (3) interface between airside and landside. All the airport facilities, let it be called components, are located either on the airside or landside. Some components require access from the airside and landside located in the interface between these two.

Airside components – Runway, taxiway, apron, Communication, Navigation and Surveillance System (CNS), Crash Fire Rescue stations (CFR/fire stations), Ground Handling workshops, aircraft engineering complex, and maintenance workshops.

Landside components – Access Road to the airport facilities, vehicle parking areas, hotels, convention centres, logistic centres, Special Economic Zone (SEZ), office complex, and other revenue generation facilities which passengers and non-passengers could use. Housing for staff can also be included.

Components which could be either on airside or landside – Air Traffic Control tower (ATC), Electrical powerhouse, water supply tanks, sewage treatment plants.

Components must be in the interface between the airside and landside –PTB, fuel storage tanks, cargo, MRO, and facilities that require access from the landside as well as the airside.

The above could be called a master list. All these may only be needed for some of the airports. Some of the components are necessary for an airport for aircraft operation. The categorization based on these will result in two groups that are required even to start with, and others are optional, which may be catered for planning purposes but may be built after some time. Some need not be catered to at all.

Airport infrastructure classification

Another way to classify is (i) essential infrastructure 'must run' an airport and (ii) other infrastructure based on business requirements. For example, infrastructure like runways and passenger terminal buildings are essential for an airport operation. However, other requirements like MRO, dedicated cargo terminal and commercial development will solely depend on business requirements.

What are the Must facilities – These are runway, taxiway, apron, PTB, the access road to the airport, and the airport utility system – power, water, and sewage. Vehicle parking area. CNS facilities, ATC tower, CFR (fire) stations, fuel storage facility, and cargo handling facility. The rest of the facilities can be called optional and decided based on the business analysis when to develop.

Figures 1.2–1.4 show the development of these components in the planning, viz. airport with single runway, apron, PTB, and other must facilities, airport with single runway, full-length

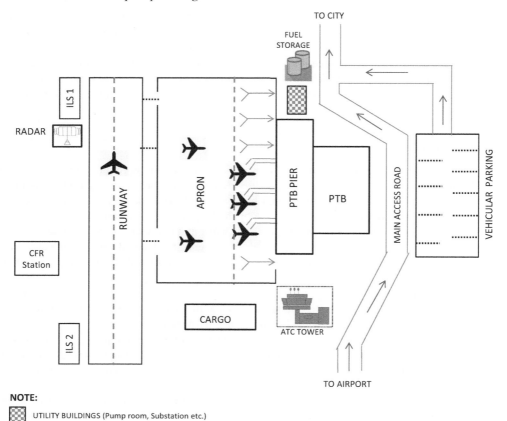

Figure 1.2 Airport with single runway, apron, PTB, and other must facilities

parallel taxiway, apron, PTB, dedicated cargo area with apron, and other must-provide facilities and airport with two runways, full-length parallel taxiway, apron, multiple PTBs, dedicated cargo area with apron, must and all other facilities, respectively.

Some of the airport-specific facilities/infrastructures are below with brief.

1   Runway – used by aircraft for landing and take-off.
2   Taxiway – parallel, entry/exit, taxi lane.
3   Type of taxiways:

   •   A parallel taxiway is parallel to the runway, and aircraft on landing exit from the runway to the taxiway so that another plane can use the runway for landing or take off.
   •   Entry/exit taxiways are the connection between parallel taxiways to the runway. It could be perpendicular or at an angle called Rapid Exit Taxiway (RET).
   •   In RETs, the aircraft moves at high speed to exit the runway as quickly as possible.
   •   Taxi lanes are taxiways but in an apron for pushing back the aircraft from the parking position to ready to start for departure. As a result, aircraft speed in taxi lanes is less compared to the movement in taxiways.

4   Apron – Where aircraft are parked, this should be closer to the PTB to connect the aircraft with a moving bridge (PBB). Accordingly, the aircraft stands could be either a contact stand

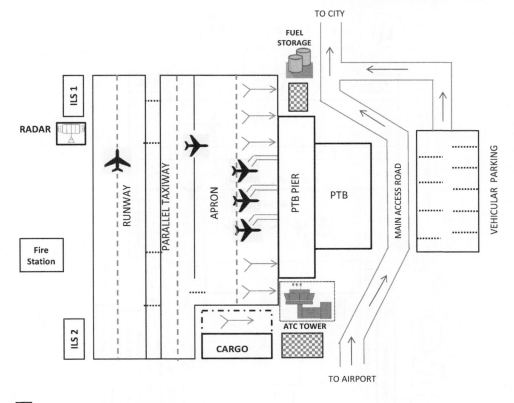

UTILITY BUILDINGS (Pump room, Substation etc.)

Figure 1.3 Airport with single runway, full-length parallel taxiway, apron, PTB, dedicated cargo area with apron, and other must-provide facilities

with PBB or a non-contact stand. Remote does not mean it is far from the PTB; these stands do not have bridges.

5 Communication, Navigation and Surveillance System (CNS) – Instrument Landing System (ILS), Doppler Very High-Frequency Omnirange (DVOR), Airport Surveillance Radar (ASR)/MSSR, Air Route Surveillance Radar (ARSR), VHF equipment, Surface Movement Radar (SMR) are part of the CNS system. A brief of these systems is as below:

- ASR is a radar system used at airports to detect and display the presence and position of aircraft in the terminal area and the airspace around airports. Whereas ARSR is for air traffic control in the air routes. The coverage of ARSR is more than ASR.
- ILS has two components – a localizer and glide path for guiding the pilot approaching the runway with the angle of approach and runway centreline.
- DVOR is an omnidirectional radar ground-based radio navigational aid that provides bearing information to aircraft to define air traffic control routes for en-route, terminal, and instrument approach/departure procedures. DVOR, when collocated with DME (Distance Measuring Equipment), provides both the bearing and slant distance of aircraft with respect to the ground station.
- VHF equipment for communication between ATC and pilots.

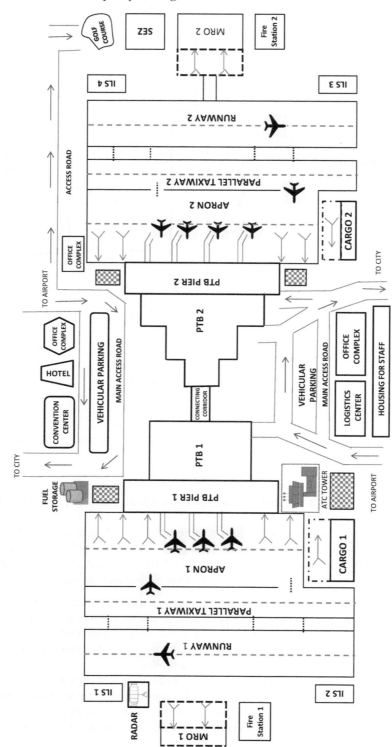

Figure 1.4 Airport with two runways, full-length parallel taxiway, apron, multiple PTBs, dedicated cargo area with apron, must and all other facilities

 UTILITY BUILDINGS (Pump room, Substation etc.)

- SMR is used to detect aircraft and vehicles in the airfield. Air traffic controllers use it to supplement visual observations.

Among all these CNS systems, the systems required for an airport will have to be examined, case to case. But for planning purposes, all these are included in this book regarding location criteria.

Meteorological systems

At an aerodrome, equipment provided to collect and share the meteorological report are:

- Wind direction indicator – wind vane.
- Wind speed measurement – anemometer.
- Temperature –air temperature, pressure, and humidity (barometric pressure sensor, AT/Rh sensor).
- Runway Visual Range (RVR) measurements – transmissometer.
- Rainfall measurement – surface observatory – rain gauge.
- Prediction of general visibility, weather conditions, and rain based on the cloud movements – Radar.

Phased development

Planning starts with forecasting passenger numbers through the airport in the next 25–50 years. The passenger numbers will be expressed annually, say 40 million passengers per annum (mppa), in the next 40 years from now. Since the assessment of the traffic is for a longer period, it is possible to identify many phases in the airport that will be developed. Say for ultimate traffic of 40 mppa; the plan is to develop the airport in 4 phases, 10 mppa in phase 1, 20 mppa in phase 2, 30 mppa in phase 3, and 40 mppa in phase 4. For simplicity, the additional passenger capacity required is ten mppa every ten years. For each of these phases, the facilities needed, and the scope/extent of the facilities are to be assessed. For example, identifying the number of runways and taxiways, the number of aircraft stands, the area of the passenger terminal building, the type and category of CNS equipment, and all other required facilities. This could be done by identifying the facilities needed for the ultimate traffic numbers, in this case, 40 mppa, and then pruning in phases to 3, 2, and finally 1.

Regarding the development of commercial assets, the traffic forecast could identify revenue sources and the relevant facilities starting from phase 1. For future phases can identify suitable locations with minimal details, as it is tough to firm up the business requirement for such a long period. Such phase-wise planning will undergo review for its relevance at that time.

The above is for greenfield airport. For a brownfield airport with a master plan, one could review the same to ensure the relevance of the planning done previously and, if required, carry out the required modifications. With technological advancement, improved aircraft performance, and many such parameters, it is necessary to review the master plan already prepared.

In this book, the airport planning description is for the conceptual design with criteria for the assessment of various facilities at an airport. Based on these criteria, it is possible to prepare the planning document with the aid of relevant documents. The planning document contains the following:

- Number, location, and length of runways, parallel taxiways.
- Distance between the runways, between the runway and parallel taxiways, and between parallel taxiways.

- Number and tentative locations of entry/exit taxiways.
- The number of aircraft stands required for ultimate traffic and their location.
- How many are contact stands, and how many remote stands?
- Category of operations.
- CNS equipment required and their location.
- Airfield Ground Light (AGL) layout.
- Distance between taxiway and apron.
- Distance between apron and passenger terminal.
- Number of PTBs, footprint required, and permissible height.
- Number and location of CFR stations.
- Location and height of ATC tower.
- Location and number of vehicular parking bays on the cityside.
- Location of a fuel storage system, type of refuelling arrangement.
- Access roads to the airport, including roads to all the facilities.
- Location of bulk utilities.
- Location of all other commercial assets/revenue-generating assets and their permissible heights.

Critical dimensions of the aeroplane for planning

Among the numerous dimensions of an aeroplane, the most important ones for airport planning are:

- Minimum runway length at a standard temperature and site elevation (termed as aeroplane reference field length).
- Wingspan.
- Outer Main Gear Wheel Span (OMGWS).
- Door levels.
- Seating capacity.
- Take-off weight.
- Overall maximum length.
- Tail Height.

For the planning of airfield layout, the aeroplanes are grouped and termed as 'aeroplane reference code', which consists of a number and a letter based on two aeroplane parameters: reference field length and wingspan.

Aeroplane reference field length, in simple terms, is the minimum runway length required for take-off under certain conditions. A number represents this, 1–4, depending on the length required.

The wingspan of the aircraft is the dimension shown below and is classified into six categories as code letters A, B, C, D, E, and F

The aeroplane code combining the two parameters is in Table 1.1.

An Aeroplane reference code combines numbers and letters, for example, 3C or 4E. If the aeroplane reference field length of an aircraft (Airbus 320-200) is 2025 m and the wingspan of this aircraft is 34.1 m, the aeroplane reference code for this aircraft – A 320/200 – is 4C. Similarly, there would be many aircraft with code 4C. Another example is the aeroplane reference code for Airbus 380–800 is 4F since the aeroplane reference field length is more than 1800 m (2779 m to be specific) and its wingspan is 79.8 m (less than 80 m).

Table 1.1 Aeroplane codes

Code number	Aeroplane reference field length	Code letter	Wingspan
1	Less than 800 m	A	Up to but not including 15 m
2	800 m up to but not including 1200 m	B	15 m up to but not including 24 m
3	1200 m up to but not including 1800 m	C	24 m up to but not including 36 m
4	1800 m and above	D	36 m up to but not including 52 m
		E	52 m up to but not including 65 m
		F	65 m up to but not including 80 m

Source: ICAO-Annex14

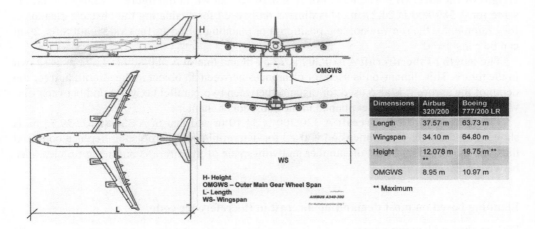

Dimensions	Airbus 320/200	Boeing 777/200 LR
Length	37.57 m	63.73 m
Wingspan	34.10 m	64.80 m
Height	12.078 m **	18.75 m **
OMGWS	8.95 m	10.97 m

** Maximum

H- Height
OMGWS – Outer Main Gear Wheel Span
L- Length
WS- Wingspan

Figure 1.5 Aeroplane dimensions

Source: Aeroplane image sourced from https://commons.wikimedia.org/wiki/File:Airbus_A340-300_v1.0.png and added dimensions. Data for the table from Airbus Website

Aerodrome reference code – Annex 14/ICAO specifies the airport planning parameters based on the aeroplane code and, accordingly, the aerodrome reference code. For example, an aerodrome reference code 4C of an airport is designed to operate aircraft up to 4C aeroplane reference code. With this, by reading the reference code of an aerodrome, one can understand the aeroplane group it can handle.

Illustrations of aeroplane dimensions

Figure 1.5 shows the OMGWS, height, length, and wingspan of aircraft along with these dimensions for two aircrafts as an example.

Runway pavement width is determined based on OMGWS. The groups of OMGWS for planning are as follows:

- Up to but not including 4.5 m.
- 4.5 m up to but not including 6 m.
- 6.0 m up to but not including 9 m.
- 9.0 m up to but not including 15 m.

For aeroplane A320/200 shown in figure with an OMGWS of 8.95 m (6 m to not including 9 m), the runway width should be 30 m, whereas for A 380/800 the OMGWS being 14.34 m (9 m but not including 15 m), the runway width should be 45 m.

Similarly, the taxiway width also depends on the range of OMGWS mentioned above. Taxiway width based on categories of OMGWS for planning is as follows.

- 7.5 m width when the OMGWS is Up to but not including 4.5 m.
- 10.5 m width for 4.5 m up to but not including 6 m.
- 15 m width for 6.0 m up to but not including 9 m.
- 23 m width when the OMGWS is 9.0 m up to but not including 15 m.

Height of the aircraft – The height of A 320/200 as shown in the figure is 12.078 m and the same for A 380/800 is 24.27 m. This dimension is used for evaluating the obstacle clearance, for example, for the runway holding position. For planning purposes for Code E aircrafts, 20 m can be considered.

The length of the aircraft A 320/200 is 37.57 m and that of A 380/800 is 72.73 m as shown in the figure. This dimension is used for clearances between an object to the aircraft and for the depth of the apron. It is also used for distance between two parallel taxiways and between runway and parallel taxiway as explained in the subsequent chapter.

The wingspan of the aircraft A 320/200 is 34.10 m and that of A 380/800 is 79.75 m as shown in the figure. This dimension is used for determining the aeroplane reference code and thus, the apron length based on number and wingspans of the aircrafts and wing tip clearance between adjacent aircrafts.

Planning based on most demanding aircraft in the reference code

For the airport planning purpose, once it is decided that the planning for the airport is, say, 4E aerodrome code, planners need to consider the most demanding aircraft in terms of the dimensions/parameters in the 4E group. The reason is that there will be some differences between the aircraft in the same code. For example, one critical parameter that varies between the aircraft in the same code is the aeroplane reference field length, which is the basis for the runway length calculation.

Category of runway operations

One more parameter to be aware of is the category of operation. When the runway operation is permitted only when the visibility is above a particular value, there is no instrument on the ground for guiding the pilot; such an airport runway is called a non-instrument runway. The operation is on 'Visual Flight Rules' (VFR). Such an operation is a non-instrument runway operation.

When the visibility is below the VFR, the instruments on the ground guide the pilot. Such a runway is called an instrument runway, and the operation is on Instrument Flight Rules (IFR). As can be seen in the subsequent description that the separation distances are more for IFR operations compared with VFR operations, and other planning parameters are also more stringent with IFR.

Depending on the Runway Visual Range (RVR) and decision height, the categories of instrument runway are

- Non-precision.
- Precision approach Cat I.

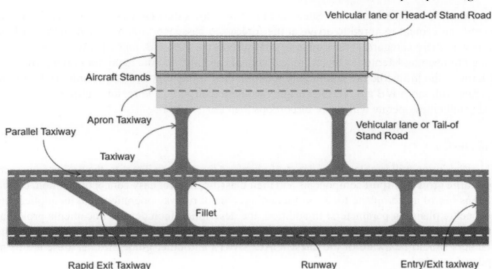

Figure 1.6 Airfield pavements layout.

- Precision approach Cat II.
- Precision approach Cat III.

The precision approach procedure is an instrument approach procedure using precision lateral and vertical guidance with weather minima as determined by the category of operation.

The instrument used for the precision approach is the Instrument Landing System, popularly known as ILS.

The non-precision approach uses VOR, which provides only lateral guidance and does not provide vertical guidance.

Example of the use of the above four parameters in the planning is as follows:

- The minimum separation distance between the runway and the parallel taxiway for Code 4C – 158 m for instrument runway and 93 m for non-instrument runway.
- Code 4E – 172.5 m for instrument runway and 107.5 m for non-instrument runway.

Annex 14 specifies the minimum distances between the runway and taxiway, between taxiways, from the taxiway to any object, and from taxi lane to object. The distances are measured from the centreline to the centreline of pavements. The category of operation is also an essential criterion for the location and height restriction of the building or structures in and around the airport.

The description and dimensions mentioned in this book for aerodrome category 4E (unless otherwise noted) and assuming Cat III instrument runway operations.

The airfield pavements of a typical airport are shown in Figure 1.6.

Aircraft fleet mix and seating capacity for planning

Aircraft types are classified as turboprop, Narrow Body (NB), and Wide Body (WB), depending on the aircraft's seating capacity. Turboprop aircraft have lesser seating capacity than narrow-body aircraft (single aisle). Wide-body aircraft are two-aisle aircraft with a seating capacity more than narrow-body aircraft. Such classification allows the planners to work out the annual aircraft movement required to arrive at the forecasted passenger numbers. The number of aircraft with these categories (for example, 20% turboprop, 70% NB, and 10% WB) that are estimated to operate determines the estimated annual capacity, and the maximum hourly numbers determine the infrastructure and facility requirements at the airport. For example, Hub airports operate with more WB aircraft than origin/destination airports, and regional airports in tier two and small cities operate with more turboprops than tier 1 airports.

Conclusion

The description will enable the readers to understand the aviation benefits, the projected passenger traffic growth, airport components and their classification for easy conceptualization, critical dimensions of an aeroplane for airport planning, type of runway operation, and its implications in specific planning parameters. In addition, the description includes the documents providing guidelines for the planning and roles and contribution by a few of the aviation organizations. Planners should be aware of the latest ICAO SARPs and other guidelines, as these are being updated regularly.

References

ATAG. (2020). *Aviation Benefits Beyond Borders*, Characteristics for Airport Planning. Aircraft Characteristics | Airbus.

ICAO. (2022). ICAO Annex 14 – Ninth Edition: Vol. I.

International Energy Agency. (2020). Energy Efficiency 2020. Energy Efficiency 2020, 105.

Technical Data from Aeroplane Manufacturers. Boeing: Airport Compatibility – Airplane.

The World Factbook – National Air Transport System – World Travel Facts. https://www.cia.gov/the-world-factbook/field/national-air-transport-system

Websites of ICAO, ACI, IATA, FAA, CASA, EASA.

Further reading

Economic Impact Study of Delhi Airport by National Council of Applied Economic Research (NCAER). https://www.ncaer.org/publication/the-economic-impact-of-the-indira-gandhi-international-airport

Want to Know What Are Airports' Codes by ICAO and IATA? Read 'Location Indicators' Doc 7910/181-ICAO.

2 Planning framework

Introduction

Passenger and cargo traffic forecasts enable the airports to be aware of the traffic in future. When reviewed with the present capacity, the airports can plan for capacity augmentation of the specific facilities/infrastructure. Similarly, the Government can initiate action for a greenfield airport with the anticipated traffic in the long term. The traffic forecast is also used by airlines and all other aviation stakeholders for them to plan their resources. The starting point for the development planning is, thus, the forecasting of the traffic. Forecast methods vary widely, but the most used in airports is the regression analysis method with different independent variables like GDP and airfare, depending on their relationship to the dependent variable. Thus, it is required to input relevant independent variables through analysis for a reasonable forecast. Forecasting being prediction requires comparing the actual traffic at frequent intervals with the forecast number, identifying the reason for the variation, and taking corrective actions. For example, traffic growth beyond the numbers forecasted based on past trends and regression can be examined by looking at the additional traffic contributors over and above these. Also, such increased growth means the need to look at the capacity augmentation plan.

The popular forecasting methods are time series analysis using the ARIMA method and regression analysis method. Both use actual past data for the analysis. Of late use of machine learning methods using the LSTM model is also in practice. The intent here is not to explain the statistics or the analytical process but practically prepare a model and apply the same to the dataset.

For the greenfield airport development with the projected traffic in the long term, it is required to estimate the extent of land needed quickly, the dimensions especially considering runway length and orientation. Multiple suitable sites can be identified with the necessary extent of land assessed. For this purpose, a matrix of specific parameters and a selection criterion is used to shortlist the best site among the identified sites. In the case of brownfield airport development, the framework is different and should be more straightforward if a master plan exists and certain conditions are met which are described.

With the land identified with parameters verified, the proposal must be submitted for Approval by the Government, whether greenfield or brownfield airport development.

Purpose of air traffic forecast

Air traffic forecast is used for:

- Infrastructure planning, financing, identifying possible traffic uncovered, and analysing business/financial model.
- Utilizing the existing assets more efficiently to increase revenue without additional infra.

DOI: 10.4324/9781003319948-2

- Preparing for the staffing requirement, organizing training, and licensing/certification.
- Ordering of aircraft, the decision about fleet mix schedule, resource allocation plan for efficient utilization, replacement, or major repair of aircraft.
- Major repairs to airport infrastructure.

The more detailed the analysis, the more accurate the projections will be, especially in the short term.

For the medium to longer term, forecasts provide an essential guide to airport planners as to when additional airport infrastructure may be required. Still, they must have regular reviews and adjustments, as necessary, to reflect any unexpected changes in market conditions.

Overestimation of the traffic will result in asset creation at a considerable capital expenditure (capex) and operational expenditure, which will impact the financials.

Underestimation means lost opportunity, which competitors may utilize or impact the service level if the throughput exceeds capacity.

Air traffic forecast is used by all aviation stakeholders, viz. airlines, airports primarily and then MRO, Fuel suppliers, GHA, cargo operators, Freight forwarders, Financial Institutions, aircraft manufacturers, aircraft leasing companies, staffing agencies, tours and travels, and training organizations.

To raise capital, as the project is based on the forecast, the forecast methodology and the results must be validated and justified, defended with valid arguments. Therefore, scenario basis i.e. low, high, and base case is the norm and base case is considered for the business viability. But the business impact on low case and the upside on the high case are to be evaluated to better prepare for such situations.

The effort required to produce a planning forecast will vary significantly from airport to airport. Considerable effort, including elaborate forecasting tools and techniques, may be warranted in the case of more complex projects. On the other hand, a more cursory update of an existing forecast may be all that is required for simpler projects. Planners should determine the appropriate level of forecasting effort during the pre-planning and scoping of the study.

The forecast can be done on the short-term, medium-term, or long-term, say 5 years, 10–15, and more than 15 years. Even this may be different for, say, airports and airlines. Short-term forecast is typically more accurate than the long term. However, business prospects based on long-term forecasts are more relevant.

Data sources

Regardless of the forecasting method used, the forecasting process examines past aviation activity patterns and other information and attempts to predict future activity based on past activity patterns. Thus, all forecasting efforts begin with gathering data about past aviation activity and additional information about the airport's market that the forecaster may find helpful in predicting future aviation activity. The following data sources are often tapped to prepare forecast information:

- Airport records.
- Socioeconomic data.
- Flight activity data.
- Passenger surveys by airlines and airports– short and medium terms.
- Aeroplane manufacturers – Region-wise, sometimes specific to a country. However, this will be for a long-term, say 20 years, with growth in %.

- IATA.
- ACI.
- ICAO.
- Airports authorities like the Airports Authority of India prepare airport-wise forecasts on short and medium terms.
- Government statistic departments based on GDP or other economic factors.

Forecasting methods

The methods could be categorized broadly as quantitative and qualitative. If past traffic data is available, the most used is the quantitative type to forecast future traffic. For example, time series data of actual past traffic can be used to forecast future traffic, assuming the trend and pattern of the past data will continue. Another method using past traffic data is to find the independent variables that have contributed to the past traffic numbers. Once that is known, regression analysis is carried out to confirm that these independent variables are significant to the dependent variable, i.e., the actual traffic numbers. After establishing the significance, the relationship form is found as linear, logarithmic, or exponential, and a suitable equation is obtained through regression. This equation is used for forecasting future traffic based on the estimated values of these independent variables in future, which will provide the traffic numbers for the future. The most used independent variable is the country's GDP. The method is based on a prediction of the independent variables; hence, the forecast accuracy depends on assessing the value of these parameters in the future. However, as an improvement to this regression type, the adjustment could be made for any specific factors for the traffic between two airports, like

- Routes that are not covered till now.
- New airports being developed or the congestion at the existing other airports.
- Impact due to regulatory approvals.
- Air service agreements.
- Discussions with airlines to understand their business plans, fleet procurement plan.
- Exchange rate variation.
- Aviation fuel price changes and others.

Gravity models assume that the air traffic between two points is proportional to the product of their populations and inversely proportional to the distance between them. Therefore, the traffic due to this factor can be used as add-on traffic to the forecast obtained through other models.

The qualitative method is used if the historical traffic data is unavailable. Theoretically, qualitative methods are experts' analysis and inputs, market research, and Delphi techniques.

Sometimes even if the historical data is available and if it is an emerging market where the potential is not fully explored may be for many reasons, such as inadequacy of infrastructure, the forecast can be developed by analysing the existing weekly traffic and identifying the domestic and international routes that are currently being operated, its frequency, and the number of airline carriers, and then carry out market research and identify the following:

- Possible increase in frequency progressively in the next 10–30 years.
- The routes that are not being served presently can be included in the forecast.
- The aeroplane fleet mix operating as of now and how these could change in the future with higher seating capacity aircraft.
- The population using other modes of transport like road or rail and their origin and destination and how some portion of these could be converted as air passengers.

Also, a SWOT analysis of the existing airport/location can identify the weaknesses which could be removed, and opportunities utilized.

Data collected in collaboration with Government, industries, and tourism organizations, the development plan for the city will also provide inputs to the traffic growth potential.

Even in quantitative techniques, it is the practice that some of the above-mentioned qualitative inputs are taken and considered along with the traffic growth projected through, say, regression analysis.

Some aspects of the forecast

Forecasts based on aggregated data have better accuracy than disaggregated datasets since they have lesser variance and a lesser random component. However, sometimes it is better to use disaggregated data, especially in the growing aviation market, as a prediction on an overall market basis may miss some regions' traffic potential. In the matured market, the aggregated forecast on a broad basis may work better.

Data with more frequency gives better prediction accuracy, and such data requires to be updated.

The short-term forecast and action taken can maximize revenue without building new infrastructure, utilize existing assets more effectively, and detect potential untapped traffic.

Choosing a fleet mix, flight schedule, major aircraft repairs, significant airport infrastructure improvements, planning for the need for additional staff, organizing training, and licence and certification are all decisions made in the medium term.

Aircraft orders, resource allocation plans, funding infrastructure, analysing business prospects, and financial modelling all benefit from a focus on the long term.

Short-term forecasts are more accurate than medium or long term, but long-term forecasts are required for business purposes.

Forecasting is by no means an exact science. As argued by de Neufville, Odoni, Belobaba, and Reynolds 'any forecast of phenomena involving people is inherently unreliable and likely to be wrong'. This means that total accuracy is impossible, and some degree of uncertainty must be expected.

Forecast based on analysis of time series data

Time series data is a sequence of data observed or being observed at a specific time interval. For example, the time interval could be weekly, monthly, quarterly, or yearly. These past data are analysed to forecast future values. Hence, the time series is time-dependent, and the dataset is univariate, meaning there can be only one variable: the passenger numbers in the traffic forecast. In contrast, the regression analysis method can utilize multivariate data sets, which are explained later in this chapter.

Forecasting using time series can be done by Moving Averages (MAs), exponential smoothing, and autoregression.

Time series data can be decomposed as:

1 **Level.** The baseline value for the series is if it were a straight line.
2 **Trend.** The series' optional and often linear increasing or decreasing behaviour over time.

3 **Seasonality.** The optional repeating patterns or cycles of behaviour over time.
4 **Noise**. The optional variability in the observations the model cannot explain.

All-time series will have a level, most have noise, and the trend and seasonality are optional. The key features of many time series are trends and seasonal variations. Another essential feature of most time series is that observations close together in time tend to be correlated (serially dependent).

Figure 2.1 shows a data set that is non-stationary.

Figure 2.2 shows a data set that is stationary.

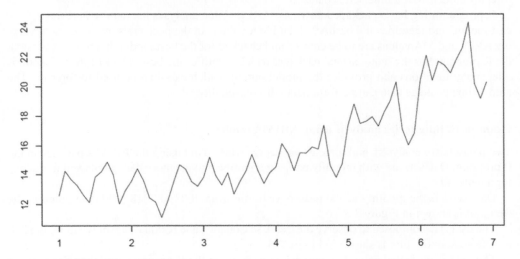

Figure 2.1 Plot of non-stationary data

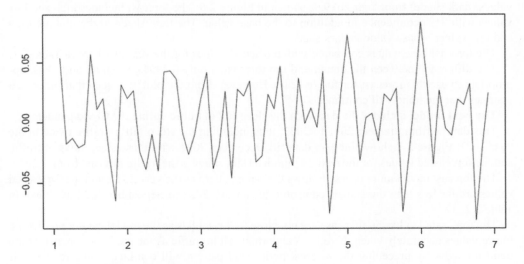

Figure 2.2 Plot of stationary data

Models using ARMA and ARIMA methods

Combining Auto-Regressive (AR) method and Moving Average MA method is known as ARMA. From the ARMA model, another one called ARIMA is created, including I, which is the differencing. Thus, combining AR, I, and MA are called ARIMA. ARIMA is a forecasting algorithm based on the idea that the information in the past values of the time series can alone be used to predict future values.

Model evaluation using the ARIMA method manually is complex and time-consuming to get the best model. However, programming packages like python or R can be used to create a forecast model from a time series dataset.

R programming has a package known as 'ARIMA' that analyses the data set, creates a forecast model, and identifies the best AR, I, and MA values. In the package's initial version, varying AR, I, and MA values are to be entered and checked for the best model. In the latest version, the R program has the 'auto. arima' package, which identifies the best values of these functions after many iterations and provides the model output, which can then be used to forecast. The auto. arima package also can perform data with seasonality.

Example of time series analysis using ARIMA model

Two datasets are analysed, and forecast values are worked out using the ARIMA package in the R program. Datasets are with monthly passenger numbers to get more data points and frequency for a better fit.

Data set 1 is the monthly actual passenger traffic from 2003 to 2018 (192 data points). The data plot is shown in Figure 2.3.

The data is decomposed to observe the trend, seasonality, and residuals as shown in Figure 2.4.

The seasonality plot is shown in Figure 2.5.

The data is modelled using the auto arima package in the R program, and then the forecast for January 2019 to February 2020 is obtained through the program. The plot, including forecast values (dark shade) from Year 2019, is shown in Figure 2.6. The forecast includes high and low values with 95% confidence in addition to the base value. The light shade in the plot are high and low values – base value in dark shade.

The forecast base values compared with the actual values for the year 2019 are in Table 2.1.

The difference between the actual and the forecast is only 0.299%, so small and, thus, appropriate to use this forecast for future years. However, from the plot, it is seen that the model assumes that the trend will continue.

The next model includes the data with the steep fall in traffic during the Covid pandemic.

This data is from the year 2011 to 2021, thus including the steep fall in traffic twice in the year 2021. Figure 2.7 shows the pax data till December 2021 with these steep lows in traffic and the forecasted values for the next 24 months. Dark shade is the traffic forecast from Y 2022.

The forecast model more or less follows the same pattern as the year 2021, and the forecasted values are far less than the actuals compared to January 2022 to September 2022 as shown in Table 2.2.

The forecasted values in this case are not close to the actuals as the model cannot predict the future values accurately when there is an abnormal fall in traffic as the model assumes that the trend immediately preceding the forecast period and pattern will continue in future. Thus, if there is no steep increase or fall in the actual values, the forecast model based on time series analysis works well.

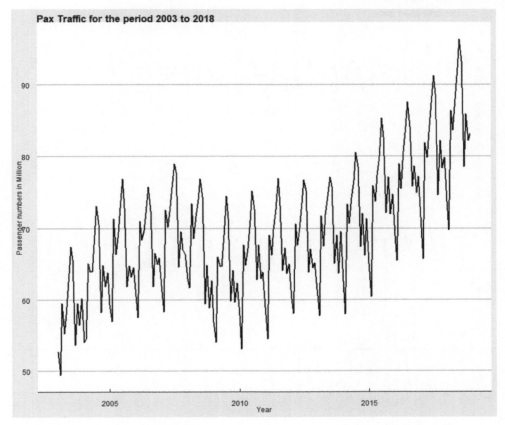

Figure 2.3 Monthly data of passengers

Causal method and regression analysis

Regression analysis is about studying one dependent variable (in this case, passenger traffic) and one or more independent variables (GDP, airfare, aviation fuel price, and population). First, independent variable (s) is chosen, which would have significance or a relationship to the dependent variable, and regression is carried out with the past traffic data.

The regression equation is the relationship between the dependent and independent variable(s) and can be linear, logarithmic, or exponential. The simplest form is a linear relationship with an equation as

$$Y = \beta 0 + \beta 1 X + u$$

where Y is dependent variable, $\beta 0$ is intercept, $\beta 1$ is Slope, X is the independent variable, and u is the error or residuals.

The exponential equation may take the form.

$$Y = A*(X)^B$$

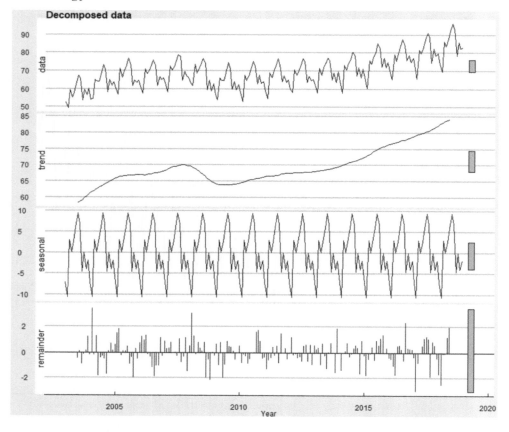

Figure 2.4 Decomposed dataset

where Y is the dependent variable, A is a constant, X is the independent variable, and B is the elasticity of the independent variable.

Natural Log Y = Natural Log A + B* (natural log X)

In this case, A is the intercept, and X is the independent variable. Elasticity is the ratio of the percent change in the independent variable to the percent change in the dependent variable. It is expected that a 1% change in the independent variable need not result in a 1% change in the dependent variable; it could be different.

Log Natural (Pax numbers) = Constant (that is the intercept) + slope (B) * Natural Log of GDP.

For future traffic forecasts, the natural log of GDP forecasted in that year is required to get the traffic numbers in log form, which must be converted to a number using inverse log.

In the time series model, the data is univariate, which is only one variable against a period, monthly or weekly, quarterly, or yearly. The assumption in the analysis and forecast was that the past values are the basis for future values, and the trend and pattern will continue. However, it would be of interest to evaluate the reasons behind the past traffic trend and patterns so that the forecasts for the future period can be more realistic.

That is the basis of the regression analysis wherein relevant independent variables which have an association with the passenger traffic growth in the past are found. In the regression analysis,

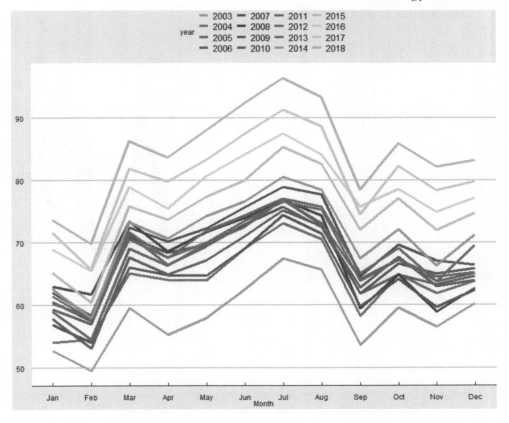

Figure 2.5 Plot showing the seasonality of the data

it is essential to find the strength of the relationship between the independent variable(s) (for example, GDP) and the dependent variable (traffic). In addition, there are tests to check the overall significance of the regression model statistically.

Such independent variables could be more than one. Regression analysis output will enable us to determine how much variation of a dependent variable (s) is explained by the independent variable(s). If it is statistically insignificant, then some other predictor variable(s) will be chosen. If significant, that model can be used to predict the future values using the regression equation with estimated future values of the independent variables.

Example of the forecast using regression analysis

The data set is of the yearly passenger traffic from 1995 to 2019, avoiding the steep low traffic in Y 2020 due to the pandemic. The dependent variable is passenger traffic. Independent variables considered are:

• Only GDP (Single variable).
• GDP and Inflation (Two variables).
• GDP, Inflation, and Product of GDP & Inflation (Three variables).

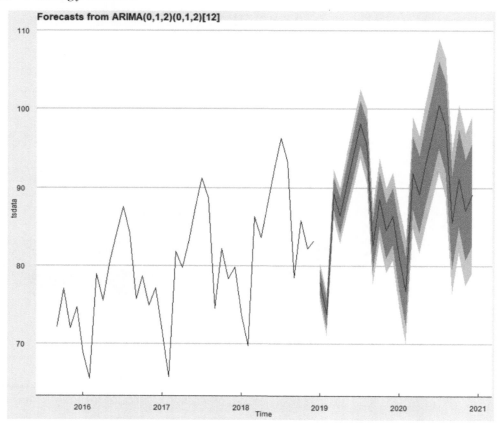

Figure 2.6 Forecasted values using ARIMA model

Table 2.1 Actual passenger and forecasted values

	Actual passenger numbers	*Forecasted values*
01-01-2019	76,725,079	77,884,127
01-02-2019	71,960,017	73,821,673
01-03-2019	90,530,076	89,269,682
01-04-2019	86,957,958	86,464,681
01-05-2019	92,359,258	90,489,355
01-06-2019	95,537,871	94,295,896
01-07-2019	99,189,775	98,209,383
01-08-2019	95,968,379	95,371,892
01-09-2019	82,833,675	82,632,016
01-10-2019	88,919,490	88,558,566
01-11-2019	82,402,530	84,594,097
01-12-2019	89,597,073	86,366,745
01-01-2020	80,594,291	80,953,131
01-02-2020	75,708,828	76,755,686
Total	**1,209,284,300**	**1,205,666,930**

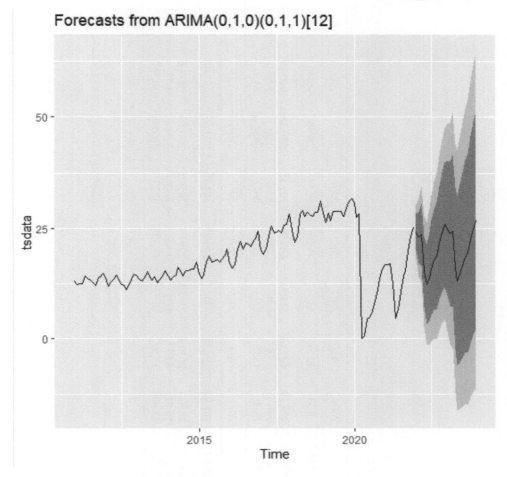

Figure 2.7 Forecasted values considering steep fall in traffic

Table 2.2 Actual passenger and forecasted values

	Actual	*Forecasted*
01-04-2022	24.34	11.19
01-05-2022	26.85	17.322
01-06-2022	25.28	18.11
01-07-2022	23.94	20.99
01-08-2022	24.68	23.31
01-09-2022	24.94	25.15
Total	150.03	116.072

Regression analysis using the three independent variables will give three results and explain how to choose the best among the three.

Table 2.3 shows the dependent and three independent variables.

Regression analysis was carried out as a first step with single, two, and three variables. The correlation between the variables is shown in Figure 2.8.

Table 2.3 Dependent and three independent variables

Year	1995	1996	1997	1998	1999	2000	2001	2002	2003	2004	2005	2006	2007
Passenger numbers in million	34.63	35.25	35.25	35.33	35.88	38.33	42.51	43.71	48.69	59.54	78.30	96.40	116.89
GDP	360.28	392.90	415.87	421.35	458.82	468.39	485.44	514.94	607.70	709.15	820.38	940.26	1216.74
Inflation	10.22	8.98	7.16	13.23	4.67	4.01	3.78	4.30	3.81	3.77	4.25	5.80	6.37
Multiplicative	3684	3527	2979	5575	2143	1878	1835	2213	2313	2672	3484	5450	7754

Year	2008	2009	2010	2011	2012	2013	2014	2015	2016	2017	2018	2019
Passenger numbers in million	108.88	123.8	143.43	159.6	159.4	169.03	190.13	223.61	264.97	308.75	344.69	341.05
GDP	1198.9	1341.9	1675.6	1823.0	1827.6	1856.7	2039.1	2103.6	2294.8	2651.5	2702.9	2831.6
Inflation	8.35	10.88	11.99	8.91	9.48	10.02	6.67	4.91	4.95	3.33	3.94	3.73
Multiplicative	10,010	14,603	20,090	16,247	17,324	18,600	13,592	10,322	11,355	8825	10,646	10,560

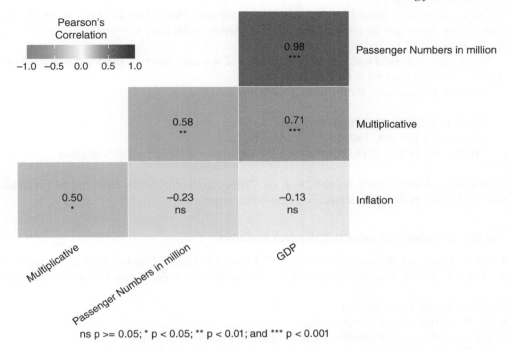

ns p >= 0.05; * p < 0.05; ** p < 0.01; and *** p < 0.001

Figure 2.8 Correlation matrix

Table 2.4 Regression analysis output with three independent variables

	GDP only (model 1)	GDP and inflation (model 2)	GDP, inflation, and product of GDP and inflation (model 3)
R squared value	0.960	0.970	0.9921
Adjusted R squared value	0.958	0.968	0.9909
Standard error	20.39	17.899	9.518
Significance of independent variables	Significant	Both GDP and inflation are significant individually as well as jointly	All the three variables are significant independently as well as jointly
Coefficients for equation			
Intercept	−22.99	2.139	−41.214
GDP	0.118	0.1169	0.153
Inflation	NA	−3.44	4.1625
GDP*inflation	NA	NA	−0.00652

It is seen from the correlation matrix that except for inflation, the other two variables have a significant correlation. Therefore, in the regression output, the p-value of inflation will be examined along with the overall significance of the variables. If jointly the independent variables are significant, the variables can be considered. The regression output parameters between the three-regression analysis are summarized in Table 2.4.

R^2 is the coefficient of determination. Its value lies between 0 and 1. Zero indicates the dependent variable variation cannot be explained by the independent variable, and 1 means 100%

of the variation is explained by the independent variable; thus, close to 100% is better. The above table shows that the regression analysis in model 3 with three independent variables best fits the data.

Some more statistical tests can be carried out, like standard error. To shorten the description, it is assumed that model 3 is the best fit.

The forecast equations for the three models are as below.

Model 1 (−22.99 + 0.118*GDP)
Model 2 (2.139 + 0.1169*GDP − 3.44* Inflation)
Model 3 (−41.21 + 0.153*GDP + 4.6125* Inflation − 0.00652* GDP*Inflation)

Traffic forecast for the years beyond 2019, i.e., 2020, can be obtained by inputting the predicted GDP and inflation for 2020, similarly, in the future years.

Another iteration with more independent variables

In the next iteration, the yearly passenger traffic from 1995 to 2021 includes the low traffic in Y 2020 and Y 2021. In this case, four models were created with independent variables as follows:

- Only GDP (Single variable).
- GDP and Inflation (Two variables).
- GDP, Inflation, and Product of GDP & Inflation (Three variables).
- GDP, Inflation, Product of GDP& inflation, GDP^2 & $Inflation^2$ (Five variables).

The regression output of these four models is summarized in Table 2.5.

Table 2.5 shows that the best model is model 4, with nearly 90% of the variation in passenger traffic can be explained by the five independent variables, and the standard error is also less. The equation for the best model is as below.

−83.527 + (0.364 multiplied with GDP) − (9.968 multiplied with inflation) − (0.01576 multiplied with the product of GDP and Inflation) − (5.801 multiplied with GDP^2 multiplied with 10^{-5}) + (1.3559 multiplied with $Inflation^2$).

Future years' traffic forecast is obtained by inputting the predicted GDP and inflation for these years. For example, assuming that for the year 2022, the GDP is 3395 and inflation is 3%, the forecasted traffic for 2022 will be 305 million.

(−83.527 + 0.364*3395) − (9.968*3) − (0.01576*3395*3) − (5.801*3395*3395*10^{-5}) + (1.355*3*3)

If the inflation is assumed to be 3.5% and GDP is 3395 for 2022, then the forecast for 2022 is 278.52 million.

The purpose of explaining various models is to impress upon the necessity to analyse the models with all the relevant independent variables. This will enable the planners to choose the appropriate forecasting model.

Choosing independent variables

The most popular and extensively used predictor variable is GDP, as many analyses have shown that passenger traffic and GDP have relationships. Also, from the example discussed, we can consider GDP, inflation, and other independent variables like air ticket fare, aviation/crude oil price, and GDP/capita, provided such variables are statistically significant to the dependent variable.

Table 2.5 Regression analysis output with five independent variables

	GDP only (model 1)	GDP & Inflation (model 2)	GDP, inflation and product of GDP and inflation (model 3)	GDP, inflation, product of GDP and inflation, GDP2 and inflation2 (model 4)
R squared value	0.789	0.799	0.829	0.9186
Adjusted R squared value	0.780	0.7828	0.8068	0.899
Standard error	45.42	45.20	42.63	30.78
Statistical significance of independent variables	Significant	GDP is significant. Inflation is not. However, jointly both are significant.	GDP is significant. Inflation and the third variable are not. However, jointly all the three are significant.	GDP and GDP^2 and product of GDP and inflation are significant. Inflation and inflation^2 are not. However, jointly all the five variables are significant.
Coefficients for equation				
Intercept	−2.0661	23.18	−28.1088	−83.527
GDP	0.096488	0.0929	0.135742	0.364
Inflation	NA	−3.4422	5.500	−9.968
GDP*inflation	NA	NA	−0.00763	−0.01576
GDP^2	NA	NA	NA	−5.801E-05
Inflation^2	NA	NA	NA	1.3559

The independent variables included in the model and their precise values influence the accuracy of the regression analysis model for future values. Furthermore, for the dependent variable's future projection (in this case, pax numbers) to be accurate, the model's equation relies on the independent variables' future values (for example, GDP and inflation). This means that to forecast the passenger traffic forecast for the next ten years, the GDP and inflation values for the next ten years are to be predicted based on reliable sources. However, the actual passenger numbers depend on the actual values of the independent variables (GDP and Inflation). Suppose the actual values of the independent variables are lower than the predicted values; for example, the actual GDP is less than that considered for the forecast. In that case, the actual traffic will be less than the forecast, and in that case, the forecast is considered overestimated. Similarly, forecast passenger numbers will be underestimated if the actual GDP value exceeds the assumed values while forecasting the traffic. Whereas inflation is inversely proportional to the traffic forecast, more inflation leads to less traffic and vice versa.

Also, some other independent variables could become significant in these ten years. Thus, it is required to review the actual traffic and compare it with the forecast every quarter, ascertain the reasons for the variation, and modify the forecast numbers.

Independent variables for passenger segments

In the example, GDP and inflation are considered independent variables. The data set has international and domestic traffic together, and the assumption was that the GDP is valid for both international and domestic passenger numbers. Another way of analysing is the traffic forecast in two parts with two sets of independent variables, one for domestic and one for international passenger traffic. Country's GDP for domestic traffic and World GDP for international traffic.

Another option for international traffic forecast, in this case, is to analyse past international traffic, identify the country of origin for most of the traffic, and apply the GDP of that respective country. For example, the international passenger traffic forecast could include the mixed value of the GDP of the countries served by the airport.

Other independent variables

Also, aviation turbine fuel prices can be considered an independent variable and tested for their significance. Another option could be to use variables very specific to the country to conduct a regression to see the significance or otherwise of the variables. For example, in airports with a majority of tourism traffic, like, Maldives, such analysis may be helpful instead of choosing variable values for all the countries.

Scenario-based traffic forecast

The forecasted passenger numbers by the method above are the base scenario, with which the business analysis can commence. As the forecast with all the models is based on past traffic numbers, we could analyse the impact on the forecast numbers, positive as well as negative, due to some of the factors mentioned below.

(i) Regulatory requirements in the country, (ii) air services agreement, (iii) exchange rate fluctuations like USD to local currency, (iv) increase or fall in oil prices, (v) political factors, (vi) feedback from airlines and tourism industry, (vii) overall global aviation market forecast, and (viii) routes served at present.

However, it is a practice to identify the upside and downside of the traffic numbers due to either there is a probability that values of the assumed independent variables may change or certain factors which are not considered in the base forecast but may happen in the forecasted period (being long term), and these may impact the traffic projections. If the impact of such analysis is significant, the forecast needs to consider such factors. If the impact is negative, the traffic forecasted numbers will be less than the base case, and if they have a positive impact, the numbers will be more than the forecasted values. Thus, the forecast will arrive at three scenarios – base, low, and high.

The traffic forecast in near terms after a drastic traffic fall, like during the SARS outbreak, economic slowdown, or the Covid-19 pandemic, will be a challenging as recovery period depends on many factors and may differ between the regions. In these situations, region-wise assessment based on several factors is required. Therefore, airports must save the data during normal and non-normal periods with hourly passenger traffic, aircraft movements, fleet mix and routes served, and load factor, among others.

Assessment of traffic potential

How to evaluate the traffic potential and how much of it is untapped. In any market, the present number of air trips per person and expected numbers in the future are good indicators of how much business and leisure travellers will want to fly. If there is a scope for significant air transport growth, the sooner we need safe, efficient airports, reliable transportation and communication networks around airports, and other types of aviation infrastructure. Knowing how the tendency to fly might change in different markets helps forecasters to predict traffic growth, and the industry can plan accordingly. 'Propensity to fly' is the parameter that can be used to identify the potential for traffic growth. The propensity to fly depends on factors like the economic health of the population, demographic changes, competition among airlines (more LCC carriers), hub-type airports, and a large immigration population.

For example, India's propensity to fly was 0.06 trips per capita, relatively low compared to some peer nations (e.g., Vietnam's propensity to fly 4× higher). Another term for the traffic potential assessment is 'resident trips' per country. Resident trip equals propensity to fly multiplied by the population. As per the report, by 2042, China will be the market with the most significant number of resident trips displacing the United States. The emerging markets are India, Philippines, Indonesia, and Russia, where resident trips are expected to increase significantly by 2042. (PwC report)

In some cases, like an island nation with limited land available, the number of hotel beds will be a constraint, which must be considered in the analysis, even though there could be unlimited traffic potential.

The top-down approach and bottom-up approach

Air traffic forecasting is more than just analysing past data and preparing and applying appropriate models. The airports need to understand the air passengers' preferences that may give inputs to the routes to be included. Airports evaluate their performance in capacity utilization, de-peaking of the traffic to utilize the facilities evenly in a day to the extent possible, and so on.

Airports can understand (i) the airlines' strategy for route development, (ii) actual load factors for various routes, and (iii) airlines' current fleet mix and their augmentation plans. Such studies will help airports to evaluate the additional traffic that are possible through the airport and included in the traffic forecast with reasonable assumptions.

Sensitivity analysis of the forecast

A simple model with a minimum number of independent variables statistically significant to the dependent variable is better than a complicated model for aviation forecast. However, since there are many uncertainties and assumptions in deriving the forecast, as already briefed it is an industry practice to prepare the forecast on three scenarios viz low (some downsides of the assumptions), base case (based on all assumptions come true) and the high case (some upsides of the assumptions). However, the business case is prepared with base case scenario numbers, and feasibility is examined. Then, sensitivity analysis with the other two scenarios, the especially low case, is reviewed to evaluate the possible financial impact and mitigation if it happens at all.

Outputs of the traffic forecast

- Number of years of forecast.
- Annual Passenger numbers for each year.
- Annual Air Traffic Movement (ATM) year wise.
- Peak-hour passenger numbers year wise.
- Peak-hour ATM numbers year wise.
- Aircraft fleet mix.
- Annual pax numbers and annual ATM numbers for low and high-case scenarios.

Utilization of the traffic forecast

Greenfield airport

Traffic forecast shows the annual passenger numbers and says, it reaches 40 million passengers in 40 years. Accordingly, the airport capacity is planned for 40 million passengers per annum. The traffic forecast may also include the annual aircraft movements, known as Air Traffic Movements (ATM), for the 40 million passengers. The ATM from the passenger traffic is derived as explained here. The traffic forecast would have identified the proportion of domestic and international passenger numbers. Also, the forecast will identify the origin and destination of the international sectors to estimate the narrow-body vs. wide-body aircraft. Let us assume the following.
Domestic traffic = 30 million and International traffic = 10 million.
Assuming the following

Fleet mix- Narrow body = 70%, Seating capacity 210, 70% load factor for domestic and 85% for international

Wide body = 30%: Seating capacity = 300, 85% load factor for international

Based on the above assumptions, the annual movement of aircraft can be calculated as shown below

Domestic = Passenger numbers/(aircraft seating capacity * load factor) = 205,000 app

International (10% narrow body and remaining wide body) = 10/10*1,000,000/ (0.1*210*0.85 + 0.9*300*.85) = 10*1,000,000/(17.85 + 229.5) = 40,428

Total ATM = 205,000 + 40,428 = 245,428 say 250,000

Thus, the annual pax number is 40 million, and the annual ATM is 250,000

Assessment of land area requirement

The planning framework starts with the number of runways required, as the runway length and minimum distance between the runways are the critical dimensions for the airport land assessment. The factors that determine the runway length is described in the subsequent chapter. While assessing the suitable site for airport planning, with little data, it is possible to assume the runway length from an existing airport in the region operating with similar most demanding aircraft operations, subject to modification for site elevation if required.

The factors that determine the runway capacity along with some indicative numbers with guidelines of ICAO/FAA are explained in the subsequent chapter.

It is usual to consider the land requirement for a minimum of two runways. The land requirement for a two-runway airport is an example with dimensions that need to be calculated to determine the length and width of the required land shown in the figure. The layout in Figure 2.9 shows two runways, two parallel taxiways per runway, aprons, and PTBs.

In the above layout, it is to be noted that the dimensions b, c, d, e, and f, similarly b1, c1, d1, e1, and f1 are to comply with the separation distances as per SARPs (minimum specified, which the planners may increase if required). Dimensions 'a' and 'a1' may be different; it depends on whether any facilities are to be located beyond the runway to the boundary. Dimensions

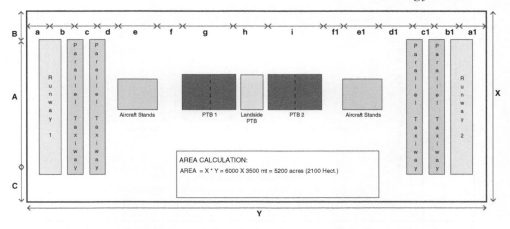

Figure 2.9 Layout with two runways, two parallel taxiways and apron

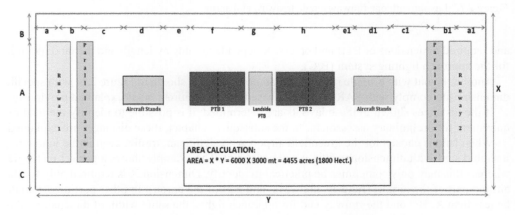

Figure 2.10 Layout with two runways, single parallel taxiway, and apron

'g', 'h', and 'i' will be decided based on the PTB area and landside area requirement. One way of quickly calculating Y is fixing the separation distances between the runways and checking whether the facilities in between the runways can be accommodated. Practice shows that if this distance is 2600 m, there will be much flexibility to accommodate the facilities, especially the orientation of the PTB, as shown. There could be many options for the orientation of the PTB together with the apron. Thus, dimension Y is dependent on the separation distance between the runways and the orientation of the PTB and apron. In comparison, dimension X depends on the length of the runway and the length (B/C) required for the approach lighting system.

The layout and the area mentioned are only for illustration. This is one of the many ways to work out a layout considering minimum separation distances between them as prescribed in SARPs.

Can a three-runway layout possible? Yes, provided the separation distances between the runways are reworked to have various modes of operations (discussed in the subsequent chapter), and the detailed working of other facilities is required. For example, airports have three runways on 5200-acre land.

Like the above, a layout with one parallel taxiway per runway is shown in Figure 2.10. In this case, dimension Y can be finalized if the separation distances between the runways are decided

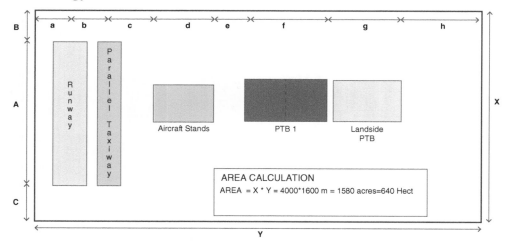

Figure 2.11 Layout with one runway, single taxiway, and apron

and required dimensions of PTB and others. X depends on runway length and the land required for the approach lighting system (B/C).

Another layout with a single runway and other facilities is shown in Figure 2.11 with specific dimensions to comply with SARPs and rest based on the requirement as explained previously.

If the distances shown in these layouts are determined, it is possible to identify the land requirement for preliminary assessment. In the subsequent chapter, these distances are explained.

When land is chosen for the greenfield airport with significant traffic, even in the long term, it should start with dimensions without any constraint. The example shows a perfect rectangle, whereas this may only sometimes be practical to identify. Dimension X is required only for the airfield part of the airport (runway, taxiways, and part of the apron). In other portions, it could be less than X. Beyond the runway end for approach lights, the same width of dimension 'a' is optional, as explained in the subsequent chapter.

Suppose there is a constraint in land availability, it is preferable to identify the land requirement for airside and landside facilities, which are all 'must requirements' for an airport and separately, other area requirements which are need-based and assessed. If the land availability is limited for commercial development, the 'project's financial viability may suffer, and this aspect is to be examined. Or part of the land can be acquired for the initial phase and the remaining land later. These could be one of the parameters for choosing the best site among many alternatives.

It is not only the dimension, but the runway orientation depends on many factors, the first and foremost being the wind direction. Therefore, when choosing the possible sites for the airport, one can consider the runway orientation of the nearest airport if the wind pattern is not readily available.

It is also explained in the master planning chapter the necessity to consider the ultimate master plan to protect the areas outside the airport boundary to clear any obstruction when the airport is taken for development with ultimate master planning facilities.

Can we reduce the distance between the runways to less than ideal? Yes, it can be reduced after examining the layout to fit in all the facilities and analyzingthe throughput capacity.

In the framework, looking at the land requirement/ways to add capacity beyond the forecast period when the traffic will be more than the forecasted numbers is a good practice.

Some examples of airports with a single runway and two runways

Single runway airports

There are two prominent airports – Gatwick Airport and Mumbai Airport. They handled more than 300,000 annual ATMs and close to 47 million annual passengers in Y 2019.

Two parallel runways airports

- Munich airport, with a separation distance of approximately 2300 m between the runways, handled close to 48 million passengers in Y 2019.
- With a separation distance of approximately 390 m between the runways, Manchester airport handled close to 30 million passengers in Y 2019. The runways are staggered.
- With a separation distance of approximately 2100 m between the runways, Oslo Airport handled close to 29 million passengers in Y 2019. The runways are marginally staggered.
- With a separation distance of approximately 400 m between the runways, Dubai International Airport handled close to 86 million passengers in Y 2019. The runways are staggered.

Airports with three runways

Kuala Lumpur Airport, with a separation distance of more than 2100 m between the runways, handled close to 62 million passengers in Y 2019

- With distances of close to 2000 m and 1600 m between the three runways, Beijing Capital International Airport handled 100 million passengers in Y 2019.
- Singapore Changi Airport added a third runway recently. The distance between two old parallel runways is app 1700 m, and it handled 68.28 million pax in Y 2019 with two runways in operation.
- Hong Kong Airport also added a third runway recently; the distance between two old parallel runways is app 1600 m, and it handled 71.42 million pax in Y 2019 with two runways in operation.

It is to be noted that the annual passenger handled is not directly proportional to the number of runways. For example, airports with more wide-body aircraft may operate fewer flights to achieve passenger numbers due to higher passenger capacity per aircraft. Conversely, an airport handling with the same passenger numbers with a narrow-body and turboprop aircraft will have higher aircraft movements. Thus, the possible number of aircraft movements in a runway system and the fleet mix decide the number of passengers that can be handled.

For preliminary planning, we can assume 300,000 annual aircraft movements with a single runway and a fleet mix with fewer turboprop aircraft, more narrow body, and some percentage of wide-body aircraft. This can result in 40–50 million passengers per annum. However, we should note that such a high volume of passengers with a single runway means zero contingency if the single runway is non-operational, even for routine maintenance, not to mention major repairs. For this purpose, practically any airport handling more than 20–30 million passengers per annum and in growth mode should plan for a standby runway. Thus, greenfield airport planning should cater for a minimum of two runways and preferably a third runway which can be planned with optimum land requirements.

The planning framework so far consists of two aspects. *First, the traffic forecast with annual passengers in, say next 40–50 years. Second is assessing the land area required to cater to forecasted traffic, primarily driven by airfield requirements.*

Identification of suitable site

The next planning requirement is to identify four or more locations/sites where such an extent of land can be made available. The following are the major parameters to be evaluated between the chosen sites.

- Identify the length and width of the sites and choose the sites which can accommodate the runways in the desired direction. Drop the sites which do not meet these criteria. Among the selected sites, create a matrix to compare the following features/evaluation of the sites.
- Identify site-wise the extent of landowners. If the Government owns most of the land for a site, it gets easier and more cost-effective for the land availability. Existing land usage includes agriculture, residential units, and factories.
- Identify the extent of relocation of existing facilities within the site chosen and approximately estimate the compensation for relocation of these facilities.
- Carry out a broad obstacle survey in and around the sites to ensure no major structures or buildings. If exists, the feasibility of relocating them and the relocation cost is to be estimated.
- Assess the existing communities and infrastructure sensitive to noise, such as schools, hospitals, a bird sanctuary, and the like, near the proposed site.
- Distance from the nearest airports and a preliminary assessment of air space restrictions, if any.
- Nearest defence airfield, if any, and their views about the proposed airport.
- Carry out a preliminary environmental assessment.
- Cityside assessment for the vehicular traffic to the city or main catchment area.
- Overall planning of the city development by the local Government.
- Topography of the sites identifying the ground profile variations.
- Soil bearing capacity of the sites.
- If the site being chosen is for the second airport for the city, the distance between the site and the existing airport, and the feasibility of a mass rapid transport system.
- Identify the area surrounding the airport free from restrictions- water bodies, sanctuary, tall structures, and natural elements like a hillock.
- Existing mass transport modes, rail or high-speed, dedicated road networks near the site shortlisted, or planned by the government to implement such schemes in future.

Comparing these major parameters for the chosen sites can lead to a maximum of two sites for the proposed airport. Among the chosen two sites, a pre-feasibility study, as described in the subsequent chapter, will enable us to select the best site for further planning.

Assessment by Air Navigation Services (ANS) providers

It is better to identify the requirement of ANS in consultation with the ANS providers and include it in the site/land assessment report. One of the critical aspects is the nearest airport in operation and its impact due to the proposed airport and the air space preliminary analysis considering the existing and proposed airports.

Brownfield development framework

The immediate focus will be the possibility of increasing capacity by improving the processes and use of updated technology. For long-term development for capacity enhancement, the first step would be to look at the approved master plan and examine if the development so far has happened as per this and, if not, the impact on the capacity addition. The approved master plan should also be reviewed to see the applicability of the same, considering present and near-future technology, Air Traffic Management practices and technology, passenger processes, and equipment. The airfield layout also requires a revisit as ICAO/Civil Aviation Authorities (CAAs) specifications are continually updated. Feedback and learnings from the operations will also be an input to the development planning. Evaluation of the obstacle limitation surfaces outside the airport is required due to additional infrastructures as per the master plan or current planning (if different than master planning). This is to ensure the surfaces are protected, and there is no violation. If there are violations and development happened affecting the surfaces, these are to be removed, or mitigation worked out before finalizing the plans for the additional infrastructures. Obstacle limitation surfaces are explained in Chapter 4.

If there is no land available for airfield capacity addition like another set of runway/taxiway systems, more so with the ideal distance between the runways, should explore all possible distances between the two runways with estimated capacities. Staggering of the runways is another option, explained in the subsequent chapter on capacity. Such a layout should also examine the capacity augmentation of the passenger terminal building and landside development, like vehicle parking spaces and access roads.

Suppose the area around the airport is fully developed and densely populated. In that case, identification of the minimum impact on the existing population and a cost and benefit analysis is required to decide on relocation of the existing affected communities. An environmental impact assessment and a new obstacle survey must also be carried out.

Greenfield airports will typically be developed away from the city and less populated areas, but then the population around the airport will increase over the years. Thus, one aspect is to be examined particularly in two scenarios, when land use planning was not strictly implemented or when the development was not planned previously and is considered now. Noise and air pollution due to increased aviation activities to the residents and noise-sensitive facilities like hospitals and educational institutions will have severe objections from the community.

Assessment of land for commercial development

One of the planning frameworks is to examine the feasibility of exploring all non-aeronautical activities by developing commercial facilities outside the passenger terminal building to enhance the financial viability and early return on investment. The dependence on aeronautical revenues could thus be reduced, as these are regulated and market-driven if not regulated. As a part of the planning framework, identifying the sources of such revenues through a market survey will enable the possible activities, which may be in phases, on a long-term basis. For this, it is essential to identify the demand and enablers of such a market. If sufficient time and data are available, this aspect could be included as a part of the selection criterion to improve the financial viability of the greenfield airport development. Greenfield airport construction will always be away from inhabited regions, but it is essential to know the business activities and access to the airport.

Approval process

Greenfield airports and the development of existing airports happen in developing countries. In-principle approval process of obtaining regulatory approval is a process adopted. However, the implementation of the development may differ between the Governments.

The Government of India, for example, has published a document titled 'Guidelines for setting up of Greenfield Airports'.

In India, the airport development process starts with the proposal submitted by the regional Government to the Central Government for getting project approval in principle, including the site identified. The proposal includes all the preliminary details of the site, as explained above, with traffic details to the Central Government, which constitutes a committee of members from relevant ministries for reviewing the proposal. Once the site identified is approved by the Central Government as suitable for establishing a new airport, the regional Government submits a detailed proposal of the airport to the Central Government, including a techno-economic study, mode of implementation like by the Government or through PPP model, implementation time. Once cleared by the Central Government, the regional Government initiates the process for implementation of the project through a competitive bid process. The Government initiated greenfield airport development starting with identifying land, as mentioned above by the Government. Once the project is approved, the methodology of the implementation, whether wholly by the Government or PPP model, is decided by the Government.

CAA, the Nation's Aviation Regulators, guides the brownfield airport development, primarily the airfield, and other relevant authorities if the development includes PTB. Prior Approval of such a proposal is required not only from the financing aspect but on technical aspects. Where there is an airport economic regulator, like in India, prior Approval of brownfield airport development is required to ensure that the capex is reasonable as the aeronautical charges are impacted by the capex. Also, a comprehensive consultation is carried out with all stakeholders regarding the expansion plan, and capacity enhancement envisaged. It is always a standard process to get the plans approved by the CAAs and the safety case while implementing the development. The safety case will assess the safety implications of developmental works on existing operations. Depending on the estimated safety index, mitigation measures are identified to avoid accidents/incidents.

Conclusion

Short, medium, and long-term air traffic forecasts are crucial for business continuity and capacity planning. Numerous approaches are utilized for traffic forecast, but none can accurately predict the future; hence, continuous monitoring of actual traffic is required to compare with projected traffic. As a result, the actual traffic volume may exceed or fall short of projections. The regression analysis approach employs numerous independent variables selected based on the airports/regions. Critical infrastructures/facilities are driven by demand. Therefore, the land required is determined based on the traffic demand and the separation distances between facilities, particularly the airfield layout, which must adhere to ICAO SARPs. A suitable location can be selected for a greenfield airport using appropriate selection criteria after evaluating the requisite land.

Assessment of land required for greenfield is based on:

- The most demanding aircraft based on traffic forecast.
- Runway length required.

- The number of runways and separation distance.
- The number of parallel taxiways.
- Minimum distances from runway centre line to fence and land required beyond the ends of the runways for approach lighting categories.

For brownfield airports, the assessment is based on a review of the existing master plan to see whether modifications would be required based on the actual traffic recorded with the aircraft type and learnings from operations. Also, it will have better visibility on future traffic growth and the necessary additional infrastructure. Stakeholder consultations also help to assess the impact on operations during the implementation, regulatory approvals required, safety assessment, and flight schedule impact.

The process for greenfield airport development may differ between Governments. However, whether it is greenfield or brownfield development, it requires clearance from applicable regulatory authorities. In addition, the brownfield airport development concept contains a safety case and implementation strategy to prevent accidents and incidents as the airport will be in operation during the implementation of the development.

Exercise

Choose any two airports, analyse the annual ATM numbers and Passenger numbers of statistics - for the last ten years, and find out pax per ATM for comparison between airports.

References

ACRP. (2010). *Airport passenger terminal planning and design*. Volume 1: Guidebook. https://doi. org/10.17226/22964

de Neufville, R., Odoni, A. R., Belobaba, P. P., & Reynolds, T. G. (2013). *Airport systems: Planning, design, and management*. New York: McGraw-Hill Education.

Morphet, H., & Bottini, C. (2013). Propensity to Fly in Emerging Economies: What Do the Trends Mean for Aviation Infrastructure Investment? 20–28. Paper published by PwC.

Solvoll, G., Mathisen, T. A., & Welde, M. (2020). Forecasting Air Traffic Demand for Major Infrastructure Changes. *Research in Transportation Economics*, 82 (November 2019), 100873. https://doi. org/10.1016/j.retrec.2020.100873

3 Airport capacity and planning

Introduction

Airport planners should know how to assess the airport's capacity and its determinants. Airfield layout planning plays a crucial role in airfield capacity, with the appropriate location of the airfield elements. Maximizing the PTB capacity is possible by designing the facilities for less than the peak passenger numbers subject to congestion within acceptable limits during these peak traffic periods. If the traffic forecast does not include the peak hour traffic, we can apply the rule of thumbs; practically, this is required during the in-principle approval of greenfield airport development when only high-level traffic numbers will be available. For Cargo facility capacity, we can apply rules of thumb during the preliminary evaluation of the project. In the case of brownfield airport development, past operational data will be available and based on which capacity augmentation planning is possible. Landside facilities shall also be planned to meet the airport's capacity. PTB capacity should enable achieving the Level of Service (LOS), for example defined in IATA ADRM. Various interventions can increase airport capacity.

Airport capacity

It is the ability of an airport to meet the demand. The airfield capacity will determine the airport's capacity in terms of the number of Air Traffic Movements (ATM) and the capacity of the Passenger Terminal Building (PTB) in terms of passenger numbers. The landside infrastructure, like approach roads and vehicle parking slots, shall match the passenger terminal capacity, and other aeronautical and commercial facilities use landside infrastructure. The description covers all the infrastructure that contributes to the capacity as these are to be understood as an airport planner.

The airfield capacity, primarily of the runway, determines the number of ATM it can handle. It can be specified for one hour and computed for one day and annually. For example, the runway capacity can be defined as 60 ATMs per hour or 900 ATM average per day or 300,000 ATMs annually. To handle 60 ATMs in one hour, other airfield infrastructure, including an adequate number of aircraft stands, should be planned and made available.

The terminal building capacity and the city-side facilities like access roads and car parks shall also be designed to match the airfield capacity.

Terminal building capacity is usually specified in million passengers per annum (mppa). For example, 70 mppa means this airport can handle 70 million passengers in one year.

The passenger traffic data published by the airports or capacity published in other documents will be in million passengers per annum, considering both airfield and passenger terminal

DOI: 10.4324/9781003319948-3

capacity. With the aggregated annual capacity, it will not be possible to decide the facilities and infrastructure required. For example, the planner needs the maximum number of ATMs estimated in a particular period, generally in one hour. With this maximum hourly traffic, it is possible to evaluate the requirement of the number of runways, number of parallel taxiways, entry/exit taxiways, and number of aircraft stands. Similarly, for a PTB, the number of maximum passengers estimated to pass through the processes in one hour is required to determine the number of processors needed for a particular waiting time and the necessary floor area to avoid congestion.

Theoretical airfield capacity

This theoretical capacity is based on many elements: infrastructure, aeroplane reference code, fleet mix, and operational procedures.

Airfield capacity, i.e., the number of ATMs that can be handled in **one hour**, depends on

1 Number of runways – if more than one, parallel or not.
2 Separation distances between multiple runways.
3 Availability of parallel taxiway.
4 Number of parallel taxiways for each runway.
5 Number of entry/exit taxiways from runway to parallel taxiway and their locations. Type of entry/exit taxiways – perpendicular or angled.
6 Number of runway holding positions.
7 Airfield layout with reference to other infrastructure, for example, PTB(s).
8 Aircraft fleet mix.
9 Air Traffic procedures.
10 Restriction, if any, in the air space.
11 Aircraft arrival/departure ratio.
12 Aircraft performance – Runway Occupancy Time (ROT), for example.
13 Mode of operations for parallel runways.

Out of all the above, SL No. 1 to 7 is for the airport planners to consider and SL No 8 to 13 is dependent on operations and not related to infrastructure planning.

Ways to quickly estimate the runway capacity on a preliminary basis

Capacities of the runway(s) can be calculated using the following documents, which provide guidelines.

1 FAA AC: l50/5060-5 – Airport capacity and delay provide capacities of the airfield based on the defined parameters. The capacities are annual as well as hourly capacity. For example, based on the fleet mix, per the AC's categorization, a single runway can handle a yearly ATM between 195,000 and 240,000. The hourly ATM can be between 51 and 98 in VFR and 50 and 59 in IFR.
2 ICAO airport planning manual (Doc 9184) provides theoretical capacities of various runway configurations in VFR and IFR operations. For example, it specifies a two-runway system with more than 1311 m separation distance annual ATM between 305,000 and 370,000 and an hourly capacity between 103–197 for VFR and 99–119 in IFR operations.

3 **ACRP's** publication 'Evaluating Airfield capacity' uses a spreadsheet. With the inputs to this spreadsheet can get the capacity. This assessment is based on inputs given to the evaluation; thus, one can get a range of capacities based on various input combinations. Also, this is a preliminary assessment and could be considered for a pre-feasibility study. The airfield layout can be assessed based on this assessment.

It is also helpful to look at the statistics of existing airports with specific airfield layouts and get to know the actual traffic they have handled. For example, single-runway airports like Gatwick and Mumbai are very popular in handling the maximum number of ATMs and passenger traffic. Since the ATM handling capacity depends on many factors, it is challenging to match with other airports. Still, one can understand how the airports perform in this capacity aspect and evaluate whether such infrastructure and procedures can be implemented. Of course, not all parameters can be adopted. For example, the fleet mix, which is decided by the airlines depending on the number of passengers and availability of aircraft and, thus, cannot be copied between the airports. Air traffic procedures, for example, can be compared and action initiated to modify these in the operations for improvement.

Similarly, infrastructures like additional entry/exit taxiways at the right location are examples that can be implemented. For detailed planning or during operations, it is possible to estimate the capacities based on actual airfield layout, traffic, fleet mix, and operational procedures using simulation tools. Such analysis can also provide the bottlenecks that restrict the capacity.

Number of runways

Configuration of the multiple runways

The minimum distance between the multiple parallel runways depends on how the runways can be utilized for operations and these are classified as follows:

I   Parallel non-instrument runways (Figure 3.1).
II Parallel instrument runways for simultaneous operations (Figure 3.2).
III Simultaneous parallel dependent approaches (Figure 3.3(a)).
IV Simultaneous parallel departures (Figure 3.4).
V   Segregated parallel approaches/departures (Figure 3.4).

I Parallel non-instrument runways

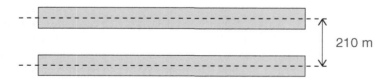

Figure 3.1 Parallel non-instrument runways. Reference – ICAO Annex 14

Non-instrument runways are meant only for VFR (Visual Flight Rules) operations, as the good visibility will enable the pilots to ensure the safety of the operations and the ATC also will have the visibility to monitor and caution/instruct the pilots. VFR operations will provide the maximum number of movements. However, VFR may not be always possible in the case of 24 hours operational airport and hence, airport capacity based on VFR operations for such an airport is not appropriate.

II Parallel instrument runways for simultaneous operations

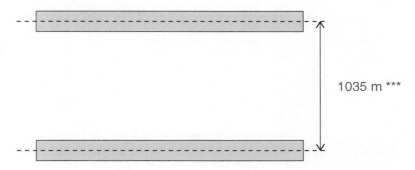

1035 m ***

Figure 3.2 Independent parallel instrument approaches. Reference – ICAO Annex 14 and Doc 9643

1035 m *** is the minimum separation distance between the parallel runways for simultaneous operation of independent runways, but ICAO specifies the type of radar equipment and procedures depending on a) when the distance is between 1035 m and 1310 m, between 1310 m and 1525 m, and finally when the distance is more than 1525 m. In practice what is considered is minimum of 1525 m for greenfield airport planning. For brownfield development, if there is a constraint in locating the runways at 1525 m, the maximum distance that is possible between 1035 m and 1525 m can be evaluated.

However, from practical point of view to locate the aprons, PTB and parallel taxiways (especially two for each runway), the required distance between the runways will have to be more than 2000 m. For this reason, greenfield airports planning considers a distance between 2000 m and 2600 m.

Thus, a separation distance between runways greater than 1525 m and ideally 2600 m provides less constraint in operations and locating the apron, terminal buildings, etc. Such configuration provides maximum capacity. This configuration supports independent and simultaneous operations of two runway systems.

III Dependent parallel instrument approaches

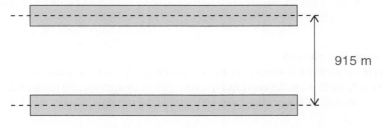

915 m

Figure 3.3(a) Dependent parallel instrument approaches. Reference – ICAO Annex 14 and Doc 9643

If (II) is not possible due to lack of land availability, this configuration with 915 m separation distance can be planned. In this mode, it is not an independent operation of the two runways as the separation distance is less than 1525 m. This configuration permits a dependent parallel approach mode of operation by achieving the separation of the aircrafts using the longitudinal distance between the arriving aircrafts. Figure 3.3(b) explains the concept.

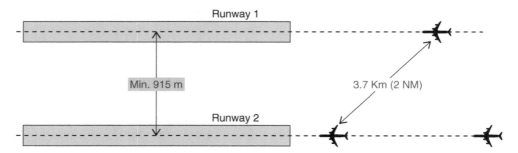

Figure 3.3(b) Dependent parallel instrument approaches with separation between arrivals. Reference – ICAO Annex 14 and Doc 9643

The above mode is for arrivals. However, for simultaneous/independent departures minimum distance can be 760 m with a defined procedure.

IV, V Simultaneous parallel departures and Segregated parallel approaches/ departures When the separation distance is 760 m, either simultaneous or independent parallel departures are permitted. Or when one runway is used only for arrival and another one only for departure, called segregated operations with a defined procedure.

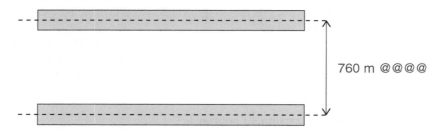

Figure 3.4 Simultaneous parallel departures and segregated operations. Reference – ICAO Annex 14 and Doc 9643

Use of Staggered runway.
    If 760 m separation distance is also not possible, the runways can be staggered as shown in Figure 3.5. In this configuration for every 150 m staggering, 30 m can be reduced, i.e., 730 m against 760 m. The staggering must be towards the runway as shown in Figure 3.5(b)

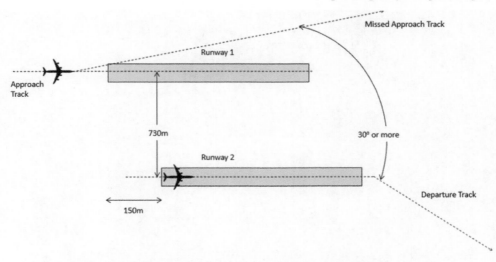

Figure 3.5(a) Staggered runways and operations. Reference – ICAO Doc 9643

From the above configurations of the runways and considering the restrictions in the operation the capacity varies. The highest sustainable capacity being when the runways are separated by more than 1525 theoretically, but more than 2000 m practically.

An example of staggered runways

Figure 3.5(b) Staggered runways at Manchester Airport
Source: Google earth

Non-parallel runways

So far, it is assumed that the runways are parallel or near parallel as defined in ICAO. However, non-parallel runways exist at some airports. These are not crossing each other within the airport, but when the take-off flight path is extended from both runways, they meet at some point

Figure 3.6 IGI Airport with non-parallel runways
Source: Google earth

(see Figure 3.6 R1 and R2). These runways' utilization is reduced as they meet away in the flight path. In these cases, one runway is usually used for arrival and the other for departure, and the departure and arrival are time separated so that the operation is not simultaneous. Some capacity addition is possible with all safety mitigation implemented and published in AIP (Aeronautical Information Publication).

Intersecting runways

Figure 3.7 shows intersecting runways. Both runways cannot be operated simultaneously. But with defined operational procedures and safety case assessment, non-simultaneous use is possible. This configuration is worse than the non-parallel runways as the capacity addition is limited with severe safety implications. However, this configuration can reduce taxi times for the terminals close to the secondary runway. The runways are not meant for simultaneous operations. Still, even a marginal capacity increase sometimes is valuable, particularly if the taxing time is also reduced and more flights can be prepared for departure. Planners don't plan for this configuration for greenfield airports.

Intersecting runways are also used when the crosswind components facilitate the operation of these runways. When the crosswind components for the main runway are more than the maximum permissible values, the main runway cannot be used for operations. If the crosswind components at this time are favourable for the cross runway, this will be operated. Orientation of the crosswind runways is chosen to use in those conditions.

Figure 3.7 Intersecting runways
Source: Google earth

Runway holding positions

The next capacity contributor is the runway holding position (shown in Figures 3.8 and 3.9) where the aircraft must stop and get clearance from ATC before entering the runway. Normally, it is a practice to identify one runway holding position. More than one runway holding position can marginally increase the number of aircraft movements in an hour.

The aircraft wait at the holding position at the busy airports, either awaiting the arrival or departure of another plane. The time taken by an aeroplane for takeoff consists of the time taken to move from the holding point to the lineup for ready to take off plus time taken by the aircraft to move from the time ATC advises for takeoff plus Runway Occupancy Time (ROT) of the departing aircraft. ROT is calculated from the time to take off instruction to the time the departing aircraft has airborne (wheels off the ground), or it passes the end of the runway. The average time considering various aeroplane codes may be 100–120 seconds. Hence, the holding point must be located appropriately so that the average time taken for departure is optimum and usually avoid backtracking on the runway. Time saved in this process will add to the capacity. Multiple holding positions thus add to the capacity. For example, see Figure 3.9 with two holding positions at the beginning of the runway.

Parallel taxiway and entry/exit taxiways

ROT is one of the factors that determine the airfield capacity. Arriving aircraft occupancy time is the time an arriving aircraft takes from the threshold position until it vacates the runway. Minimizing the ROT will allow another aircraft to commence the takeoff roll or another arriving aircraft to be cleared to land. This can be facilitated by constructing a parallel taxiway and locating the runway exits at appropriate locations connecting to the parallel Taxiway. As there are several types of aircraft, from turboprop to wide body, the location of these exits will also be different (wide body requires more runway length to de-accelerate than a turboprop). Also, exit taxiways

Figure 3.8 Runway holding position. Photograph by AMA

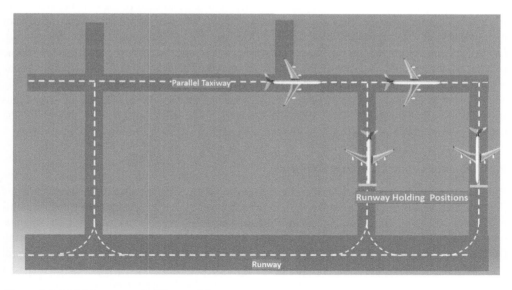

Figure 3.9 Multiple runway holding positions

at an angle instead of perpendicular to the runway clear the aircraft faster as the aircraft need not slow down too much before entering the exit taxiway. Such angled exits are called 'Rapid Exit Taxiways' (RET). Software is available for checking the average ROT with the aircraft fleet mix and RET locations as inputs. The aim is to get an average ROT of 50 seconds. Even at the airports in operation if the airfield capacity analysis shall include ROT. Similar to arrival ROT, for departing aircraft the ROT is the time taken from instruction to depart and the aircraft clears the runway. This time can be minimized by entry taxiways from parallel taxiway to runway, not only at the runway beginning but also at intermediate entries.

Assuming there is no parallel taxiway at the airport, the arriving aircraft must backtrack on the runway to reach the apron. Similarly, departing aircraft spend more time on the runway. Thus, this would affect the capacity. It may be essential to have multiple parallel taxiways to support the runway capacity.

The location of the PTB(s) is also contributing to the requirement for parallel taxiways. Apron configuration, apron taxi lanes, and simultaneous aircraft movement in the apron also increase the capacity. The PTB's location on one or both sides of the parallel runways and aircraft crossing the active runway affects the capacity.

Figures 3.10(a) and 3.10(b) explain the concept and more description in a subsequent chapter. Similarly for the other direction of landing as shown in Figure 3.10(b)

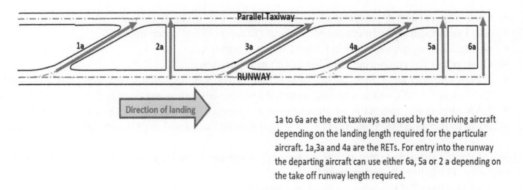

1a to 6a are the exit taxiways and used by the arriving aircraft depending on the landing length required for the particular aircraft. 1a,3a and 4a are the RETs. For entry into the runway the departing aircraft can use either 6a, 5a or 2 a depending on the take off runway length required.

Figure 3.10(a) Entry and exit taxiways

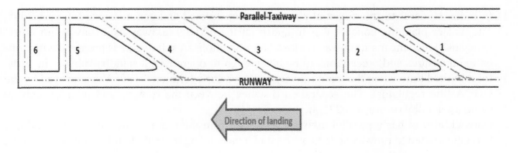

Figure 3.10(b) Entry and exit taxiways

Separation distance between runways

Why are the minimum separation distances of parallel runways under IFR operations more than VFR operations for approaches? The reasons are that operational safety is dependent on the accuracy of the surveillance radar monitoring system. Also, the ability of controllers to intervene when an aircraft deviates from the approach track guided by the Instrument Landing System (ILS) and the precision with which aircraft can navigate to the runway, and the reaction time by the controller, pilot, and aircraft. (Visit the Los Angeles airport website and read the notes to see how the capacity of the airport differs from IFR to VFR.)

Parallel runways with separation distance less than 760 m

The next one to be discussed about airfield layout contributing to capacity is the parallel runways for simultaneous operation with a separation distance of less than 760 m. Previously, it was mentioned that ICAO specifies the minimum separation distance must be 760 m for simultaneous operations under Instrument Meteorological Conditions (IMC). FAA has specific operational guidance for airports with less than 760 m separation distance between parallel runways. Such runways are called Closely Spaced Parallel Runways (CSPR). For example, San Francisco International Airport has CSPR at 230 m distance and operates on IMC with parallel approaches under very specific conditions – called Simultaneous Offset Instrument Approaches – approved by FAA.

Example of airports with CSPR

- CDG airport (384 m separation).
- São Paulo/Guarulhos International Airport (Brazil) (375 m separation).
- Shanghai Hongqiao Airport in China (360 m separation).
- Guangzhou Baiyun Airport in China (400 m separation).
- Toronto airport has CSPR at 305 m and had 27 runway incursions between year 2012 and 2017 as per TSB Canada and has provided specific mitigation measures.
- LAX airport has two pairs of closely spaced runways, one pair at 213 m (the airport's proposal to increase the separation by 79 m is approved) and another pair with 260 m separation.

With specific procedure and safety assessment, there seems to be some way out to increase the capacity. These are all airport specific.

Can the parallel taxiway be used as runway?

Yes, and described in the subsequent chapter.

Three airports with the concept of parallel taxiway as a standby runway are as follows:

1 In India, Hyderabad International airport was constructed and commissioned in year 2008. The master planning concept was to construct the parallel taxiway as a runway for emergency use when the main runway is closed for operations. A safety case is prepared with mitigation measures and precautions to be taken even to operate as a standby runway in VMC for a limited time when the main runway is closed for operations. This was approved by the DGCA (the regulator). The separation distance between the runway and parallel taxiway (used as standby runway) is 225 m.
2 Gatwick airport has a parallel taxiway at 198 m from the main runway centreline and this was constructed to runway specifications and hence, being used as standby runway when the main runway is closed for operations for few hours (for example routine maintenance).

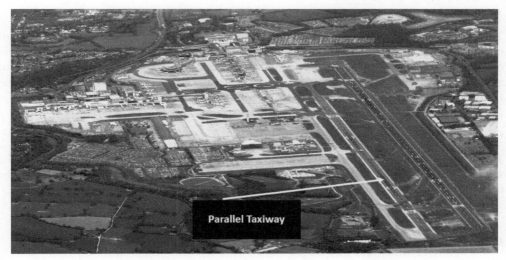

Figure 3.11 Airport diagram of Gatwick Airport

Source: https://upload.wikimedia.org/wikipedia/commons/2/21/Gatwick_Airport_%2850850159593%29.jpg

3 Mactan Cebu International Airport in the Philippines has constructed a second parallel taxiway between runway and first parallel taxiway. The second parallel taxiway is designed and constructed as a runway for stand-by operations, like Hyderabad airport described above.

In the master planning chapter, it is explained why the minimum distance as per ICAO between a parallel taxiway and runway may not be practically sufficient always. Thus, there is an option for a greenfield airport to be planned with a parallel taxiway at a greater distance than the minimum as per ICAO. For example, suppose this distance is at least 210 m with runway specifications. In that case, this parallel taxiway can be used as a standby runway in VFR, when the main runway is not in operation. In future, there is a possibility to operate as a runway under certain conditions together with the main runway.

Runways separated by less than 760 m are called CSPR. This concept will gain popularity as constructing the second runway at a far distance for a marginal increase in capacity or at airports where a second runway for independent simultaneous operations is impossible because of the unavailability of land or the cost of acquiring land is exorbitant. Incremental capacity or as a standby runway can be used if the parallel taxiway location and specifications are deliberated and decided at the time of planning.

More attention is paid to the airfield layout design, more on runway and taxiways, since it is challenging to modify or add infrastructures on the airside, especially in busy airports, if necessitated due to capacity improvement. Due to restricted working hours for addition or modifications, the capital expenses also will be very high in a brownfield airport development. For some works, the airfield may have to be closed, meaning rescheduling the flights, which will attract criticism from airlines and passengers. Also, air safety concerns will have severe consequences due to safety breaches. Airside and aircraft operations are subject to strict regulatory controls.

Apron stands

The apron stands are located close to the passenger terminal. The basis for the determination of number of stands for the required capacity is discussed in the subsequent chapter. The number of stands for the same airport capacity could be different depending on the turnaround time of aircrafts. Turnaround time of aircrafts will be more for hub airports when compared with Origin Destination Airports. Also, if airline(s) use the airport as a base for its operations.

Capacity of Passenger Terminal Building (PTB)

To the pre-feasibility assessment, the PTB overall area would suffice without going into the system aspects of the passenger and baggage processing. Based on PTB area requirement for the traffic forecasted, the location can be identified and safeguarded for future expansion as well.
   The PTB area can be split up as below.

Departure process

Check-in processing (conventional manned, self-service kiosks, and self-bag drops).
Passport control.
Security screening (passengers and cabin bags).
Gate holding – seating.
Number of Gates to board the aircrafts.
Restroom facilities.

Arrival process

Passport control.
Baggage carousels.
Customs inspection.
Meeters and greeters.

Common areas

Queuing areas in all the processes.
Circulation space and common areas.
Corridors for level changes – arriving/departing.

Services

Rooms for all services (electrical, mechanical, ITC, etc.).
Airline lounges.
Retail stores.
Duty-free retails.
F&B.
Medical centre.
Airline offices.
Regulatory authority offices.
Baggage handling areas (make up and break up).

Land side

Vehicle drop of lanes – arrival and departure.
Vehicle parking slots.

Peak hour capacity

For determining the infrastructures on the airside, landside, and PTB, it is necessary to decide on the number of passengers (for PTB and landside) and the number of aircraft movements (for airfield) in a specific period, generally for one hour. The highest number (passengers and aircraft movements) represents the peak hour demand and, consequently, the required capacity in one hour. Therefore, the traffic forecast study can include hourly traffic; from that, the highest traffic volume is selected. When the traffic forecast analysis does not have hourly traffic, another approach is to extract the peak hour demand from the annual traffic projection using the rules of thumb.

Could the required infrastructure/facility be determined based on the peak hour traffic volume, or could it be slightly less? It could be less to optimize the capital and operational expenditures, but congestion during such peak traffic periods must be tolerable/acceptable. The logic here is that the infrastructure/facilities will be utilized only during peak hours if they are designed for peak capacity. It is a compromise between low congestion during peak periods and severe underutilization during non-peak periods. Typically, the airfield infrastructure is intended to accommodate peak-hour traffic. In contrast, it is standard practice to construct PTBs with a marginal lesser capacity than the peak hour passenger volume.

Peak hour capacity assessment from annual numbers

The following are the methods for the peak hour traffic assessment of the PTB. There is no standardization on this.

FAA methodology (AC 150/5360- 13A)

Average Day of the Peak Month (ADPM) is a common methodology used to identify existing and forecast future peak activity. In this methodology, first identify the peak traffic month. Say it is 30,000 passengers in a month. Per day passenger numbers in that month are 1000. In that month, identify the day in which the passenger numbers are close to 1000 and in that day, identify the hourly peak passenger numbers for the 24 hours and choose the highest passenger numbers out of the 24-hour traffic.

Design day traffic is the average day activity worked out as per ADPM. To find the peak hour traffic numbers, a flight schedule for this design day traffic, forecasting the flight schedules, aeroplane code (for seating capacity), and load factor. From the design day flight schedule, the highest traffic numbers in one hour can be found out which will be the peak hour traffic numbers. Since the assumption of the fleet mix and number of aircrafts are part of this assessment, can get the peak hour ATM also.

IATA methodology

In this methodology, peak month is identified. In the peak month, busy day is found out, which is the second busiest day in an average week of that month.

Example

Let us say the peak passenger traffic in a month at an airport is 30,000. Average passengers per week is 7500. In the peak month, out of the four weeks in that month, identify the weekly passengers which is close to 7500. Say it is 7700 in the second week. In that week, plot the daily passenger numbers for all the seven days. Out of these seven-day traffic, identify the second-highest traffic of the day. Take the second highest traffic number, which is per day, plot hourly traffic for 24 hours and choose the highest hourly traffic and that traffic number is the peak hour traffic number for facility design.

Some more methodologies

UK adopts **Standard Busy Rate** (SBR), which corresponds to the 30th busiest hour in the study year. Paris airports use the 40th busiest hour. To work out, the 30th or 40th busy hour requires passengers forecast every hour for one year and when arranged in descending order, from highest to lowest, the passenger numbers at the 30th or 40th hour as the case may be is considered as peak hour traffic.

Busy Hour Rate (BHR) is the peak hour passengers that correspond to the 95th percentile of the passengers per hour worked out for one year. Meaning an airport designed for this passenger numbers will experience congestion only for 5 percentiles. In this arrange the hourly traffic in year and calculate the sum of the top volumes amount to 5% of the annual volume.

Among all the methods above, IATA methodology is mostly used by the planners. In all these methodologies, the planner needs to have the historical traffic data. The peak hour traffic for future periods is based on the current peak level of operations and requires adjustments for future increased traffic numbers. For a greenfield airport, a preliminary flight schedule is to be prepared and from this the peak day and peak hour traffic numbers are derived. This can be converted to a peak hour factor and compared with other airports in the region or similar passenger profile to validate the assumption.

Preparing a flight schedule for a new airport means many assumptions and takes considerable time and effort. One practical method is to use a peak hour factor based on rules of thumb depending on the annual traffic numbers. Say, for example, a peak hour factor of 0.021% means for 10 million annual passenger numbers, the peak hour passengers are 2100. Similarly, if the yearly passenger number is 30 million, the peak hour passenger is 6300 when the peak hour factor is 0.021%. The peak hour ATM can be estimated with peak hour passengers as above, with an assumed fleet mix and average passengers per flight. Alternatively, like passenger numbers, use a different peak hour factor for ATM and estimate the peak hour ATM from the annual ATM numbers. Thus, both peak-hour passengers and peak-hour ATMs can be worked out. This peak hour factor decreases as the annual traffic grows, and the factor will stabilize beyond some numbers. For example, peak hour traffic of 6300 derived from a 0.021% peak hour factor for 30 million annual passenger numbers. For 50 million annual passenger numbers, with the same 0.021% factor, the peak hour passenger numbers will be 10,500. Whereas if the factor is reduced to 0.018%, the peak hour numbers will be 9000 passengers. Thus, between the two factors, the lower one requires a lesser increase in additional infrastructure from a peak of 6300 passengers to 9000 passengers. The additional traffic will be accommodated during non-peak hours. Increasing the peak hour traffic requires infrastructure and facilities to be expanded substantially, incurring more capex and operational expenditure, and leaving the non-peak hours with much lesser traffic than peak hour traffic.

The peak factor example is given in Table 3.1

The numbers are only illustrative.

Table 3.1 Peak hour factor

Annual passenger nos	Peak hour factor
More than 20 million	0.031%
15 million to 20 million	0.035%
1 million and below	0.56%
Annual ATM nos	**Peak hour factor**
More than 300,000	0.081%
100,000 and below	0.20%

PTB area

The number or quantity of processing equipment (check-in, passport control, security equipment etc) depends on the number of passengers that will be in the queue at a time, maximum permissible queuing time and average processing time per passenger. If more queuing time is permitted, lesser processing equipment is required, but this will increase the area requirement as more passengers will be in the queue. For example, check-in process being the first process, it is required to estimate how many of the peak hour passengers will enter the queue at a time. For this either i) estimate the numbers in every 15 min in peak hour and consider the max value or ii) assume 70% of peak hour passengers. Based on this and with permissible queuing time the number of processors can be decided. For example, an airport with a maximum number of tourists can expect more passengers in groups to reach the airport at a time by coaches, etc., than an airport with business travellers. For the subsequent processing, say passport control, the input passenger numbers are the output passenger numbers from Check-in. Whereas arrival passport control is different as maximum passengers from a flight will reach the process at a time.

There are three components for determining area requirements for the processing area. One is the area occupied by the processing equipment within the passenger areas; the second is the queuing area which is the space per passenger multiplied by the number of passengers. The third component is the circulation area around the processes and the subsequent processing. Figure 3.12 is an illustration of the check-in area consisting of three zones viz., the area occupied by the check-in system, including the baggage belt, passenger queuing area, and circulation space. Figure 3.12 illustrates about two check-in counters.

The security hold area mainly depends on the number of passengers to be catered for seating, the space occupied by the seating, circulation, and queuing area for boarding.

Similarly, the arrival area consists of arrival corridors from the boarding bridges or remote parking. In addition, the area occupied by passport control systems, queuing, circulation space, space occupied by baggage reclaim belts and distance between the belts, circulation area around the baggage reclaims belts, exit through customs area, and meeters and greeters' area.

In addition to the processing area, the requirement for services, commercial, etc., as mentioned previously to be included. The retail area to be developed in the PTB, office spaces, and services areas are all airport specific. The commercial area depends on the business case, with a separate study conducted for the extent of such requirements. One can consider 70% for operational purposes, 20% for retails, and 10% for services.

What happens if the actual passenger during the peak is more than the estimated peak numbers? The queuing time increases, and the area becomes congested.

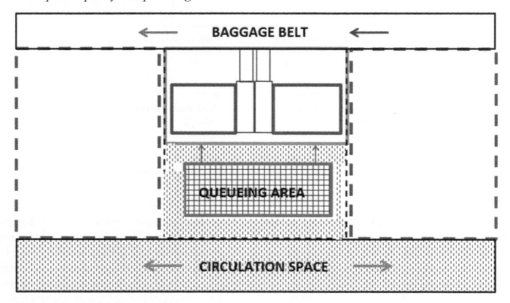

Figure 3.12 Check-in area showing one module of two counters with queuing area and baggage belt and circulation area

Level of Service

IATA ADRM provides guidelines called LOS space-time matrix, with area per passenger vs. queuing/waiting time, and classifies the design as either optimum or suboptimum or over design, based on the values. For example, check-in area process LOS is as follows:

Area per passenger in sqmt – 1.8 over design, between 1.3 and 1.8 optimum, less than 1.3 sqmt sub-optimum.

Maximum waiting time in minutes – less than 20 minutes overdesign, between 10 and 20 optimum, and more than 20 minutes sub-optimum.

The above guideline can be used for designing the PTB and while the PTB is in operation, these LOS parameters can be verified and classified. Especially when both the parameters are sub-optimum level, the service is classified as underperformed.

If it is not possible to calculate the detailed breakdown of the PTB area requirement during the initial analysis of the airport development, the practice (no uniformity, left to the government to decide and provide guidelines) is to consider 8000–10,000 sqm per million passengers per annum. For an airport planned for 40 million passengers per annum, the PTB area will be approximately 320,00–400,000 sqm. Another thumb rule based on peak hour passengers is 20 sqm per PHP for domestic and 25 sqm for international. Considering the peak hour factor of 0.030, for 40 million passengers per annum, the PHP is 12,000. Based on PHP considering only domestic passenger operations, it would be 240,000, and for international, it would be 300,000 sqm. For preliminary planning, a higher number can be assumed. Thus, assuming 400,000 sqm in three levels, the PTB location can be identified in the master plan with a footprint of 130,000 sqm. Such thumb rule can be cross-checked with the airport in operation in the region. IATA's guideline is area per peak hour passenger is 'not exceeding' and does not specify the minimum area per passenger.

When the PTB is commissioned, it may be in the 'overdesign category' as the design takes consideration of traffic at least five years later. However, how much is this requires review to ensure the facilities are not so much over designed in the implementation stage.

Busiest five top airports in Y 2019

- Atlanta International Airport – Annual passengers handled 110+ million – five runways.
- Beijing Capital International Airport – Annual passengers handled 100+ million three runways.
- Los Angeles International Airport – Annual passengers handled 88+ million – four runways.
- Dubai International Airport – Annual passengers handled 86+ million – two runways.
- Tokyo Haneda Airport – Annual passengers handled 85+ million – four runways.

Cargo terminal

Like passenger traffic forecasts, cargo forecasts based on past data can be worked out using methodologies, including regression analysis. In addition to normal growth in line with increased aircraft movements, adjustment factors for the following could be potential growth areas.

1 Industrial development around the airport.
2 The products which are time sensitive for delivery, like perishable items and pharmaceutical products.
3 High-value precision items which require careful handling, etc.
4 Planned Special economic zones.

Discussions with the local government and industry chambers of commerce will provide more input.

Some considerations for planning

Turnaround time of dedicated cargo aircraft will be very high, in the range of 4–5 hours, unlike passenger aircraft. The capacity calculation should consider this after discussions with airlines/ cargo operators. If belly cargo is substantial, it requires lesser cargo storage capacity. Transfer cargo traffic needs to be ascertained, for example, mail. Cooling off or cargo dwell time must be verified with the authorities, which impacts the capacity and sizing. This will be different for international and domestic. Capacity for truck parking, offloading, and unloading bays requires special considerations. The operation planned – fully automatic or semi-automatic, or manual – should be considered for sizing.

Cargo ATMs

From the annual cargo traffic in MT, we can find the number of ATMs by dividing, say, 300 (instead of 365 days) and assuming average tons per aircraft (say 50 Tons or as per the current quantity). ATMs are based on this and by estimating the appropriate fleet mix in consultation with the airlines or cargo operators for dedicated freights. The belly cargo proportion is calculated based on the current level. As per the forecast, the operation for the ultimate capacity should be the basis for the sizing, as automatic handling requires more height. The capacity calculation on the airside includes the number of aircraft stands, wide body and narrow body ratios, storage area for cargo handling equipment, and the terminal area, including special requirements like cold storage and landside requirement. Include the office areas for cargo agents and regulatory authorities.

IATA provides guidelines for cargo terminal building areas of 5–17 sqm per ton, depending on the type of operations. ACI provides a guideline of about 70,000 sqm for 100,000 MT of cargo capacity. The area of the cargo terminal building also depends on whether it is shared among multiple operators or a single agency operating as a shared facility.

Busiest top 5 Cargo handling airports

Hong Kong Airport	4.80 million MT
Memphis airport	4.32 million MT
Shanghai Pudong Airport	3.63 million MT
Louisville Muhammad Ali Airport	2.79 million MT
Incheon Airport	2.76 million MT

Airport capacity on landside

There are two requirements – vehicle parking area and access road. For integrated PTB, the peak hour passenger numbers should be split between international and domestic. The split between domestic and international is required explicitly if the peak hour passenger numbers do not coincide with optimizing the needed landside area.

Depending on the passenger profile, we can identify the type of vehicle and number of passengers for each type, giving the total number of each type of vehicle. For example, if the airport handles majorly tourism traffic, it is expected to have more coaches, at least 20 passengers per vehicle. On the other hand, we can assume one passenger per cab for business and four passengers per cab for leisure travellers.

If passengers park and fly, we must add this population segment to the car park capacity.

With the passengers per vehicle and the total number of peak hour passengers, it is possible to find the population of vehicles during the peak hours. The proportion of vehicles may be like – coaches 25%, cars 10% (long term parking), taxis 55%, and minivans 10%. With the number of vehicles and dimensions of each type of vehicle, we can estimate the area for vehicle parking. To this, we can add 50% for the vehicle circulation. Depending on the total area required, it is possible to decide whether to plan for surface parking or multilevel parking. Along with the population of passenger vehicles, the vehicle population of the staff of the airport, government authorities, airlines, tenants, and the number of visitors is to be estimated and included.

The number of vehicular lanes near the PTB depends on the number and type of vehicle, the vehicle's dwell time at the kerb, more for coaches and less for cabs, and vehicle length.

We can convert the vehicle population with various types to equivalent car units. This provides the number of car units in the peak hour, which will be the basis for calculating the number of lanes required in the access road to the airport. Lane capacity is specified in the number of car units in standard guidelines and LOS.

Level of service for roads

To evaluate the acceptability of the service level on roads, the Highway Capacity Manual (HCM) defines the LOS from A to F, where A is the best LOS, and F is the worst. The actual volume/

capacity of the road, i.e., congestion, for the specific speed limit, is the basis for the LOS. HCM defines the conditions defining the LOS. The number of lanes is planned to achieve LOS 'C', which 'Represents a constrained constant flow below speed limits, with additional attention required by the drivers to maintain safe operations. Comfort and convenience levels of the driver decline noticeably'.

Assuming the speed permissible is 25 miles per hour and four lanes, the capacity of each lane is 740 vehicles, and the total capacity is 2960 vehicles. As said previously, the number of vehicles and the vehicle types are converted to a common scale called per unit car. Assuming the per unit car population is, say, 2000, then the LOS = 2000/2960 = 0.67, whereas it should not exceed 0.59 to achieve LOS C. Thus, five lanes are required that will give a capacity of 3700 units and the LOS = 2000/3700 which is 0.54 and since less than 0.59 for LOS C, the road with five lanes is acceptable.

Ways to increase the airport capacity

Following are the possibilities/options to increase the existing airport capacity, with minimal capex:

1 In the case of PTB capacity, we can review the current process, number of processing equipment, number of boarding gates, and the queuing area available. Evaluate the utilization of these on an actual basis and, identify the process improvements additional infrastructure required, and try to accommodate these within the building area.
2 We should also examine the latest technology adopted at other airports, which can increase the capacity. For example, increasing the number of self-check-in kiosks and self-bag drops reduce the processing time and thus increases the capacity. Self-check-in for cabin bag passengers can be installed at the kerb side and, therefore, does not require an additional floor area in the check-in hall. Using technology in passenger processing, like facial recognition from entry to boarding, adds to the capacity.
3 Using the non-peak hours for additional capacity does not require any additional infrastructure. Say the passenger throughput in 24 hours is as shown in Figure 3.13.

   a In the figure, it is seen that there are four peak hours with 9000 passengers. The theoretical capacity could be more than 9000, say 11,000. One of the primary reasons for such a difference is the passenger load factor as per capacity calculation and actual load factor. Another possibility is that the actual fleet mix could differ from the assumed fleet mix. Hence, one should evaluate the actual peak hour capacity utilization from annual capacity.
   b It is also seen that there are many hours, other than four peak hours, where passenger numbers are less. Thus, throughput is less than the capacity at these hours. Capacity can be increased if these non-peak hours can be utilized for additional demand. During the slot allocation, we should meet the additional traffic demand with hours other than peak hours. This is called de-peaking. Assuming it is possible to increase the number of ATMs during non-peak hours, this will increase the capacity.

4 Analysis, including simulation tools, can be used to evaluate the capacity without additional infrastructures, for example, with modified air traffic control procedures. Similarly, PTB simulation tools are available to assess the capacity, which can suggest if the improvements are possible without the expansion of the PTB.
5 Even a temporary building could be added depending on which process area is short of the capacity by actual measurement of waiting time and queuing area at each process. There are practical examples of airports adding a building only for the arrival carousel area and in line

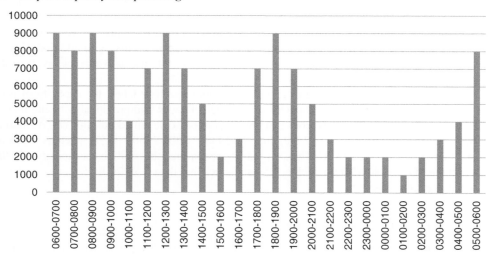

Figure 3.13 Actual hourly passenger numbers in a peak day

with the master plan so that the same structure could be integrated with the overall expansion of the facility later. Similarly, we can add a check-in area if this is the constraint for the additional capacity.

6 For the airfield, we can look at the capacity vs. demand of apron stands and runway capacity. Runway capacity review will include time taken by the aircraft moving from runway to apron on landing and vice versa for departure and identify where there are delays due to lack of infrastructure or procedures. Increasing the number of aircraft stands should be easier if the land is available and there is a master plan.

7 Air traffic procedures could be examined, including the separation distances between aeroplanes as prescribed and as actual. Benchmarking with similar traffic airports could give inputs. Airports nowadays implement Airport Collaborative Decision Making (ACDM) process, which brings all the stakeholders on board to achieve operational efficiency and thus reduce delays and increase capacity.

8 For capacity-constrained airports, which cannot increase the airfield capacity since additional land cannot be acquired, can evaluate aircraft operation with a mix of VFR and IFR operation, and some airports operate under this mode. Based on meterological data of many years, it is possible to identify how many hours VFR is possible for a number of days/months in a year. Also, the airlines should be able to operate under VFR without the aid of instruments, and an appropriate procedure is required to be described.

9 The mode of aircraft operation with multiple runways is another factor to examine. A mixed mode of operations is when both the runways are used for arrivals and departures. The mixed mode of operation enables more capacity since it is possible to insert a departure between two arrivals. Semi-mixed mode also adds to capacity.

Airports always try to sweat the asset by utilizing the resources with the highest efficiency and increasing the capacity to meet the demand. However, major infrastructure additions mean huge capital expenditure, funding requirements, and increased operational expenditure. Also, the capacity that is worked out, say, ten years back requires reassessment due to improved passenger processes and airfield and aeroplane technology. For example, the newer version of narrow-body aircraft has more seating capacity than a few years ago. This helps airfield capacity increase, and such marginal PTB capacity increase should be possible with minimal interventions.

Conclusion

Airport capacity depends on airfield capacity and the PTB capacity. It is required to arrive at the peak hour capacity of the airfield and the PTB from the annual capacity basis of the traffic forecast. There are rules of thumb for deriving the same. The theoretical capacity depends on many design elements and operational factors. Hence, when comparing the capacities of two airports, it is required to understand these two aspects and look at the differences before concluding. The airfield components are designed for peak hour demand. In contrast, facilities/area of PTB is designed for less than the peak hour demand knowing that there could be acceptable congestion during those periods. This approach can optimize the cost. In addition, to augment an existing airport's capacity, it is required to review the operational procedures and other aspects. If they can be modified/improved, capacity addition is possible without significant capex.

References

ACRP. (2012). Evaluating Airfield Capacity – Report 79. In ACRP. https://doi.org/10.17226/22674

Airport Curbside and Terminal Area Roadway Operations. (2010). In Airport Curbside and Terminal Area Roadway Operations. https://doi.org/10.17226/14451

FAA. (1983). Advisory Circular – Airport Capacity and Delay (Issue 150/5060-5).

IATA ADRM (11th ed.). (2019). IATA.

ICAO. (1983). Manual on Simultaneous Operations on Parallel or Near Parallel Instrument Runways (SOIR) – Doc 9643. ICAO.

ICAO. (1987). Airport Planning Manual. ICAO.

ICAO. (2022). ICAO Annex 14 – Ninth Edition: Vol. I.

Additional reference material

ACRP's Airport Passenger Terminal Planning and Design, Volume 1: Guidebook, chapter VII Landside facilities planning.

ACRP Report 4 (48), which documents recent trends in airport ground access.

4 ICAO SARPs for planning

Introduction

ICAO's Standard and Recommended Practices (SARPs) play an important role in aviation, bringing uniformity in planning, design, maintenance, and operations. Some States may meet specific requirements differently, but the States inform the ICAO of such deviations, which are published, and information disseminated with all operators globally. ICAO has a rigorous process for SARPs formulation, including its amendments based on user feedback and consultations. SARPs, primarily from ICAO's Annex 14, are the basis for airport planning, and the planners also should consult with the State's regulations and adopt them in the planning.

Obstacles in and around the airport constitute a significant safety hazard; hence, planners should carefully evaluate compliance with SARPs. The shape, height, and extent of these surfaces vary and, therefore, properly mapped around the airport location and assessed.

A zoning map around the airport with all the Obstacle Limitation Surfaces (OLS) marked in the map with height permissible at different locations helps the developers to be aware of such limitations while proposing the development for approval.

ICAO standards and recommended practices

SARPs adopted by the ICAO Council under the provisions of the 'Convention'. The convention was signed in Dec 1944 in Chicago by 52 signatory states and is known as Chicago Convention. The convention contains 96 articles and 22 chapters. First, it provides for the establishment of ICAO and specifies the rights and obligations of the States. For example, it provides for mutual recognition of airworthiness certificates, personnel licences, etc., under Article 33. States agree to implement in their National Regulations the SARPs and procedures adopted by ICAO for uniformity. It specifies that it is State's obligation to notify ICAO if it finds it impracticable to implement any SARPs. As of year 2019, ICAO has 193 countries, including all UN member states.

SARPs are defined as below by ICAO

Standard: Any specification for physical characteristics, configuration, matériel, performance, personnel, or procedure, the uniform application of which is recognized as necessary for the safety or regularity of international air navigation and to which **Contracting States will conform in accordance with the Convention**; in the event of impossibility of compliance, notification to the Council is compulsory under Article 38.

DOI: 10.4324/9781003319948-4

Recommended Practice: Any specification for physical characteristics, configuration, matériel, performance, personnel, or procedure, the uniform application of which is recognized as desirable in the interest of safety, regularity, or efficiency of international air navigation, and to which **Contracting States will endeavour to conform in accordance with the Convention**.

(The highlighted sentence explains the difference between these two terms)

Is it compulsory for the States to confirm the Standards prescribed by ICAO? If a State is unable to comply with a specific Standard, the State will have to notify the differences between the ICAO standards and the national regulation and practices. As described in Chapter 1, ICAO is not a regulatory authority, and they do not implement the standards or recommended practices. These are the responsibilities of the Civil Aviation Authority (CAA) of respective States. Similarly, suppose the State is unable to implement the recommended practices of ICAO. In that case, they are advised or invited to file the differences with ICAO, especially if the differences are important for the safety of air navigation. ICAO does not mention that States shall file the differences in case of recommended practices. In addition to filing with ICAO the differences in SARPs, they should be included in Aeronautical Information Services (AIS) publication. This ensures that such differences are known to all the States and stakeholders.

Why SAPRs?

SARPs are the means to bring uniformity in the specifications, materials, configuration, etc., among all the airports in the world so that when the pilot, whichever airport he flies, sees the same information. Examples are a uniform pattern of airfield pavement marking, candela output, and configuration of airfield ground lighting. Such uniformity among the airports will provide an easy understanding and evaluation of information by the pilots.

How does ICAO develop standards and procedures for international civil aviation?

The development of SARPs and Procedures for Air Navigation Services (PANS) follows a structured, transparent, and multi-staged process – often known as the ICAO' amendment process' or 'standards-making process'. This involves several technical and non-technical review bodies, either within or closely associated with ICAO (working groups, task forces, committees, panels, etc.), and generally composed of State and industry Subject Matter Experts (SMEs). New items are added to the ICAO Work Programme after formal reviews by ICAO's Secretariat, Air Navigation Commission (ANC: the main technical advisory body to the ICAO Council), and the 36-State ICAO Governing Council.

Specific matters to be assessed are derived from multiple sources, including accident investigation report recommendations, ICAO assemblies, regional bodies, individual States, and industries. Once an expert group has submitted its recommendations on a specific work programme item, these are reviewed by the ANC and then transmitted to States and industry for review. The ANC considers all relevant feedback and fine-tunes its final recommendation for the ICAO Council's ultimate consideration and possible adoption. Final ANC recommendations would also include complete impact assessments and implementation plans.

What makes SARPs so effective today, and how can they ensure international civil aviation's safe, efficient, and orderly growth in the coming years? The answer lies in aviation's four 'C': **Cooperation, Consensus, Compliance, and Commitment**. Cooperation in the formulation of SARPs, the consensus in their approval, compliance in their application, and commitment of adherence to this ongoing process.

SARPs **cover all technical and operational aspects of International Civil Aviation**, such as

- Safety.
- Personnel licensing.
- Operation of aircraft.
- Aerodromes.
- Air traffic services.
- Accident investigation.
- Environment.

There are a total of 19 Annexes to the Chicago Convention 19 Ann specify the SARPs.

- *Annex 1 – Personnel Licensing*
- *Annex 2 – Rules of the Air*
- *Annex 3 – Meteorological Service for International Air Navigation*
- *Annex 4 – Aeronautical Charts*
- *Annex 5 – Units of Measurement to be Used in Air and Ground Operations*
- *Annex 6 – Operation of Aircraft*
- *Annex 7 – Aircraft Nationality and Registration Marks*
- *Annex 8 – Airworthiness of Aircraft*
- *Annex 9 – Facilitation*
- *Annex 10 – Aeronautical Telecommunications*
- *Annex 11 – Air Traffic Services*
- *Annex 12 – Search and Rescue*
- *Annex 13 – Aircraft Accident and Incident Investigation*
- *Annex 14 – Aerodromes*
- *Annex 15 – Aeronautical Information Services*
- *Annex 16 – Environmental Protection*
- *Annex 17 – Security: Safeguarding International Civil Aviation Against Acts of Unlawful Interference.*
- *Annex 18 – The Safe Transport of Dangerous Goods by Air*
- *Annex 19 – Safety Management*

The Annex pertaining to airside of the aerodrome are:
Annex 3, Annex 6, Annex 10, Annex 11, Annex 14, Annex 15, and Annex 18. Among these Annex 14 is the central focus for the airside planning for an airport. In this chapter, the SARPs from Annex 14 are briefed. In the subsequent chapter on master planning, Annex 10 will be touched upon for the location of CNS equipment.

For detailed design and planning, all the other relevant SARPs of the other Annex will have to be understood and incorporated. For example, passenger security and baggage security provisions are included in Annex 17.

Planners can view the document – How to Build an ICAO SARPs – in ICAO's website.

For airport planning, the aviation regulations are mostly applicable to airside facilities, in view of aeroplane operations.

SARPs from Annex 14 for airside planning are briefed in tabular form

Planning requirement	Standard (S) or recommended practices (R)	Brief SARPs
Orientation of the runway	R	Specifies in terms of permissible cross-wind components and usability factor
Best location of runway among many options in the selected orientation	R	Consider the permissible longitudinal and transverse slope. Specifically applicable for sites where the ground profile is undulating and involves huge cut and fill.
Length of runway	R	Length to meet the operational requirement of aeroplanes to operate at the airport and by applying all correction factors.
Separation distance between centrelines of runways	R	Specifies minimum distance for non-instrument; instrument runways – dependent, independent, and segregated operations
Separation distance between runway centreline and parallel taxiway centreline	R	Specifies minimum distance depending on instrument and non-instrument runway. Also depending on aerodrome reference code
Separation distance between centrelines of parallel taxiways	R	Specifies depending on aerodrome reference code
Separation distance between any object (including aircraft wing tip) and taxiway centreline	R	Specifies minimum distance depending on aerodrome reference code
Separation distance between any object (including aircraft wing tip) and taxilane centrelines	R	Specifies minimum distance depending on aerodrome reference code. This distance is less than that of taxiway as above. This distance may need to be increased when jet exhaust wake velocity may cause hazardous conditions for ground servicing
Separation distance between taxilane-to-taxilane centrelines	R	Specifies minimum distance depending on aerodrome reference code. Less than distance between taxiway to taxiway
Permissible height and location of structures, buildings, etc. from runway	Standard	Specifies depending on the type of runway operations and aerodrome reference code
Maximum permissible longitudinal slope of runway and taxiway	R	Specifies depending on the numeral of aerodrome reference code.
Sight distance when there are slope changes	R	Unobstructed line of sight is required for certain height and distance. These parameters are based on letter of aeroplane reference code.
Maximum permissible transverse slope of runway and taxiway	R	Specified depending on the letter of aeroplane reference code. Not less than 1% slope to avoid water stagnation. Flat portion allowed in runway, taxiway junctions. Transverse slope should be substantially the same throughout the length
Permissible transverse slope on runway shoulder	R	Specifies maximum of 2.5%

(Continued)

Planning requirement	Standard (S) or recommended practices (R)	Brief SARPs
Runway turn pad	Standard	Required for code D, E and F when there is no taxiway connected at the runway end. This is to avoid 180 degrees turn on the runway
Runway turn pad	R	For code letters A, B, and C
Sizing of turn pad	Standard	Based on OMGWS group of the aeroplane
Shoulder for turn pad	R	Required and the width to cover the outer engine of the most demanding aircraft
Runway Strip	Standard	Required
Length of runway strip	Standard	60 m beyond the end of runway for Codes 2, 3, and 4. 30 m for code 1 if non-instrument runway and 60 m if instrument runway
Width of runway strip from centreline of runway for precision runway	Standard	140 m for Code 3 or 4 70 m for Code 1 or 2
Width of runway strip from centreline of runway for non-precision runway	R	140 m for Code 3 or 4 70 m for Code 1 or 2
Width of runway strip from centreline of runway for non-instrument runway	R	75 m for Code 3 or 4 40 m for Code 2 30 m for Code 1
Grading of runway strip	R	The strip has two portions – part of the width is graded and beyond that it is non-graded. For example, out of 140 m strip width, 75 m from runway centreline is graded, and remaining 65 m is not graded.
Objects on runway strip	Standard	Not permitted for precision runway except those required for air navigation and these must be frangible and meet the requirement.
Whether open storm water drains permissible in the airfield.	R	To consider the location and design which may damage the aeroplane. Drain covers are recommended. Drain structure should not protrude the surface to avoid damage the aircraft. Open drain may be permitted in the non-graded portion of runway
Longitudinal slope and transverse slope of runway strip	R	Runway strip has two parts. (1) Graded portion and (2) non-graded portion. For graded portion Maximum permissible slope specified based on numeral of aerodrome reference code
Runway End Safety Area (RESA)	Standard	Codes 3 and 4. Required for Codes 1 and 2 if it is instrument runway. (For Codes 1 and 2 non-instrument runway it is recommended)
Dimension of RESA	Standard	Width – 2 times the width of runway. Length – 90 m from strip for Code 3 or 4. Reduced width for other Codes
Dimension of RESA	R	Length – 240 m from strip for Code 3 or 4. Reduced length for other Codes. Reduced length acceptable if arresting system is installed. Permissible slope specified
Objects on RESA	R	Not permitted
Taxiways	R	To be provided

(Continued)

Planning requirement	Standard (S) or recommended practices (R)	Brief SARPs
Number of exit and entry taxiways	R	To be provided to expedite aircraft movement from and to runway. Rapid Exit Taxiways when traffic volume is high
Width of taxiways	Standard	Depending on the OMGWS.
Taxiways on bridges	Standard	There are very specific requirement including width of the bridge and access to fire vehicles.
Taxiway shoulder	R	Required for Codes C, D, E, and F. Width depends on the code letter
Taxiway strip	Standard	Required for taxiways except taxilane
Objects on taxiway strip	R	Not permitted. Drain provision is like the specifications for drain on runway strip
Width of the taxiway strip	R	Distance from centreline is the same as specified separation distance between taxiway centreline and object
Grading of taxiway strip	R	Specified depending on OMGWS of aeroplanes
Slopes of taxiway strip	R	Specified depending on the Code letter of aerodrome
Apron Size	R	To cater for maximum anticipated traffic
Slope on apron	R	Required to prevent accumulation of water. Not to exceed 1%
Clearance between aircrafts and between aircraft and any object in apron	R	Minimum clearances specified based on Code letter. 3 m for A and B, 4.5 m for C and 7.5 m for D, E and F. Distances for Codes D, E, and F can be reduced subject to certain prerequisite, which normally not considered during planning.
Isolated aircraft parking position	Standard	Required to establish
Location of isolated aircraft parking position	R	Provides guidelines. Away at maximum distance possible and not less than 100 m from any building, etc.
De-icing/anti-icing facilities	R	Required at airports where icing. Conditions are expected to occur. ICAO Doc 9640 for more guidance
Size and number of De-icing/anti-icing pads	R	Provides guidelines. additional information in ICAO Doc 9157 Part 2
Strength of de-icing/anti-icing pads	R	For traffic density at the airport and consideration like an apron for static loading
Clearance distances on a de-icing/anti-icing pad	R	As per the recommended clearances for aircraft stands. Provide increased clearances for bypass configuration considering taxilane an object. Similarly, if it is close to taxiway.
Environmental considerations	R	Surface drainage design to ensure no mixing with normal surface drain to avoid groundwater pollution
Location	R	Either at aircraft stands or at place for which provides guidelines and requirement. Should clear obstacle limitation surfaces, not to affect navaids performance and clear view from ATC tower

(Continued)

Planning requirement	Standard (S) or recommended practices (R)	Brief SARPs
Slopes on de-icing/anti-icing pads	R	Maximum longitudinal slope as little as practicable and transverse slope not exceeding 1%
Rescue and fire fighting	Standard	Shall be provided for airports with commercial air transport operations
Response time (response time is the prime criteria to locate the place where the rescue and fire fighting vehicles are to be positioned)	Standard	Response time is the time taken for the vehicle to reach any point on each runway in operation and ready to apply 50% of the discharge rate. The timing is 3 minutes as standard, and 2 minutes is recommended to reach any point of operational runway. For other parts of the movement area, 3 minutes is the response time as a recommended practice
Location and number of fire stations	R	Fire vehicles are housed in a fire station. The location is decided based on a calculation to show that the response time is achievable. Thus, to achieve the required response time some airports may require more than one fire station, one main and other(s) satellite.
Aerodrome category	Standard	Specifies the aerodrome category specifically defined for fire and rescue services. Aerodrome category is dependent on two dimensions of the aeroplane, its overall length and maximum fuselage width. There are 10 categories. This is to decide the number of firefighting vehicles and quantities of extinguishing agents depending on the category.
Number of fire fighting vehicles	R	Depends on the aerodrome category. One vehicle for category 1 to 5, two vehicles for 6 and 7 category and three vehicles for category 8 to 10. Fire station building area requirement is dependent on this.
Emergency access roads	R	Required for minimum response time. Access up to 1000 m from threshold or at least up to airport boundary is recommended.
Location of runway holding position	Standard	Specified depending on the Code number of aerodrome reference code and type of runway operations- Instrument, Non-precision, Precision approach Cat I, II and III and take off runway
Airfield ground lighting configuration	Subsequent chapter describes the SARPs, and brief requirement is described. The description also will briefly touch up on power supply requirement.	

(Continued)

Planning requirement	Standard (S) or recommended practices (R)	Brief SARPs
Width of runway	R	Depends on numeral in aeroplane reference code and OMGWS
Strength of runway	R	To withstand the traffic – type of aircraft and annual movements.
Shoulders for runway	R	Required for airports with Code letter D, E and F. Specifies the total width of the pavement including the runway width

Airport planners should be familiar with the above SARPs as these requirements guide the planning. When the requirement in ICAO is read, it is easy to understand if it is a standard or recommended practice. Wherever the requirement is mentioned as 'Shall' it means it is a standard, and if it is mentioned as 'Should', it is a recommended practice – also titled as 'Recommendation'.

There could be some differences between ICAO SARPs and CAA's regulations. The following are an example of a few countries. However, the intent of the ICAO SARPs is maintained by the CAAs.

CAA (UK)

Refer to differences in ICAO SARPs and Procedures published by CAA (UK) in this link GEN 1.7 DIFFERENCES FROM ICAO STANDARDS, RECOMMENDED PRACTICES AND PROCEDURES (ead-it.com)

One example is aerodrome reference code parameters. CAA (UK) is different than ICAO SARPs. CAP 168 of CAA (UK) publication titled 'Licensing of Aerodromes'. This document does not differentiate between SARPs. Also, certain explanations are given for the requirement specified.

CASA (Australia)

Like CAA (UK), CASA has also filed the differences and the document is in this link http://www.airservicesaustralia.com/aip/aip.asp. One example is RESA length requirement which is different from ICAO Annex 14. Also, most of the specifications are standards, mentioned as 'must' and few are mentioned as 'preferred' (an example being RESA length). In the preferred matter, thing or value is not complied with, the aerodrome manual must contain:

a   A statement to that effect.
b   The reasons for non-compliance.
c   The alternative matter, thing or value that is complied with.

FAA

FAA publishes Advisory Circulars for planning, design, and operations. The differences between FAA AC and ICAO Annex (more specifically Annex 14) can be viewed online and the link is GEN 1.7 Differences from ICAO Standards, Recommended Practices and Procedures (faa.gov)

Airports in the United States are for the most part owned and operated by local governments and quasi-government organizations formed to operate transportation facilities. The Federal Government provides Air Traffic Control (ATC), operates, and maintains NAVAIDs, provides financial assistance for airport development, certifies major airports, and issues standards and guidance for airport planning, design, and operational safety.

There is general conformance with the SARPs of Annex 14, Volume I. At airports with scheduled passenger service using aircraft having more than nine seats, compliance with standards is enforced through regulation and certification. At other airports, compliance is achieved through the agreements with individual airports under which Federal development funds were granted; or, through voluntary actions.

For example, aerodrome reference code in FAA

In the United States, the Airport Reference Code is a two-component indicator relating the standards used in the airport's design to a combination of dimensional and operating characteristics of the largest aircraft expected to use the airport. The first element, Aircraft Approach Category, corresponds to the ICAO PANS-OPS approach speed groupings. The second, Airplane Design Group, corresponds to the wingspan groupings of code element 2 of Annex 14, aerodrome reference code.

EASA

EASA has also field the differences and available in the weblink "Cooperation with the International Civil Aviation Organization (ICAO) | EASA (europa.eu)"

The table of compliance checklist is published Annex wise. The table provides information, clause wise as below.

Differences – No or Yes. If differences exist, it provides information such as whether the level of implementation is (i) more exacting or exceeded (ii) different in character or other means of compliance (iii) less protective or partially implemented or not implemented (iv) significant difference.

Obstacle Limitation Surfaces (OLS)

Annex 14 SARPs are fundamentals for airfield planning to identify the dimensions of airfield pavements and layout and provide classification of the runway operations and the airfield requirement matching with these. With these, it is possible to work out the minimum length and width of the land required to develop the airfield components. The OLS is another essential aspect of airport planning, whether greenfield or brownfield, which is part of Annex 14.

One of the critical aspects of airport planning is to understand the limitations in and around the airport due to structures and buildings in terms of their location and maximum permissible height in order not to pose a safety risk to aircraft operations. ICAO Annex 14 specifies that when a new instrument runway is being located, particular attention needs to be given to areas over which aeroplanes will be required to fly when following instrument approach and missed approach procedures to ensure that obstacles in these areas or other factors will not restrict the operation of the aeroplanes for which the runway is intended.

The surfaces are established to provide protection for the plane in the event of any exceptional circumstances/emergency, such as a missed approach, engine failure, tyre burst, and human error.

The surfaces are as follows:

- Outer conical surface.
- Outer horizontal surface.
- Conical surface.
- Inner horizontal surface.
- Transitional surface.
- Approach surface.
- Takeoff climb surface.

The below-mentioned 'inner' surfaces are for controlling the height of aircraft, navigational aids, and vehicles which will be close to the runway.

- Inner transitional surface.
- Inner approach surface.
- Balked landing surface.

For a **precision approach runway**, the surfaces to be considered for height evaluation and zoning are as follows:

- Conical surface.
- Inner horizontal surface.
- Approach surface.
- Transitional surface.
- Inner surfaces.

Height evaluation

Analysis of existing or proposed buildings or structures or even a naturally tall object like a hillock is based on three criteria. First is the OLS mentioned in Annex 14, and second is specified in PANS-Aircraft Operations (PANS-Ops). The third one is the protection surfaces of the Communication, Navigation and Surveillance (CNS) equipment so that their performance is not affected due to the presence of structures, buildings, or objects. The first part is covered in this description, and the third criterion is covered in the chapter on master planning. The PANS-Ops procedural requirement needs to be examined in detail later during the detailed design phase of the development and hence not included in this book. (PANS-Ops is used for designing the instrument flight procedures and specifying minimum safe altitude for each procedure segment. Once a new airport site is identified based on these provisions or examination of these surfaces for a new runway in an existing airport, designers will be able to work on the procedures based on other parameters like navaids available, aeroplane speed, etc.)

OLS provides the permissible height of the obstacles in a volume of airspace. The permissible height varies from the location of the obstacle from the defined points, depending on the surface.

This chapter description is based only on ICAO Annex 14 SARPs. Annex 14 defines the obstacle that includes temporary as well as permanent and mobile objects located in an area intended for the surface movement of aircraft, i.e., on the ground or extending above a defined surface. The purpose is to protect the aircraft in flight or objects outside the defined surface above, which has been assessed as a hazard to air navigation.

As the surfaces with height and their area of coverage from the airport are permanent, it is a practice to publish these as zoning maps around the airport and make them available to the public. This helps the local Government and developers/builders/approving authorities understand the requirement of permissible height at various locations around the airport. In addition, this helps everyone with height limitations specified by the authorities (within 20 km of the airport location) at the places where they intend to put up a structure or building. While ensuring that the proposed height is permissible per the zoning map, they submit it to the authorities for approval. This makes the process transparent, more manageable, and less time-consuming.

The following are the various surfaces based on location, height permissible, and datum elevation for calculating the allowable height depending on the flight phase in operation.

Outer horizontal surface

Any object or tall structure which are 30 m in height over the ground elevation at the location and 150 m above the aerodrome elevation, within a radius of 15 km from airport, is required to examine with PANS-OPS procedures for instrument approach. (Aerodrome elevation is the highest elevation of landing area of the runway.)

Conical surface

The purpose of the conical surface, together with the inner horizontal surface (described below), is to protect airspace for visual circling prior to landing. The limits of the conical surface comprise a lower edge coincident with the periphery of the inner horizontal surface and an upper edge located 100 m above the inner horizontal surface (45 m above datum elevation) sloping upwards and outwards from the periphery of the inner horizontal surface. It covers two circles of 6100 m radius drawn from runway end and a tangent parallel to the runway. It is like inner horizontal surface with 4000 m radius.

Both the above surfaces are for defining procedures for flight operations and hence are not discussed in this chapter. However, while evaluating a site for a greenfield airport existing tall structures or objects up to 20 km from the site are required to be listed out and examined on a preliminary basis.

Inner horizontal surface

This surface protects the airspace during the flight's visual circling before landing. It also provides protection for circuiting aircraft following an instrument approach, balked landings, or the visual final approach for IFR (Instrumental Flight Rules) operations.

It is a surface in the horizontal plane at 45 m above the airport. Within this surface, the maximum permissible height is 45 m above the datum elevation. The boundaries of this surface, shape, and extent, around the airport are depicted in Figure 4.1(a) for a single runway and Figure 4.1(b) for parallel runways separated by 2000 m.

ICAO Annex 14 SARPs specifies that **the height of the inner horizontal surface shall be measured above an elevation datum established for such purpose**. Thus, datum elevation is not clearly specified in ICAO, and it refers to Airport Services Manual Doc 9137 Part 6. This

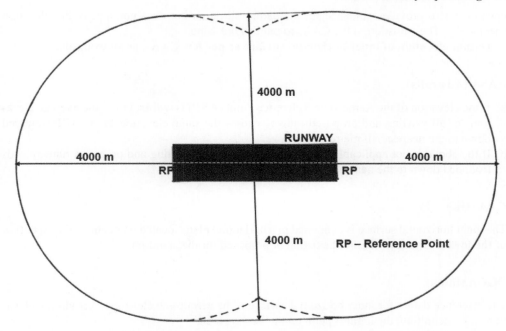

Figure 4.1(a) Inner horizontal surface for a single runway. Reference – ICAO Doc 9137 – Part 6

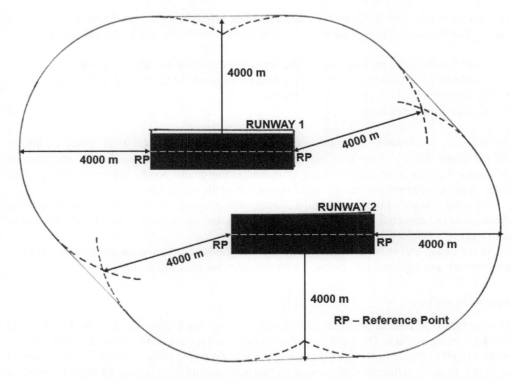

Figure 4.1(b) Inner horizontal surface for two parallel runways in an airport. Reference – ICAO Doc 9137 – Part 6

document also provides guidance for the datum elevation but does not specify the elevation specifically. Thus, it is left to the CAAs to publish the same.

Datum elevation of inner horizontal surface as per few CAAs, as an example.

CASA (Australia)

a) If the elevation of the Aerodrome Reference Point (ARP) is within 3 m of the average elevations of all existing and proposed runway ends – the same elevation as the ARP (rounded down to the nearest half metre).
b) If the above is not applicable, the average elevation of existing and proposed runway ends (rounded down to the nearest half metre).

CAA (UK)

The inner horizontal surface is contained in a horizontal plane located 45 m above the **elevation of the lowest runway threshold** existing or proposed for the aerodrome.

DGCA (India)

The reference datum for inner horizontal surface is the aerodrome elevation. Aerodrome elevation is, by definition, the highest point on the landing area.

EASA specification

The height of the inner horizontal surface should be measured above an established elevation datum. The elevation datum used for the height of the inner horizontal surface should be:

- The elevation of the highest point of the lowest threshold of the related runway; or
- The elevation of the highest point of the highest threshold of the related runway; or
- The elevation of the highest point of the runway; or
- The aerodrome elevation.

For relatively level runways, the datum elevation determination is not critical. When the threshold elevations differ by more than 6m, the datum elevation should be based on the factors such as elevation of the most frequent used altimeter setting datum points, minimum circling altitudes in use or required and the nature of operations at the aerodrome.

For more complex inner horizontal surfaces, with runways on different levels, a common elevation is not essential, but where surfaces overlap, the lower surface should be regarded as dominant.

As the datum elevation for the IHS differs from State to State, this should be considered by the planners and appropriately fix the datum elevation for evaluation of objects.

Approach surface

This surface is to protect the flight path during landing. See Figure 4.2 showing the plan and elevation of the surface. The surface is like a funnel, and it ends at 60 m from threshold with a width of 280 m (equal to width of the runway strip) and it is in three sections for a total length of 15,000 m, first section 3000 m, second section 3600 m, and third section 8400 m. The surface diverges on plan at 15% on either side. The width of the surface is 280 m, 60 m away from

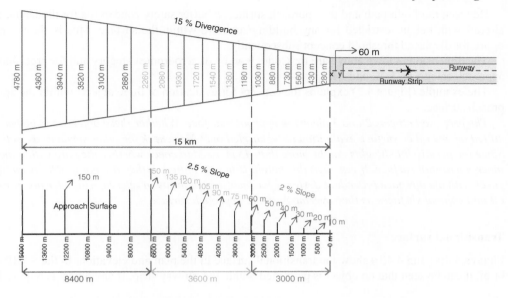

Figure 4.2 Approach surface. Reference – Annex 14/ICAO

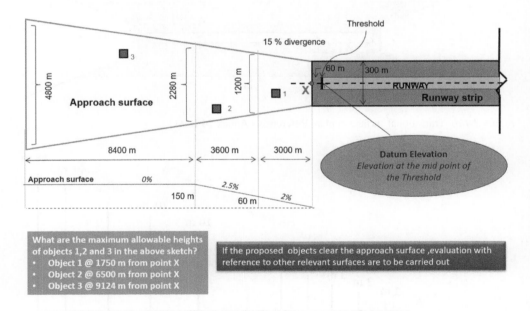

Figure 4.3 Evaluation of objects in approach surface

threshold and width increases @ 15% on either side, thus 1180 m at 3000 m, 2260 m at 6600, and 4780 m at 15,000 m.

In elevation, the slope of the surface is 2% for the first section and 2.5% for the second section, and continues the same height as that of at the end of the second section till 15,000 m.

The datum elevation for this surface, from which the permissible height will be calculated, is the elevation of midpoint of threshold (Figure 4.3).

Between the flight path and the approach surface, a buffer safety zone exists for the landing aircraft with height restricted for any building/structure within the surface. This is shown in figure for displaced threshold concept subsequently.

The dimensions shown above are for Codes 3 and 4 of aerodrome category and for precision approach categories I, II, and III.

The example (Figure 4.3) explains the concept for evaluation of three objects within the approach surface.

The proposed objects 2 and 3 clear the approach surface. Whether these objects can be permitted or any other surface evaluation to be carried out? Yes, check for other surfaces as well. Since the permissible heights can be more than 45 m, need to check whether they are within the inner horizontal surface. If yes, then this height is not permitted. If they are not in IHS, need to check with the airspace procedure designer for their acceptability in reference to outer horizontal and conical surfaces as they overlap with the approach surface.

Transitional surface

Figures 4.4(a) and 4.4(b) show the transitional surface in the plan and elevation. In the SARPs brief, it can be seen that no object is permitted within the runway strip. If any object is required

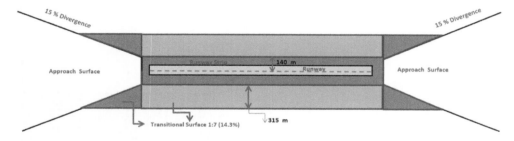

Figure 4.4(a) Transitional surface in plan. Reference – Annex 14/ICAO

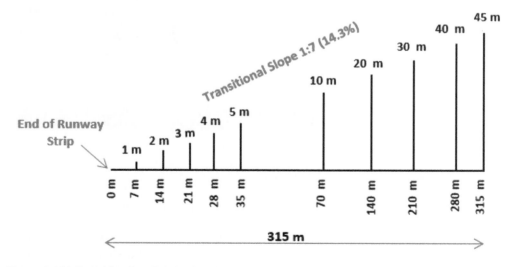

Figure 4.4(b) Transitional surface in elevation

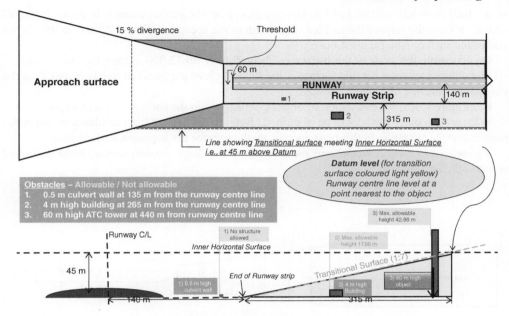

Figure 4.5 Evaluation of objects in transitional surface

to be located in the strip for air navigation purposes those objects must be frangible. Hence, the transitional surface commences from the end of the runway strip parallel to runway centreline. The permissible slope for the surface is 14.3% (for Codes 3 and 4 and for precision approach categories), meaning for every 7 m from the strip, the height permissible is 1 m. This surface ends with the inner horizontal surface which is at 45 m height. Thus, the surface extends up to 315 m (45*7).

The datum elevation for the surface, between the runway ends, is the point on the runway centreline extended perpendicular from the location being extended. Beyond the runway end, till the approach surface the datum elevation is the ground elevation at the extended runway centreline. The surface as seen extends up to a certain point in the approach surface boundary. In this portion (i.e., dark fill abutting approach surface in Figure 4.4(a)), the datum elevation is the height of the approach surface at that location.

Together with the transitional surface, the approach surface defines the volume of airspace that shall be kept free from obstacles to protect an aircraft in the final phase of the approach-to-land manoeuvre.

See the example in Figure 4.5 for the evaluation of objects falling within the surface.

Also, object 3 height being 60 m and within inner horizontal surface means maximum permissible height is only 45 m. Planners should note the height means the height over the elevation of the runway centreline. In this case, the assumption is that the runway centreline elevation and the ground elevation at the object locations are the same.

Take-off climb surface

This surface is to protect the aircraft during take-off phase. It starts at 60 m from the end of the runway with a width of 180 m. The surface on plan diverges at 12.5% on either side for 4080 m at which the width will be 1200 m. Beyond this point, the surface extends to a total length of 15,000 m from the start of the surface. The width of the second section is 1200 m width till the end of the surface (see Figure 4.6(a)).

On elevation, the slope of the surface is 2% uniformly till 15,000 m from the start point.

The datum elevation for this surface is the highest elevation between points X and Y on the extended centreline of runway.

See Figure 4.6(b) for evaluation of objects falling within the surface, as an example.

What are the other surfaces to be examined? Refer to the answer for a similar question in approach surface example. In this case, include evaluation for the approach surface also.

*Assuming **a runway is meant only for take-off** (no landing), the **only surface to be evaluated** is take-off climb surface.*

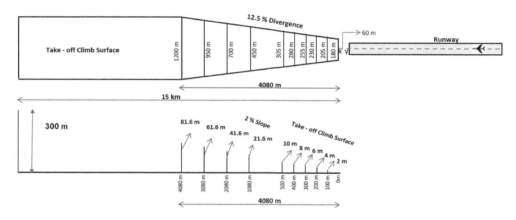

Figure 4.6(a) Take-off climb surface in plan and elevation. Reference – Annex 14/ICAO

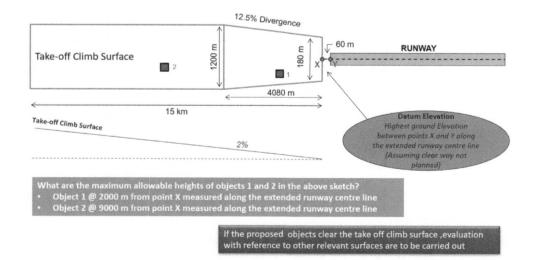

Figure 4.6(b) Evaluation of objects in take-off climb surface

Inner transitional surface, inner approach surface, and balked landing surface

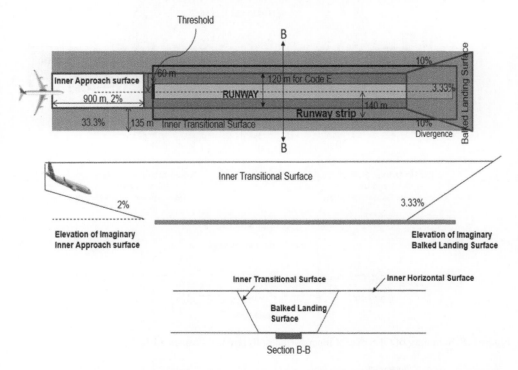

Figure 4.7 Inner transitional, inner approach and balked landing surface. Reference – Annex 14/ICAO

The surfaces discussed so far above are the controlling criteria for the height of the buildings or structures in and around the airport. These 'inner' surfaces mentioned herein are for controlling the height of aircraft, navigational aids, and vehicles which will be very close to the runway. These surfaces along with balked landing surfaces are combinedly called as obstacle free zone. These are applicable only for precision approach categories of runway operation.

See Figure 4.7 for these surfaces in plan and elevation, showing the dimensions and permissible slope. The permissible slope of the inner transitional surface is 33.3% (meaning 1 m height for every 3 m).

One example of the use of the inner transitional surface is the runway holding position where the aircrafts/vehicle hold and gets ATC clearance before entering the runway. Since they will be parked very close to the runway, the location should clear the permissible slope criteria.

Location of runway holding position based on inner transitional surface compliance is explained in the chapter on master planning.

All the surfaces except the inner surfaces are summarized in Figure 4.8.

Slope and dimensions of these surfaces will vary with aerodrome reference code and whether the runway is used for visual, non-precision, or precision approaches. The dimensions mentioned are applicable for Codes 3 and 4 and for precision approaches and these are more stringent than applicable for non-precision or non-instrument runways.

The concept of datum elevation, permissible height, and the elevation of the location where the height permissible is being evaluated is to be understood. Figure 4.9 is for a transitional surface as an example. The height permissible within the transitional surface triangle in that location is measured from the elevation of the runway centreline.

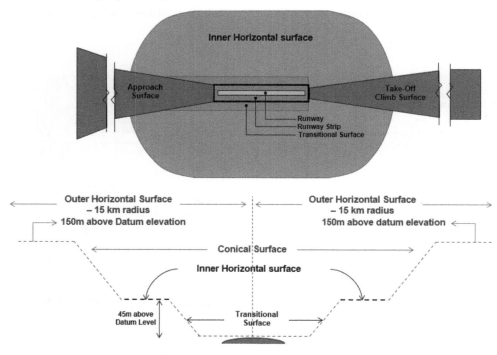

Figure 4.8 Summary of OLS except inner surfaces. Reference – Annex 14/ICAO

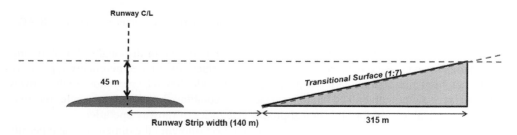

Figure 4.9 Concepts of datum elevation

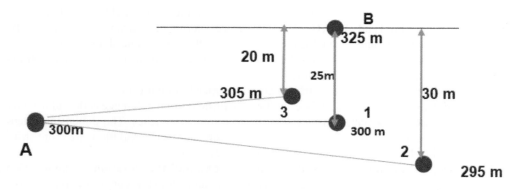

Figure 4.10 Same datum elevation but varying ground elevation of the object

Figure 4.10 shows varying ground elevation at the location of the objects with the same datum elevation. Location 1 in the figure is where the ground elevation and the datum elevation are equal. Whereas at location 2 the ground elevation is lower than the datum elevation and at location marked 3 the ground elevation is higher than the datum elevation.

Let us assume the datum elevation (at A) is 300 m AMSL in all the three cases above. The height permissible for this datum elevation is say at location B in all the three cases is say 325 m AMSL.

In case 1, the datum elevation A and the location elevation at location 1 are the same. Hence, as the height permissible is 325 m AMSL, location 1 will allow 25 m height.

In case 2, the datum elevation A and the elevation at location 2 are not the same. The elevation at 2 is 295 AMSL. As the height permissible is 325 m AMSL, height permissible at location 2 will be 325–295 = 30 m as the location elevation is below the datum elevation.

In case 3, at location 3 the elevation is 305 m AMSL, higher than location A. In this case, height permissible at location 3 will be 325–305 m = 20 m.

All the elevations considered and published in AIP will be Above Mean Sea Level (AMSL). Thus, in the no objection certificate permitting the objects the authority will mention the height permissible AMSL and the height in m from the ground elevation at that point in AMSL.

OLS and category of operations and aerodrome reference category

The stringent requirement is for precision approach and aerodrome reference categories 3 and 4. **The surfaces are same for aerodrome reference categories 3 and 4 for all the three precision approach categories I, II, and III.** The surface dimensions are the least for non-instrument runways, as the operation is in good visibility and in VFR procedures. The surface dimensions for non-precision runways codes 3 and 4 are the same as that of precision runways code 3 and 4, except inner surfaces are not applicable and the conical surface has lesser height for code 3.

The least requirement in terms of aerodrome reference category is for code 1. Remember the code numbers 1–4 is depending on the aeroplane reference field length which is the least for code 1 and the highest for code 4. This is the basis for the dimensions of OLS along with type of approach.

An example is given in Table 4.1 for code 4 aeroplane reference code with category of operations for approach surface.

Approach surface

Table 4.1 Approach surface details

	Non-instrument runway	*Non-precision approach runway (Code 3/4)*	*Precision approach runway (Code 3/4)*
Width at the start of the surface	150 m	280 m	280
Distance from threshold	60 m	60 m	60 m
Divergence	10%	15%	15%
Length of the first section	3000 m	3000 m	3000 m
Slope	2.5% for code 4/3.33% for Code 3	2%	2%
Length of the second section	**Not applicable**	3600 m	3600 m
Slope	**Not applicable**	2.5%	2.5%

Reference – Annex 14/ICAO.

Mitigation for objects protruding the surfaces

If an existing object protrudes the surfaces, practically more serious ones are those in approach, transitional and take-off climb surfaces. In the case of objects which are necessary but penetrating inner horizontal surfaces, it is a practice to carry out an aeronautical study and identify the probability of collision with aircraft using the collision risk model. IHS is basically for protecting aircraft on visual circling, so it should be possible to mitigate through the definition of visual procedures and identify the object through marking and lighting, both day and night. A common obstacle protruding the IHS in an airport is the ATC tower, whose height may exceed 45 m from the datum elevation for covering multiple runways.

In the case of objects protruding the approach surface, the object is required to be removed. If that is not possible, it is to be examined whether by reducing the object height appropriately, the object will clear the surface. If both are not practicable, determine whether infringement can be avoided by displacing the threshold. If this option is possible, then we need to examine whether the reduced landing length is sufficient for the most demanding aircraft, considering all aspects like wet runway, etc. Then, when the runway threshold is displaced, this part of the runway can be used for take-off.

In the case of objects protruding take-off climb surfaces, the first two options above for the approach surface must be examined. If both options are ruled out, the runway end for the take-off can be moved backwards, thus reducing the take-off distance available, and the revised take-off distance's sufficiency for most demanding aircraft is to be assessed.

Generally, objects infringing transitional surfaces are not allowed.

In addition to the above, any objects which are immediately outside the surfaces but may impact safety performance are to be removed. A safety risk assessment is carried out in these cases and identifies the safety index. Also, any past safety breaches in other airports and the learnings will be valuable.

Concept of threshold and displaced threshold

Figures 4.11–4.14 provide the threshold concept.

The minimum height above the threshold has to be 15 m. The slope of the approach surface is 2% whereas the flight path is 3 degree or 5% slope. In the Figure 4.11, the obstacle height is within the 2% slope and hence permissible and hence, the threshold is at the runway extremity. The vertical surface between the approach surface and the flight path is the buffer zone in order to take care of abnormal operation and still the object is not a safety breach.

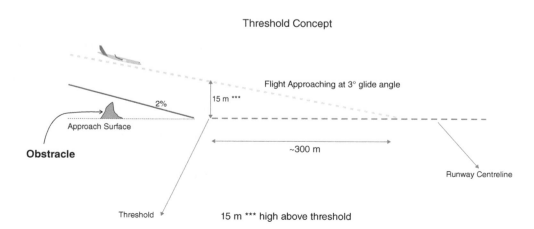

Threshold Concept

Figure 4.11 Obstacle not protruding the approach surface

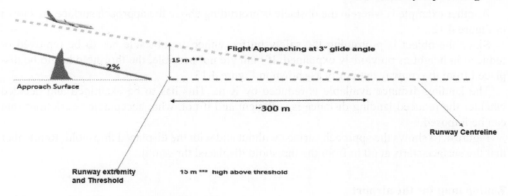

Figure 4.12 Obstacle protruding approach surface

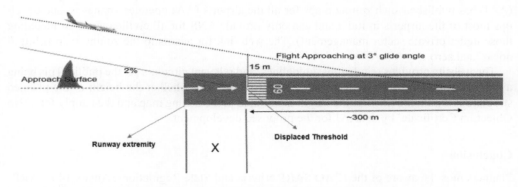

Figure 4.13 Displaced threshold enables obstacle clear of approach surface

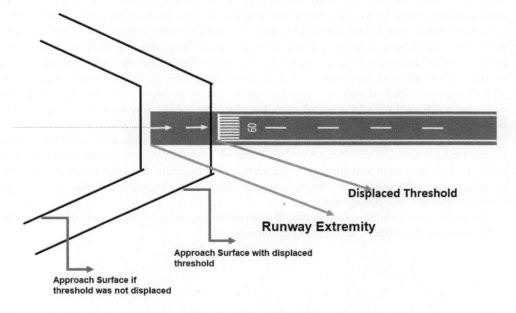

Figure 4.14 Approach surfaces with and without threshold displacement

Another example is wherein the obstacle is protruding above the approach surface, as shown in Figure 4.12.

Since the object is protruding the safety buffer, either the obstacle has to be removed or reduced in height as previously explained. If both are not possible, the threshold has to be displaced from the runway extremity as shown in Figure 4.13.

The landing distance available is reduced by X m. This has to be examined and decided whether the reduced landing distance is sufficient and if not, what acceptable restrictions that can be imposed.

Figure 4.14 shows the approach surface without and with the displaced threshold. Remember that the surface starts at 60 m from the threshold/displaced threshold.

Zoning map for the airport

The zoning map around the airport will show all the surfaces from the runway(s) with colour coding of the permissible height of these surfaces. In India, the Airports Authority of India (AAI) has published such zoning maps for all the airports (AAI operates, manages, and develops most of the airports in India and can only provide ANS for all civilian airports, including those under private sector management). The web link for access to the zoning map is http://nocas2.aai.aero.

The website provides regulations, guidelines, and relevant circulars for the public. This being a public document, the developers can themselves evaluate whether the height of the planned structure is within the permissible height mentioned in the zoning map and then apply for a 'No Objection Certificate' by the AAI for the proposed development.

Conclusion

Planners must be aware of the ICAO SARP criteria and State Regulations. Annex 14's SARPs provide principles to determine the configuration of the airfield interns of the separation distances between the airfield pavements, the maximum/minimum permissible slope, and obstacle-free area on either side of the runway and taxiway (known as strips). After finalizing the airfield layout, especially the runway, it is required to examine the structures, objects, etc., in and around the airport and fix the heights permissible with distances from the runway for future development. Thus, as a first step, the height of buildings and structures, existing and proposed, within and around the airport, will be evaluated by examining the various surfaces created for this purpose. These surfaces, known as OLS, are defined with different heights, areas, and shapes. This chapter provided an overview and examples of these surfaces. It is seen that the datum elevation is different for all surfaces; hence, the planners should know the elevation specific to the surface being evaluated.

Similarly, the extent of the surface is also different. Therefore, while evaluating the objects for the acceptability of the height in a specific location, it is essential to assess their conformance to all surfaces instead of verifying only one surface. For example, the inner horizontal and approach surfaces may overlap at some locations. In this case, we must consider the lesser height permissible in the overlapping area.

A map of various surfaces surrounding the airport that serves as a zoning map will be helpful to the planners, developers, and approving authorities.

References

Airports Authority of India. www.aai.aero

FAA. (2022). *Airport Design AC No: 150/5300-13B*. https://www.faa.gov/airports/engineering/airport_design/.

ICAO. (1983). *Airport Services Manual Part 6 – Control of Obstacles – Doc 9137*.

ICAO. (2022). ICAO Annex 14 – Ninth Edition: Vol. I.

Ministry of Civil Aviation, G. of I. (2020). *Ministry of Civil Aviation (Height Restrictions for Safeguarding of Aircraft Operations)*.

Parafield Airport. (2017). Parafield Airport Master Planning 2017.

For the zoning map visit this link

D:\FINAL ZONING MAP-WGS SYSTEM\hyderabad\hyderabad version 1.0\colour coding map of hy-derabad.dwg Model (1) (aai.aero)

5 Master planning

Introduction

Airport master planning enables orderly development with minimal disturbance to operations and wasteful expenditure due to abortive works. There are more benefits to preparing master planning by following certain principles. With separation distances and clearances prescribed as a minimum in Standard and Recommended Practices (SARPs) of Annex 14, along with OLS, a master plan is prepared. Horizontal and vertical geometry enables the planners and approving authorities to view the conceptual design of the airport. The minimum separation distances between the airfield pavements may have to be increased to have operational flexibility, thus adding to the capacity.

Annex 14 SARPs provide guidelines for fixing the runway orientation and determining the runway length for the most demanding aircraft. The number of runways and taxiways can be assumed based on the rule of thumb and carefully benchmarking with the existing airports to approve the greenfield airport development. During detailed design, these can be firmed up with phased development. In the case of brownfield airport development, feedback from operations and a simulation using an appropriate tool can be beneficial.

In the case of other buildings, whether for aeronautical or nonaeronautical purposes, evaluation of OLS is essential and located in the master plan. The Passenger Terminal Building (PTB) and cargo facility size for the preliminary assessment could be done with the rule of thumb and provision made in the master plan.

By adopting a master planning concept, a phased development of the airport facilities is possible with the least hindrance to operations and minimal abortive works while augmenting the airport capacity.

Master planning

ICAO defines an airport master plan as one that presents the planner's conception of the ultimate development of a specific airport. It effectively presents the research and logic from which the plan evolved and artfully displays it in a graphic and written report. Master plans are applied to the modernization and expansion of existing airports and the construction of new airports, regardless of their size or functional roles.

Master planning exercise primarily identifies the ideal location of various aviation-related facilities that are required for aircraft movement, passenger and cargo handling, safety, and other support facilities. The non-aviation-related facilities – like hotels and convention centres – will also be in the master plan. Certain non-aviation-related facilities can be planned for use by the airport and non-airport users if situated appropriately. Master planning exercise involves

DOI: 10.4324/9781003319948-5

consultation with all the airport stakeholders, from airlines to Regulatory Authorities and Government agencies like immigration, customs, and security to get their inputs, suggestions, and comments.

Facilities or infrastructure to be incorporated in the master plan are as follows.

Airside

- Airfield pavements – runway (s), taxiways (parallel taxiway (s), entry/exit taxiway (s), Rapid Exit Taxiway (s) [RETs], and apron including head of stand and tail of stand roads.
- Perimeter roads.
- Stormwater drains.
- Perimeter fence (security fence).
- Communication, Navigation and Surveillance system (CNS) – instrument landing system, DVOR, VHF, etc.
- Equipment for meteorological services.
- Airfield Ground Lighting (AGL) system for airfield pavements.
- Power supply substations for all airside infrastructures and facilities.
- Ground Handling Equipment (GHE) workshops.
- Airlines engineering workshops.
- Maintenance Workshops and stores.
- Ground support vehicle workshops.
- Aircraft Rescue and Fire Fighting (ARFF) stations or fire stations.

In the interface between airside and city side

- Passenger terminal building (s).
- Cargo terminal building.
- Aircraft MRO (Maintenance, Repair and Overhaul).

Land side

- Car parks – surface/multilevel.
- Main access road and approach roads to all the facilities PTB, cargo, etc.
- Cargo warehouse.
- Airport main utility systems – power, water, and sewage treatment plants.
- Commercial development – offices, hotels, convention centre, etc.
- Housing for staff.
- Offices for airlines, airport administration, customs, immigration, security, etc.
- Hotels, convention centres, logistic centres, SEZs.

Either on airside or landside

- Airport Surveillance Radar and Secondary Surveillance Radar (ASR/MSSR).
- Air Routes Surveillance Radar (ARSR).
- Air Traffic Control (ATC) tower and technical building.
- Aviation fuel storage.
- Inflight catering facility.

The purpose of the master plan

To ensure that

- The facilities are sized to handle the ultimate forecasted traffic.
- The entire land parcel for the airport is optimally utilized.
- The facilities are located at the right location so that these do not require relocation in the phased development.
- The facilities can be built in phases where possible/feasible. The impact due to expansion/development is minimal, with the least abortive work and operational hindrance.
- Environmental restrictions, if any, are considered in locating the facilities.
- Obstacle Limitation Surfaces (OLS) around the airport site are evaluated while locating the runway. The runway location must be reviewed if structures penetrate the OLS. If unable to shift the runway location, the possibility of removal of such structures is to be evaluated. If such structures cannot be removed, reducing the height of the structures should be examined. If neither the removal nor reducing the structure's height is possible, then the master plan will identify the mitigation measures or operational restrictions due to these obstacles. Such operational restrictions' acceptability must be examined and documented in the master plan.
- Regulatory guidelines are adhered to – for example, minimum distance from the PTB to long-term car park spaces.
- Critical and sensitive areas of CNS equipment are considered while locating the facilities so that these areas are not infringed upon. Such infringement affects the performance of the CNS equipment.
- Facilities and their scope and area requirement for each development phase, from the initial to the ultimate phase, are worked out and incorporated.
- Airside development plans comply with SARPs. The airside planning precedes the planning of other facilities.
- The master plan aligns with the airport's business plan to generate more commercial revenues.

Phase wise development

For a green field airport development, an ultimate master plan can be prepared considering the extent of land available. This will show, for example, how many runways and taxiway systems can be developed. From this ultimate master plan, the facilities' phase-wise development is arrived at. The number of phases can be determined based on the traffic forecast for a specific period. Airport facilities are sized to cater for the anticipated/forecasted traffic in the first ten years; subsequent phases can be between 5 and 10 years. Proper planning will ensure flexibility in expanding these facilities and caters for phased development aligned with traffic growth. Like aviation-related facilities based on traffic forecast, the non-aviation-related facilities on the city side, like hotels, etc., will be progressively taken up for implementation based on the business forecast.

For a brownfield airport development, the available master plan must be reviewed to ensure it meets the present scenario. If no master plan is available, expansion of the existing facilities or new facilities is to be taken only after a master plan is prepared to cater for the ultimate capacity of the airport with phase wise development plan.

The master plans are typically reviewed once in five years to incorporate any required changes based on the consultations with the stakeholders and the airport's own experience during the operations.

The steps for identification of facilities and infrastructures

1 Traffic forecast and the traffic projection in terms of origin – destination passengers, transfer passengers, domestic–international split. The traffic forecast will also include the aircraft fleet mix and the number of Air Traffic Movements (ATM). Usually, when the forecast is done, the passenger numbers and ATM numbers will be on an annual basis and the forecast horizon of 30–50 years. From the yearly numbers, hourly traffic, particularly peak traffic, will have to be worked out as the sizing of many facilities depends on peak passenger and ATM numbers.
2 Determine the airfield infrastructure requirement viz.

   • Runway length, width, and number of runways.
   • Number of Parallel taxiways.
   • Number of exit and entry taxiways between runway and parallel taxiway including RETs.
   • Number of apron stands required.
   • Location of stormwater drains.
   • AGL system requirement, specifically the approach lighting requirement.
   • CNS systems that are required and their location.
   • Appropriate location of ATC tower and its height.
   • Location of Rescue and Fire Fighting (RFF) stations (fire stations).

3 Location of PTB, conceptual design, and the ultimate footprint required to meet the traffic forecast.
4 Location of cargo terminal building, the ultimate footprint required to meet the traffic forecast. Identify the cargo apron requirement based on freighter-only aircraft movements.
5 Aviation fuel storage tank farm location, size, and associated buildings.
6 Vehicle parking on city side – surface (or multi-level building) and number of vehicle slots and location.
7 Other buildings like catering building, utility building, and commercial development have a lot of flexibility and options for locations, but the area requirement for these is to be estimated and appropriately located, which will cater for the ultimate traffic projection with phased development.

The location and height of all the buildings in airside and landside should comply with the requirement specified in the previous chapter.

In this chapter, the location and sizing for the following facilities/components at the airport will be described.

• Airfield components including apron.
• PTB.
• Access road to the airport.
• Airport main utilities system – power, water, and sewage.
• Vehicle parking area.
• CFR stations.
• Fuel storage facility.
• Cargo handling facility.

CNS facilities and ATC tower are described in the subsequent chapter. All the other facilities can be sized and located based on the criteria described here.

Airfield components are depicted in the figures below with briefs.

1 Runway and its shoulder and strip.
2 Runway End Safety Area (RESA).
3 Entry/exit taxiways.
4 Parallel taxiway and its shoulder and strip.
5 Apron.
6 Aircraft stands.
7 Apron taxiway.
8 Apron taxi lanes.
9 Stormwater drains.

Figure 5.2 shows the cross-section of runway.

Shoulder: An area adjacent to the edge of a pavement so prepared as to provide a transition between the pavement and the adjacent surface.

Runway shoulder and taxiway shoulder dimensions depend on the aerodrome code.

Threshold is the beginning of that portion of the runway usable for landing. Threshold and the runway beginning could be at the same location. Or the threshold may be displaced from the runway beginning. Hence, displaced threshold is a threshold not located at the extremity of a runway. Threshold may have to be displaced from the runway beginning if there are some obstacles in the approach surface (which was discussed in Chapter 4). The implication of the displaced threshold is that the landing distance available for the aircraft gets reduced to the extent of the displacement of the threshold from the runway end.

It is to note that the runway pavement between the end and threshold can be used for take-off but not for landing.

Runway strip: A defined area including the runway and stop way, if provided, intended: (a) to reduce the risk of damage to <u>aircraft running off a runway</u>; and (b) to protect aircraft

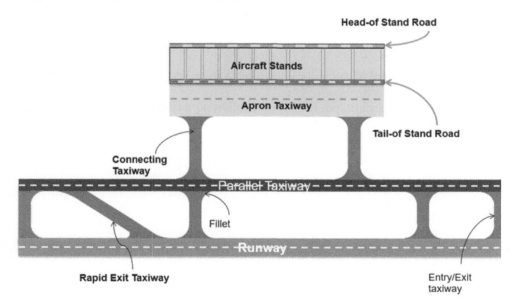

Figure 5.1 Airfield components

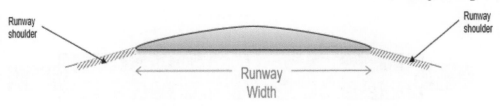

Figure 5.2 Cross-section of runway

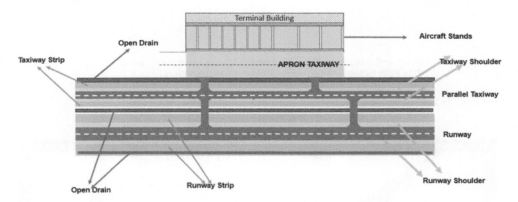

Figure 5.3 Airfield components including strips and drains

flying over it during <u>take-off or landing operations.</u> The strip includes the runway pavement and shoulder, and its width is measured from the runway centreline on either side of the runway. The strip has two portions, graded part closer to the runway and non-graded beyond that. The strip extends laterally up to 60 m from runway end.

RESA: An area symmetrical about the extended runway centreline and extends beyond the runway strip. The purpose of the RESA is primarily intended to reduce the <u>risk of damage to an aeroplane undershooting or overrunning the runway.</u> RESA starts from the strip and extends for a distance as specified in SARPs and its width is twice the width of the runway.

Objects on the strip and RESA

Due to their purpose of reducing damage to the aircraft in the event of aircraft not staying on the runway, **no objects are permitted in the runway strip** except those that are needed for navigation purposes or for safety. Such objects if installed in the strip should meet the frangibility requirement. Similar requirements apply for RESA. See Figure 5.4 for RESA.

Some of the airports may/do not have adequate land (or some other existing obstacle like water body may prevent establishing RESA) to provide RESA to the required length as per SARPs (90 m Standard and 240 m Recommended Practice). One option is to reduce the runway length to accommodate RESA. If the landing distance of runway length cannot be reduced for operating the most demanding aircraft, the guidance is to provide an arresting system. For more details may refer to FAA – Engineered Material Arresting System (EMAS). (Engineered Material Arresting System (EMAS) | Federal Aviation Administration (faa.gov)) and EASA's 'Certification Specifications and Guidance Material for Aerodrome Design'.

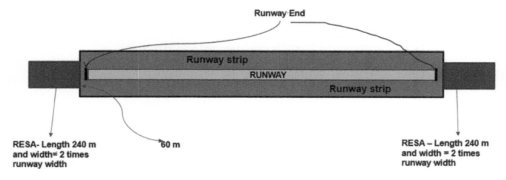

Figure 5.4 Airfield components with RESA Reference – Annex14/ICAO

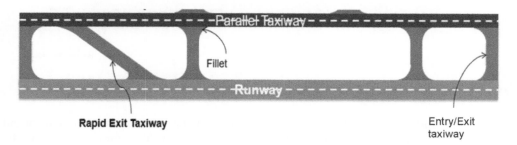

Figure 5.5 Airfield components with entry/exit taxiways

(Aircraft incidents/accidents statistics, specifically runway overrun, and their investigation report of such occurrences will highlight the importance of RESA).

Runway entry and exit taxiways are shown in Figure 5.5. Aircraft use exit taxiways for exiting from the runway to parallel taxiways. RETs being at an angle, the aircraft vacates the runway faster than perpendicular taxiways. Thus, the runway occupancy time is less and adds to the runway capacity. Note that RETs are **generally not** used for entering the runway from the parallel taxiway. Perpendicular taxiways can be used for entering the runway or exiting the runway.

Parallel taxiway and other taxiways

Width of the taxiway is as specified in SARPs. Taxiway shoulder width and strip width like runway are all specified in SARPs.

SARPs for apron taxiways are the same as that of parallel taxiways. Whereas the SARPs for the taxi lanes are different. Taxi lanes are routes bounded on either one or two sides by aircraft parking positions, by which aircraft can only gain access to these parking positions. As the aircraft speed is very less in the taxi lanes compared to taxiways, the clearance from taxi lanes to any object (including aircraft) is less than that of taxiway. However, the number of aircraft stands served by a taxi lane is restricted to say six stands so that the aircraft while taxiing does not pick up speed.

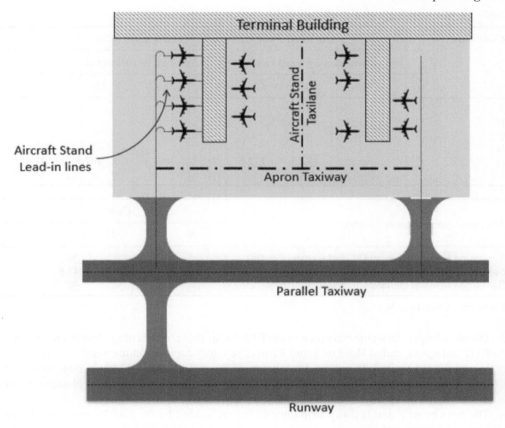

Figure 5.6 Airfield components with parallel taxiway and apron taxiway and taxilane Reference – Doc 9157/ICAO

Figure 5.6 depicts the taxiways and taxi lanes.

SARPs of Annex 14 provide the minimum distance between the runway centreline and taxiway centreline and between the taxiway centreline and to taxiway centreline. It also specifies the minimum clearance between the taxiway centreline to the object and the taxilane centreline to the object. The distances vary depending on the category of runway operation (instrument or non-instrument) and aerodrome reference code number. (Recollect that the aerodrome reference code numeral is based on the wingspan of the aeroplane, which is the basis of the separation distances.)

These are shown in Table 5.1 with values indicated for code E just as an example.

Planners to note the following.

1 For planning at this level, no constraint is imposed. For example, the tail of stand road (it requires additional pavement construction and land) may be included now and can be reviewed during detailed design for its necessity.
2 Length of the aircraft. Normally the maximum length of the aircraft in that aerodrome code is considered. Consider 80 m as the maximum length of code 4E for master planning purposes.

Table 5.1 Minimum separation distances

Code letter	Distance between taxiway C/L and runway C/L (m)							
	Instrument runways code number				Non-instrument runways code number			
	(1)	(2)	(3)	(4)	(1)	(2)	(3)	(4)
A								
B								
C								
D								
E	—	—	**172.5**	**172.5**			107.5	107.5
F	—	—						

Min separation distances for t/ws	Code					
	A	B	C	D	E	F
Separation between taxiway C/L and taxiway C/L (m)					76	
Separation between taxiway C/L and object (m)					43.5	
Separation between taxilane C/L and object (m)					40	

Reference – Annex 14/ICAO.

3   Distance from aircraft nose position to the PTB facia. This consists of vehicular lane between PTB and apron, called Head of Stand Road. The width depends on the number of lanes and bypass lanes required. However, a minimum of 10 m is considered. Apron edge to aircraft nose may add another 10 m. In total, 20 m can be considered at the time of planning at this level and can be optimized during detailed design.
4   The runway strip and taxiway strip dimensions are guided by the SARPs, and these lie between the pavements.
5   Stormwater drain for the runway runoff and taxiway runoff will have to be accommodated between the pavements.

Image of head of stand road and tail of stand roads are shown in Figures 5.7 and 5.8.

Stormwater drains

Normally open drains are considered between runway and taxiway and between taxiways. In the apron covered drains are considered. For the horizontal geometry and layout, the exact location of drains/their design is not important since the drains are within the separation distances (see Figure 5.9).

Location and number of entry/exit taxiways

In the chapter on capacity, it was mentioned that the number, location, and type of exit taxiways from runway to parallel taxiway contribute to the capacity. In the master planning, it is required to indicate these and during the detailed design, the exact location of the exit taxiways can be finalized and implemented. There are examples of operating airports adding exit taxiways to

Figure 5.7 Head of stand road. Photograph by the author

increase the capacity based on fleet mix and actual runway occupancy time. As the airfield lay-out and fleet mix at the airports are not the same, it is required to be carried out using appropri-ate tool (software for the simulation is available) to design the exit taxiway configurations. An example of the exit taxiway for different aircraft is shown in Figure 5.10(a).

When the aircraft lands in the direction shown in the figure, it can use any one of the exits from 1a to 6a, depending on the aircraft speed and the runway surface condition. Large aero-planes require a greater landing length of runway, and wet runway requires more runway length

Figure 5.8 Tail of stand road. Photograph by the author

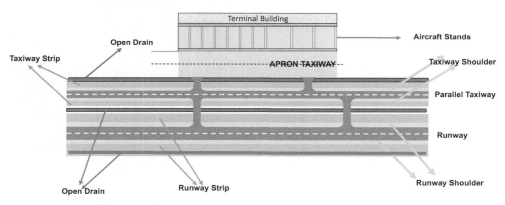

Figure 5.9 Open stormwater drains

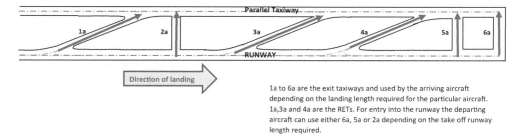

1a to 6a are the exit taxiways and used by the arriving aircraft depending on the landing length required for the particular aircraft. 1a,3a and 4a are the RETs. For entry into the runway the departing aircraft can use either 6a, 5a or 2a depending on the take off runway length required.

Figure 5.10(a) Exit taxiways

than a dry runway. Runway surface friction value also plays a significant role for the use of exit taxiways. The capacity addition is when the landing aircraft vacates the runway early means the next arrival or departure can be allowed. Thus, less runway occupancy time means more ATM and capacity. Thus, the angled exit taxiways allow faster vacation of runway as the aircraft need not slow down before exiting like in perpendicular taxiways. Thus, exit taxiways 1a, 3a, and 4a are called RETs. At the same time, the exit taxiway 2a can be used by aircraft which miss RET 1a, instead of exiting through which 3a increases the runway occupancy time. Similarly, taxiway 5a. Possible to insert a perpendicular taxiway between 3a and 4a.

For example, in the figure, 1a, 3a, and 4a will be located for the exit of turboprop, narrow body, and wide body, respectively. For the planning at this level, the exit taxiways (perpendicular and angled) and numbers at tentative location are sufficient to incorporate in the master planning drawing.

Similarly for aircrafts landing in the direction shown in Figure 5.10(b)

Perpendicular taxiways will be used for departing flights entering the runway from the parallel taxiway.

There are stipulations of minimum and maximum angle of RET with the runway and minimum length of the straight distance of the RET. The minimum distance between two consecutive RETs is also specified. The RETs must not be close enough to each other, which may confuse the pilots while exiting at high speed.

The runway holding position is the location where the aircraft and vehicles will have to stop and get ATC's clearance before entering the runway. This location is marked and lighted. The location depends on the aeroplane code, basically to be clear of the inner transitional surface explained in Chapter 4. The concept is shown in Figure 5.11(a) for code E aircraft.

Figure 5.11(b) shows the runway holding positions on airfield layout plan.

Figure 5.10(b) Exit taxiways

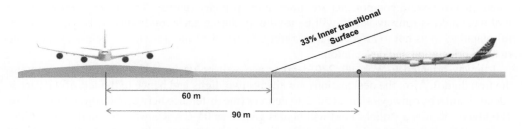

Figure 5.11(a) Location concept of runway holding position. Reference – ICAO/Annex14

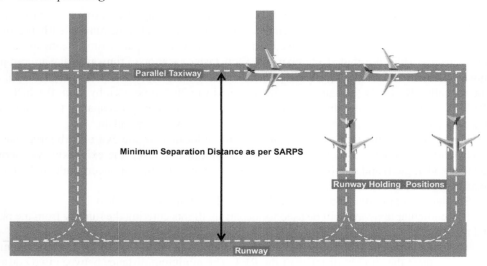

Figure 5.11(b) Runway holding positions on airfield layout plan

Criteria for locating the facilities at the airport

Runway orientation, location, and length

The runway is to be oriented along with the wind direction. However, it would be impossible to always ensure total alignment with the wind direction. Thus, SARPs recommend the permissible cross-wind components depending on the aerodrome code. Therefore, smaller aircraft with lesser cross-wind components and wide body with higher cross-wind components. For this, historical wind speed, direction, and pattern at the sites selected for an airport are why multiple sites are identified for a greenfield airport. These should be examined based on the data from the meteorological department for several years, and the wind rose diagram is plotted to identify the appropriate runway orientation. If these data are unavailable for the exact site location, data from nearby locations could be used for the study. The principle is that 95% of the time, the runway must be useable, meaning 5% of the time, the cross-wind component could exceed the permissible speed. However, it may not be possible to achieve the 95% usability of the primary runway for smaller aeroplanes but having large numbers. In such cases, the airport can plan for another runway according to the cross-wind direction, which can be used for smaller planes when the cross-wind components are more in the primary runway. This is why some airports will have a cross runway which will be used only during such conditions. This requires careful planning so as not to affect aviation safety. Figure 5.12 the description below explains the runway orientation and designation.

Runway-oriented E-W is 90–270 degrees and will be designated as 09–27, by removing the first digit 0. Also, the designations are always two digits and hence to the left of 9 a zero is added. Similarly, runway oriented 50–230 degrees (the difference between the directions will be 180 always as it is a straight line) will be designated as 05–23. Runway-oriented 140–320 degrees will be designated as 14–32. The direction is with reference to magnetic north and arrived after rounding off to the nearest 10 degrees. If it is say 147 degrees, the runway orientation will be 15–33. For example, 149 degrees will also be 15–33 runway orientation. A runway oriented north-south will be designated as 18–36 (36 not 00). Also, the designation starts with the lower

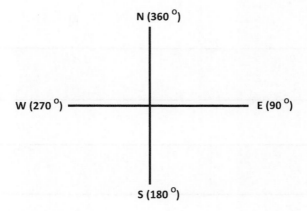

Figure 5.12 Runway orientation

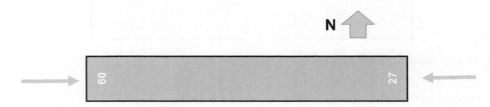

Figure 5.13 Runway designation basis

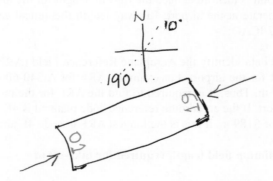

Figure 5.14 Runway orientation 01–19

value for example 18–36, 09–27, 15–23, and 10–28. Also, in the aviation nomenclature runway 10–28 is called as runway 10 and runway 28 as if there are two runways, to identify two directions of take-off or landing.

On the runway pavement, the runway designations will be marked. 09–27 runways will be marked as shown in Figure 5.13. This is because when the aircraft is approaching towards east the pilot will see on the compass 90 degrees and similarly while approaching towards west, the compass will read 270 degrees.

Runway 01–19 will be like this in Figure 5.14.

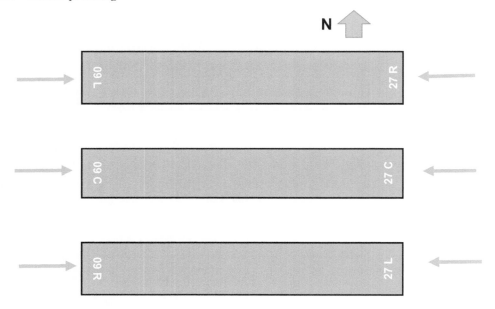

Figure 5.15 Multiple parallel runways and their designation

Two or more parallel runways will be designated as shown in Figure 5.15.

Ruwnay length calculation methodology

Once the best orientation is identified, need the runway length for the most demanding aircraft that is expected to operate at the airport. Runway length theoretical calculation is as below, described in Doc 9157/ICAO:

- From the technical data identify the Aeroplane Reference Field (ARF) Length for the most demanding aircraft for the airport. For example, ARF for A 340-600 is 3189 m and for B 777-300 it is 3140 m. Thus, it is required to find the ARF for the most demanding aircraft planned at the airport. If the aerodrome reference code planned is 4E, the ARF for the planning purpose will be 3189 m, if this is the longest ARF in code 4E aircraft group.

ARF length is the **minimum field length required for take-off at**

- Maximum certificated take-off weight.
- Sea level.
- Standard atmospheric conditions.
- Still air.
- Zero runway slope.
- The ARF length chosen is required to be corrected for the site elevation above mean sea level, temperature, and runway slope.
- The correction factor for the site elevation is 7% increase over the ARF length mentioned above for every 300 m it is more than the mean sea level. For example, if the site is 500 m above mean sea level, the correction factor is 0.07*500/300 = 0.117. Assuming the basic length is X m, with elevation correction it would be 1.117 times the basic length.

- The temperature to be considered here is not the maximum ambient temperature at the site. 'Aerodrome Reference Temperature' is to be used. The aerodrome reference temperature is the monthly mean of the average daily temperature for the hottest month of the year plus one-third of the difference between this temperature and the monthly mean of the maximum daily temperature for the same month of the year.

  Correction factor for the calculated aerodrome reference temperature is 1% for every 1 degrees over standard atmospheric temperature. Assuming the aerodrome reference temperature is 30 degree Celsius. The standard atmospheric temperature at 500 m AMSL is 11.75 degree Celsius. The difference is 18.25 degrees, @ 1% per degree, the runway length calculated with site elevation will increase to 1.117*1.1825 times the basic length.

- For runway slope, the correction required is to increase the length by 10% for every 1% slope. During the preliminary planning, we may not have the finalized runway slope, hence can consider 1% which is the maximum slope that is permissible. That is 10% more.

- Considering the elevation, temperature and slope, and temperature, **the actual runway length required would be** $1.117*1.1825*1.1* X = 1.453* X$. Where X is the ARF length or the basic length.

- If the basic runway length is say 3200 m in this case, the actual length required is 4650 m.

One important aspect to note here is that the runway length calculation assumes that the aircraft is with the Maximum Takeoff Weight (MTOW) permitted by the aeroplane manufacturers. This weight is based on all the loads (passenger and cargo load), including the fuel weight. The quantum of fuel in the MTOW is the fuel carried by aircraft to operate at the maximum range (flying distance) permissible. So, if the aircraft range is reduced, the fuel takeoff will also decrease, thus reducing the aircraft's takeoff weight, which will be less than MTOW. Thus the runway length requirement will also reduce. Aeroplane manufacturers in the technical data provide charts for each aeroplane indicating the payload vs. range and payload vs. takeoff runway length required. For example, an aircraft requiring a 3000 m long runway at sea level and zero runway slope with a MTOW of 350 MT. If the takeoff weight is reduced to 300 MT, the runway length required at sea level and zero runway slope will be approximately 2200 m. So, the planners, in consultation with all stakeholders, can decide whether the airport being planned with the most demanding aircraft is for the maximum range possible or can choose a lesser range and, thus, lesser runway length required. Or one can decide that the planning is to develop an airport with no constraints at the time of planning and during the asset's life.

Similarly, the landing length of the runway is also required to be calculated.

Once the runway length is calculated above, the associated components required can be added as below:

Lengthwise, the maximum length of the land required is for the runway. Beyond the ends of the runway, 60 m length is necessary for the runway strip and 240 m for RESA (Recommended, otherwise 90 m as per Standard) and a width twice the width of the runway is required. Further land requirement depends on the type of approach lighting system that is planned. However, a maximum length of 1000 m from the runway end and a width of 120 m should be sufficient.

Location of runway

Having determined the runway's orientation and length, the next step is to locate the runway at the appropriate location within the site and in the identified orientation. This is based on the airfield layout coordinated with PTB.

Based on the airfield layout with appropriately located airfield pavements, the horizontal geometry discussed previously is worked out with all the separation distances. With this, it is possible to determine the minimum depth/width needed with parallel taxiway (s), apron, and aircraft stand all the depths plus the terminal building. However, if the airport is planned with two runways, it is required to plot all the pavements, and PTB and the total depth required are calculated and checked with the available at the site.

The locations of the airfield pavements and primarily PTB can have many alternatives, and all of these are to be evaluated and identify the best location which provides sufficient depth for all the facilities. For example, if the runway is east-west oriented, the location can be changed in the North-South direction, but the runway orientation is maintained in an east-west orientation.

The next would be to see the ground profile from the runway to the apron at the airfield pavement location. If the ground profile is too undulating, the best location laterally by marginal shifting is possible, similarly east-west direction also to some extent without sacrificing the crosswind limitations.

The next step is to plot the OLS from the identified final runway location. If the development is greenfield, there are no structures within the airport site boundary; even if there are, these will be removed. Thus, it is required to identify all the existing objects/structures/buildings outside the airport boundary, falling within the transitional approach, take-off climb, and inner horizontal surfaces. See Chapter 4 to recollect these surfaces' shapes, distances, and surface slopes. Some adjustments to the east-west runway location can be made if objects protrude from any surfaces. If unable to reduce the height or remove the obstacle, which is infringing OLS, the mitigation measures mentioned in Chapter 4 are to be examined, which may impact operations. In the case of brownfield airport development, if the master plan is available, that will show the location of the second runway, which can be reviewed starting from OLS both within and outside the airport with all the surfaces and ensure that OLS criteria will be met.

Multiple runways

In the chapter on capacity, various configuration of runways with minimum separation distances and the utilization for operations based on the configurations was described. That could be taken as a starting point, and then with parallel taxiway(s), apron configuration, and PTB can determine the distance between the runways. A preliminary flow of aircraft from the apron to the runway and vice versa will be required if the runways are staggered.

Declared distances

The runway length is calculated as above and for publishing to the airlines and other stakeholders, the declared distances as below are to be specified in the AIP.

Take-Off Distance Available (TODA), Landing Distance Available (LDA), Take-Off Runway Available (TORA), and Accelerated Stop Distance Available (ASDA)

TODA= LDA = TORA = ASDA if the runway threshold and ends are in the same location as shown in Figure 5.16.

Figure 5.16 TORA. Reference – Annex14/ICAO

If the threshold is displaced (refer to Chapter 4 why this may be required), the LDA will get reduced by the distance of displacement from the beginning of the runway.

If the threshold is displaced by say 400 m for a runway length of 2300 m

TODA = TORA = ASDA = 2300 m, whereas LDA = 2300–400 = 1900 m

The displacement could be only for one approach or for both approaches.

Figure 5.17 shows the displaced threshold for one approach with the declared distances.

Assuming **the other approach** threshold is not displaced, Figure 5.18 shows the declared distances.

There is a concept of stopway and clearway which are defined (ICAO) as below.

Stopway is a defined rectangular area on the ground at the end of take-off run available prepared as a suitable area in which an aircraft can be stopped in the case of an abandoned take-off.

Clearway is a defined rectangular area on the ground or water under the control of the appropriate authority selected or prepared as a suitable area over which an aeroplane may make a portion of its initial climb to a specified height.

ICAO SARPs mention that the inclusion of detailed specifications for clearways/stopways is not intended to imply that these are to be provided. Stopway and clearway are not paved surfaces like runway, but this is the length available beyond the end of the runway for purpose mentioned in the definition.

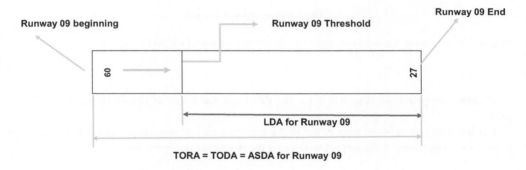

Figure 5.17 LDA with threshold displaced. Reference – Annex14/ICAO

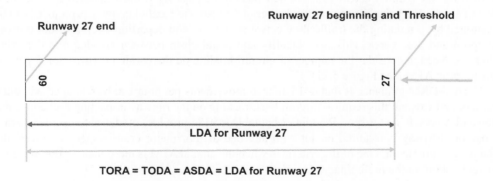

Figure 5.18 LDA without displaced threshold. Reference – Annex14/ICAO

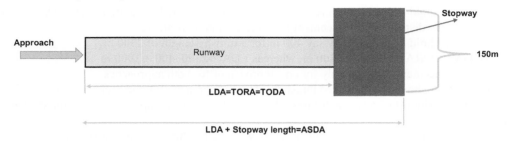

Figure 5.19 Declared distances with stopway. Reference – Annex14/ICAO

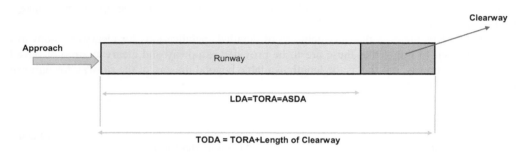

Figure 5.20 Declared distances with clearway. Reference – Annex14/ICAO

If these are provided that will alter the declared distances as shown in Figures 5.19 ad 5.20.

Declared distances at the airport for all the runways and all approaches provide information to the pilots operating at the airport will know the distances for operations.

Parallel taxiways

As the name implies, parallel taxiway is constructed parallel to the runway at the appropriate separation distance as described previously, with distances not less than as per SARPs. Whether to plan for one parallel taxiway or two depends on the peak ATM to be handled and the location of apron. The principle to decide whether more than one parallel taxiway is required can be examined by simulating the traffic flow between arriving and departing aircrafts from runway to apron and vice versa. This is to identify and avoid clash between arriving and departing aircrafts. Need to consider the number of aircraft holding on the parallel taxiway for departure during peak ATM (see Figure 5.21).

IATA, ADRM guidance is that 0–15 aircraft movements per hour can be managed without a parallel taxiway, but this requires aircraft backtracking on the runway impacting fuel consumption and delays. ICAO Airport Planning Manual Doc 9184 provides guidance to decide whether a parallel taxiway is required or not with any one of four major criteria specified meets the planning requirement. One of the criteria is when the annual ATM is more than 50,000 which is easier to adopt in the preliminary planning.

Figure 5.21 Departing aircrafts lined up in parallel taxiway

Source: Wikipedia commons

The necessity for second parallel taxiway with more than 20–25 aircraft movements per hour requires a careful study to analyse the impact of clashes between arriving and departing aircraft, affecting on-time performance and might create a congestion in apron. This also depends on the airfield layout. The master planning can consider two parallel taxiways for an airport expected to handle more than 25–30 million passengers per annum as a thumb rule. However, when to construct the 2nd parallel taxiway can be decided through a simulation study for the specific airport layout and the number of aircraft movements at the airport.

Depending on the traffic and direction of runway use, it is possible to construct part parallel taxiway to start with and add full length later. If there is no parallel taxiway or part parallel taxiway the number of aircraft movement, especially bunched movement will be restricted. In that case, there must be sufficient gap between two flights either arriving or departing or a mix. Figure 5.22 shows an airport with a part parallel taxiway.

Multiple parallel taxiway

This requirement is explained by figures along with apron taxiways. Description of apron taxiways is covered under apron.

Figure 5.23 shows runway with one parallel taxiway. Also, it is seen that the apron is located such that there is sufficient and equal length of parallel taxiway on either side is available. This will allow number of aircrafts to be lined up for departure and several arriving aircraft can enter the apron without waiting in the queue.

Figure 5.24 shows runway with one parallel taxiway, but the apron is on one side of the runway and thus, will allow number of aircrafts to be lined up for departure for the direction shown whereas the number of arriving aircraft will have some limitations in capacity as there is less taxiway length for queuing or there will be a clash between the arriving and departing aircrafts in the parallel taxiway.

Figure 5.22 Airport diagram for part parallel taxiway

Source: Wikipedia commons

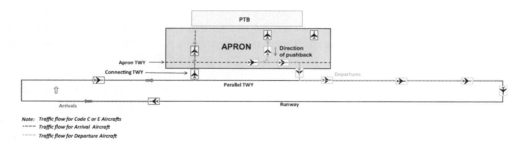

Figure 5.23 Runway with a single parallel taxiway

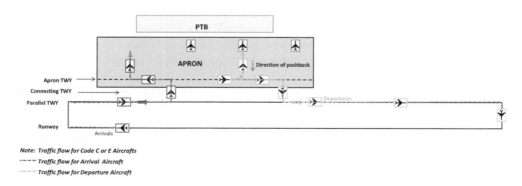

Figure 5.24 Runway with single parallel taxiway but apron on one side of runway

Figure 5.25 is with one runway and two parallel taxiways. With this, the taxiway will have adequate capacity but the congestion can happen in the apron for the movement of aircraft, meaning the apron taxiway capacity could be a constraint. This is because the push back of the aircraft and incoming aircraft to apron will use the same apron taxiway and depending on the stand allocation and number of movements either the push back has to be delayed for the incoming aircraft to reach the stand or the incoming aircraft has to wait.

Figures 5.26(a) and 5.26(b) are with one runway and two parallel taxiways and multiple apron taxiways, for adequate capacity. The apron taxiway is configured with three taxiways for simultaneous movement of aircraft with either taxiways 1 and 3 with code C aircraft OR one code E in apron taxiway 2. Figure 5.26(a) shows two code C aircrafts in outer apron taxiways, whereas Figure 5.26(b) shows one code E aircraft in the apron taxiway 2.

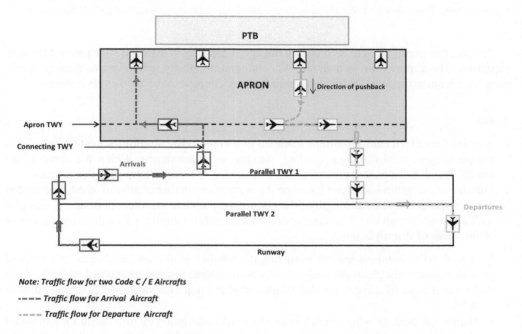

Figure 5.25 Runway with two parallel taxiways

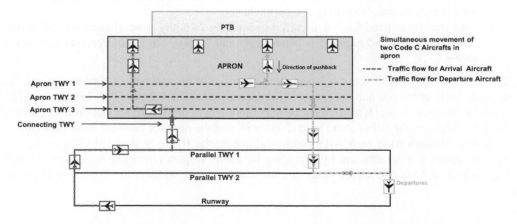

Figure 5.26(a) Runway with two parallel taxiways and 3 apron taxiways for two code C movements

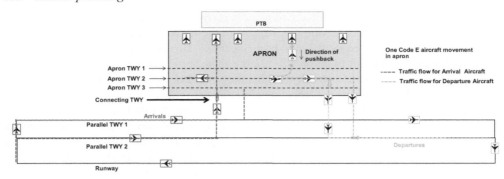

Figure 5.26(b) Runway with two parallel taxiways and 3 apron taxiways with one code E movement

The last two configurations will ensure the apron capacity is matched with parallel taxiway capacities. The airport with such an airfield configuration mostly will have two runway operations for adequate capacity. Apron and apron taxiway concepts have been explained next.

Apron

1 A defined area on a land aerodrome intended to accommodate aircraft for loading or unloading passengers, mail or cargo, fuelling, parking, or maintenance. Within the apron is the aircraft stand, a designated area on an apron intended to be used for parking an aircraft.
2 The size of the apron is decided based on the maximum number of aircraft stands required at one time (to determine the length of the apron) and the maximum length of aeroplanes (for width/depth of the apron). The number of aircraft stands required can be calculated using **one of the rules of thumb** below:

- If peak ATM numbers are not available, the number of aircraft stands can be estimated with annual throughput passenger numbers in million passengers multiplied by 3. For a 25 mppa capacity airport, number of aircraft stand required for master planning purpose is 75.
- Number of peak arriving aircraft in one hour (A) multiplied by turn round time in hours (T) multiplied by the utilization factor (U) of apron. If peak arriving aircraft numbers are not available, multiply 0.7 with the peak ATM numbers. Add number of stands required for example overnight parking and maintenance.
- Each stand is utilized for 7–8 aircraft movement in 24 hours' time. If there are 350 movements, aircraft stand required is between 45 and 50 plus other requirements mentioned above.

The length of the aircraft stand is based on the number of aircraft parked simultaneously, the aeroplane reference code and the specified minimum separation distances between aircraft. The depth of the apron is decided based on the maximum length of the aircraft that must be parked, the apron taxiway, the tail of stand road if required, and the distance between these elements.

Apron configuration as MARS: With Multiple Apron Ramp System (MARS) configuration, the apron is more efficient by providing flexibility to park either one wide-body aircraft (say codes E or F) or two narrow-body aircraft (codes C). The width of the MARS stand can be

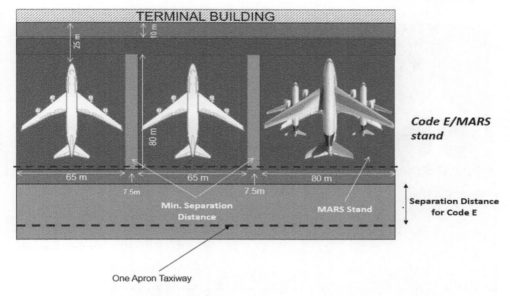

Figure 5.27 Apron taxiway for Code E aircraft

80 m against 65 m for code E-only stand. With a 65 m stand width, only one code E or one code C can be parked; whereas with an 80 m MARS stand width, the flexibility is increased to park either one code E or two code C. MARS stand is provided with two passenger boarding bridge – for code E two bridges (one for front door and the second for middle door) and the same PBBs are designed to cater for code C aircrafts one each.

The minimum separation distance between aeroplanes, called wing tip clearance, is 3 m for codes A and B aircraft, 4.5 m for code C, and 7.5 m for codes D, E, and F aircraft. If a road is planned in between the aircraft stands, these distances are to be increased.

The depth of the apron also depends on the number of apron taxiways. The options available are one apron taxiway with all clearances meant for code E aircraft taxiing, as shown in Figure 5.27.

Best practice

For large airports, the other option is three apron taxiways. Figure 5.28 shows the configuration. The two outer taxiways are designed with a separation distance for code C aircraft. The middle taxiway can be used by code E aircraft. In this configuration, either

One code E aircraft can taxi in the middle taxiway.

OR

Two code C aircraft **simultaneously taxi** in the outer taxiways.

Note the OR here. Code E aircraft must taxi only in the middle taxiway that too when the outer taxiways on either side do not have aircraft movement. In busy airports, such configuration allows simultaneous movement of two code C aircraft from and to the apron and from and to parallel taxiways. This adds to the capacity.

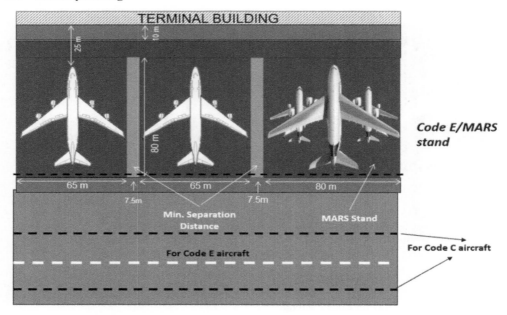

Figure 5.28 Multiple apron taxiways

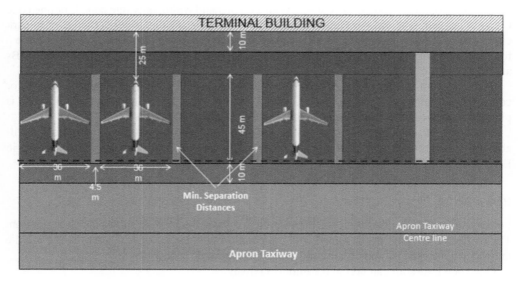

Figure 5.29 Code C apron with single apron taxiway

Configuration for simultaneous movement of two code E aircraft is also possible with additional pavement width and requirement of more clearance to the aircraft stand.

Code C aircraft stand dimensions are shown in Figure 5.29 with a single apron taxiway.

The depth of the apron shown above needs to be validated for docking passenger boarding bridges. Docking a bridge for code C aircraft requires more PBB length to maintain permissible

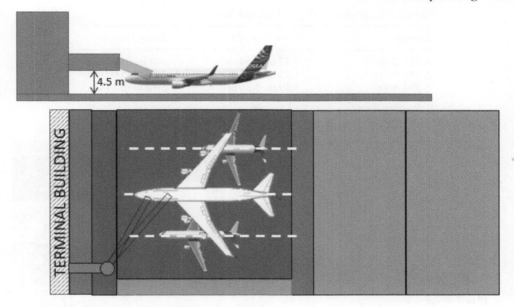

Figure 5.30 Apron dimensions to suit PBB slope

slope of the bridge for comfortable wheelchair movement and for stress-free walking. The length is decided based on the height of the node building and aircraft's door height.

See the concept in Figure 5.30.

The same two bridges shown in Figure 5.30 are designed to dock with code C aircrafts. Node position of PBB to consider extended and retracted lengths (to ensure clearance for home position of PBB with aircraft).

It is required to revalidate the apron dimension in relation to height of fixed ramp house which will provide the required clearance between fixed walkway and the vehicular lane, shown as 4.5 m in Figure 5.30.

Also, it is required to check the PBB docking with all intended aircrafts with their door heights to ensure recommended slope of PBB. Consider the slope of apron as well, the slope will be away from the terminal building. Recommended slope of PBB is 1:14 and the slope should not exceed 10%. Photograph showing the PBB docked with aircraft is shown in Figure 5.31 and the slope mentioned can be understood.

Door heights of some aircrafts as an in Table 5.2.

Wide-body aircrafts can be docked with two PBBs, whereas narrow-body aircrafts with only one PBB.

In summary, apron dimensions are based on:

a   Peak-hour aircraft stand demand.
b   Turn round time of the aircraft.
c   Fleet mix at the airport.
d   Contact/remote stand requirements based on traffic forecast.
e   Night parking requirement.
f   Additional requirements like general aviation aircrafts.

Table 5.2 Examples of height of aircraft door

Aircraft	Door 1 height	Door 2 height
A 321–200	3.47 m–3.50 m	Not applicable
A 340–600	4.73 m–4.78 m	4.88 m–5.00 m
A 380–800	5.10 m–5.36 m	5.12 m–5.34 m

Reference – Airbus.

Figure 5.31 Aircraft docked with PBB. Photograph by the author

g Buffer capacity for aircraft parked due to maintenance.
h GHE parking/storage.
i Clearances between aircraft and between aircraft and object.
j Number of apron taxiways.
k Docking PBBs with allowable slope.

The space occupied by the GHE in apron at an airport is an example in Figure 5.32.

Having located the runway, taxiway, and apron, the horizontal geometry of the airfield layout as a summary of airfield infrastructure is shown below:

Figure 5.33 shows the horizontal geometry dimensions with a single parallel taxiway. The separation distances as minimum specified in SARPs may have to be increased for operational efficiency and flexibility which is explained in the subsequent chapter.

Figure 5.34 shows two parallel taxiways.

Thus, the width of the airfield up to the PTB can be determined.

Land requirement beyond the ends of runway

The required length of the land beyond the runway end is shown in Figure 5.35, a similar requirement is applicable for the other end of the runway.

RESA dimension is 300 m length (240 m from strip) from runway end and of two times the width of the runway, thus the width of RESA is 90 m. Approach lights start from the threshold (hence it overlaps with RESA) and here it is assumed that the threshold is at the runway

Figure 5.32 Apron with GHE storage. Photograph by the author

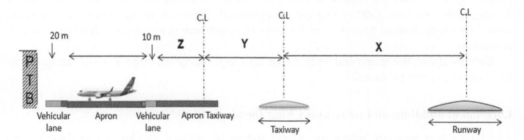

Figure 5.33 Horizontal geometry dimensions with a single parallel taxiway

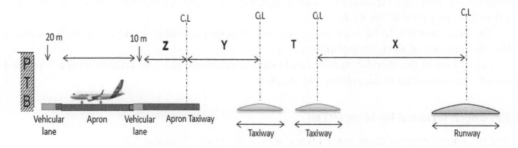

Figure 5.34 Horizontal geometry dimensions with two parallel taxiways

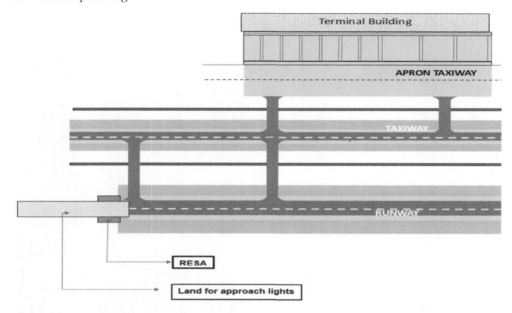

Figure 5.35 Length of land required beyond the end of runway

extremity (not displaced). The land required for Cat I approach lights is 1000 m in length and width of 120 m preferably. If the runway length is, for example, 3600 m, considering Cat I approach lighting at both the approaches the length of land required is 5600 m. If the land length is marginally less than 5600 m that can be examined. However, in this description, it is assumed for unconstrained development for code 4E aerodrome in precision instrument category operations.

With the above, the length and width of the land required for the airfield layout can be calculated and the layout prepared.

Location of buildings and structures within the airport

Any building or structure within the airport should be planned and located to comply with SARPs regarding clearances from the runway, taxiway, and apron. Also, these heights shall be examined to comply with OLS specified in SARPs. Structures or objects, whether existing or proposed in the approach/take-off climb surfaces, require careful analysis even if they comply with OLS as these are exposed to more damage, as most of the accidents happen during the take-off or landing phase of the flight.

The third criterion to be examined is that the proposed buildings or structures will not affect the performance of the CNS equipment.

Let us look at the specific facilities and evaluate criteria 1 and 2 mentioned above. The third criteria are described in the subsequent chapter.

Passenger Terminal Building (PTB)

The passenger process flows in a PTB are shown in Figures 5.36 and 5.37.

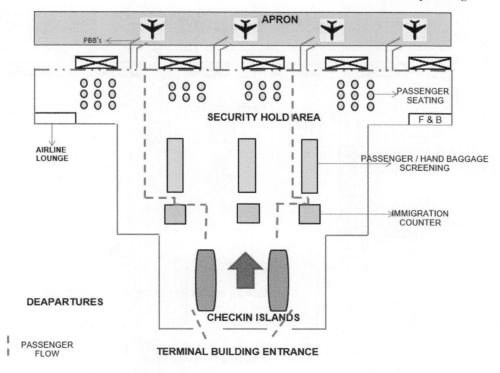

Figure 5.36 Departure passenger process flow in PTB

PTB should be located close to the apron for servicing the passengers' boarding or deboarding from the aircraft through aerobridges. Even for non-contact stands (without bridges), the PTB must be close to the apron as possible for quick service.

With the identified location, the permissible height of the building is decided, as this is one of the buildings at the airport closer to the runway. The horizontal distance from the runway/ taxiway/apron will generally exceed the minimum distance requirement for medium to large airports, i.e., beyond the strips. However, this aspect requires review.

As PTB will be a tall structure, it requires a detailed study about complying with OLS (The same principle of horizontal distance from airfield pavements and permissible height requirement is applied for all the other buildings and facilities planned at the airport).

The permissible height of the PTB is to be decided based on evaluating two surfaces – transitional and inner horizontal surfaces. The datum elevation is to be finalized for all the OLS, as discussed in Chapter 4. While calculating the permissible height, finding the ground elevation at the location where the PTB is planned to be located is required.

Transitional surface

This surface starts from the runway strip, and for every 7 m, a height of 1 m is permissible. Suppose the PTB location is 280 m from the strip, i.e., 420 m from the runway centreline. In that case, the height acceptable at the location is 40 m above the datum elevation of the transitional surface. Assuming the datum elevation is 345 m AMSL, the height of the PTB at the site should

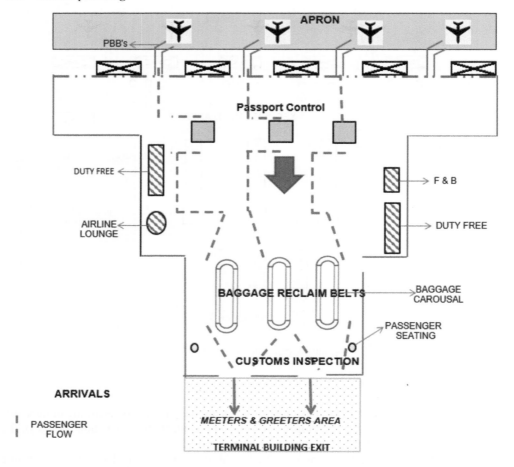

Figure 5.37 Arrival passenger process flow in PTB

be less than 385 m AMSL. If the ground elevation at the PTB location is 345 m AMSL, a 40 m high building is permissible.

In the second scenario, assuming the ground elevation is 350 m AMSL at the PTB location, PTB can have a maximum height of 35 m at the identified location whose ground elevation is 350 m AMSL as the height cannot exceed 385 m AMSL.

Inner horizontal surface

It extends about 4 km from the runway, and the height permissible is 45 m above the datum elevation of the surface. Assuming a case where the surface datum elevation is the same as that of the transitional surface (345 m AMSL), then the maximum height permissible is 390 m AMSL. When the building or structure falls within more than one surface, the lowest height acceptable per the individual surface will be applicable. In this case, as per the transitional surface criteria mentioned above, the building height permissible is 385 m AMSL, whereas the acceptable height is 390 m AMSL for inner horizontal surface. The lower height allowable is as per the transitional surface criteria, which is 385 m AMSL (40 m above 345 m); hence, the building height must be less than 385 m AMSL at this location. Similarly, in the second scenario, 35 m high building is possible at the location whose ground elevation is 350 m AMSL.

For all the buildings and structures within the airport land, OLS for the above two surfaces with principles as described can be examined and decide the permissible height at the proposed location.

From the above, one can understand that if the airport site ground profile has significant variations, it is essential to work out the horizontal geometry first, starting from the runway finished level to the taxiway finished level and then to the apron to PTB ground level. With significant variations in ground profile, there could be many options for the finished ground profile of various facilities, and from the multiple options the one which will result in the optimum cut and fill of the ground will have to be chosen.

PTB area requirement

While there are no standards for minimum area per peak hour passenger, planners come across many thumb rules. Some of these are:

1   Area per peak hour passengers **to be at most** 25 sqm for domestic and 35 sqm for international operations.
2   Domestic 22–23 sqm per pax, international 27–28 sqm per passenger, and integrated building 24–25 sqm per passenger.
3   14 sqm per domestic passengers and 17 sqm per international passengers.
4   15 sqm per domestic passenger and 30 sqm per international passenger.

Higher area requirements are airport specific. For example, a hub airport with considerable transit passengers and dwell time at the airport, for example, Dubai, Changi, and Hong Kong, requires more space than an airport handling majorly origin-destination passengers. Also, higher area requirements are justified for airports where frequent disruption may occur. For example, possible flight delays due to inclement weather result in congestion in the terminal.

Types of Baggage Handling Systems (BHSs), such as automatic sorters and long-term storage of transit passengers' bags, require more space than simple systems. Hub airports will also have many large airline lounges and commercial areas like shops and F&Bs. In addition, some airport terminals have hotels within the PTB. All these requirements are required to be considered in the next stage of evaluation of airport planning.

For preliminary assessment and master planning purposes, the following may be considered as only the footprint required for earmarking the location at this stage with an initial floor plan with concepts like many levels of PTB.

Domestic – 15 sqm per peak hour passenger.
International – 20 sqm per peak hour passenger.

Area assessment based on annual passenger traffic

If the peak hour passengers are unavailable and only annual passenger numbers are estimated, the practice is to consider 8000–10,000 sqm per million passengers per annum. We can firm up the area requirement when more information is available during the detailed design.

Thus, for 40 million passengers per annum, the PTB area required is approximately 320,000–400,000 sqm. Considering 400,000 sqm in three levels, a footprint of 150,000 sqm can be marked in the master plan with 300 m width and 500 m length. The area also depends on the percentage of aircraft stands planned as contact stands, as the area requirement will increase if

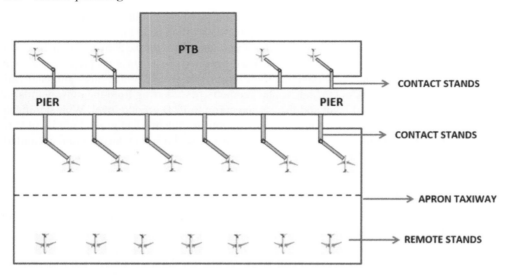

Figure 5.38 PTB with contact stands and remote stands

more stands are with PBBs. Figure 5.38 shows a terminal building layout with linear piers for contact stands and a few remote stands.

Shape of the building with options, pros, and cons are briefed in the subsequent chapter.

If multiple PTBs are planned, the location and area are to be calculated based on the capacity of each PTB in million passengers per annum or peak hour passenger numbers and sized. In the case of multiple terminals, the apron is to be ideally co-located with each terminal.

Total area assessment based on peak hour passengers and processing areas

We can also work out the PTB area requirements for each passenger process and baggage process with peak hour passenger numbers and, thus, the area required for operations. For the space needed for services, offices, stores, commercial activities, etc., if detailed working is not possible during the preliminary working, practice shows that the area of the PTB is approximately in the ratio of 60%–70% for passenger processing and operations, 20%–30% for services and 10% for commercial activities. We can compare this split-up with similar regional airports and review this during the detailed design stage. This option of bottom-up working of area requirement will be more accurate than considering per sqm for annual passengers. ADRM/IATA provides guidelines for arriving at each processing areas based on the passenger numbers. **In the preliminary planning, it is best practice to decide the number of levels and floor-to-ceiling height of the PTB of these levels, especially considering the BHS and conceptual design of the passenger boarding bridge to maintain the slope within the permissible limits.**

Landside planning

For the ultimate capacity of the airport being planned, whether greenfield or brownfield, ground access planning is required to be prepared. Such planning shall also include airport access beyond the airport boundary. For this purpose, a ground access plan shall be prepared and submitted to the government with access requirements from city, business, and tourism centres to and from the airport with the number and type of vehicles in a day and peak hour.

Multi-modal transport, like mass transport by rail or bus, should be planned and accordingly incorporated in the airport master plan and city master or urban plan with specific timelines for implementation in phases. Such a plan should also indicate the relocation of facilities required in the city and plan the city development incorporating the transport system for the airport traffic. For example, the city may need additional subways, flyovers, etc.

At the airport, it is required to plan a required number of lanes of the access road from the airport boundary to PTB and other buildings like the ATC tower, cargo, MRO, and hotels. With the access road, it is required to identify the location of vehicle parking, rail station, or mass transport parking area. It needed to be planned from the parking areas to the PTB and vice versa. It would be better if it is conceptualized whether the rail station is to be integrated with the terminal or separated and interconnected. Similarly, the location of multilevel vehicle parking and access to and from PTB are also to be decided. Such planning gets complicated for airports with multiple terminals. It is required to plan an Automatic People Mover (APM) system between the terminals or a dedicated bus transport between the terminals on a separate road.

The access road from the airport boundary to all other airport facilities must be planned. A main access road will lead to various buildings at the airport. The number of road lanes is based on the number of vehicles passing during peak hours. A minimum of three lanes is required without a median/divider between the two directions. If there is a median/divider between the two directions, two lanes on either side of the divider are required to have a bypass in case of a breakdown of the vehicle.

Planning the road network to the PTB is essential to have unhindered traffic flow to the PTB.

The number of vehicular lanes in front of the PTB for passenger drop-off is required to be evaluated based on the dwell time of the vehicles for drop/pickup of the passengers, the length of the vehicle, and the space between the vehicles. A separate bypass lane can be planned between the two lanes. The width of the road shall cater for cars, taxis, and coaches. The road network shall also include from and to the car park from the PTB. Also, the number of lanes depends on whether arriving and departing passengers reach the terminal at the same level or two different levels. For example, an airport with more than 10 million passengers per annum capacity is usually planned with departure at an elevated level and arrival at a lower level. Therefore, the number of vehicular lanes at each level must be evaluated based on peak arriving and departing passengers.

Illustrative example

Proportion of vehicle – taxi 60%, coach 10%, and cars 30%.
Number of passengers – taxi 4, coach 30, and cars – 2.
Dwell time – taxi – 3 min, coach – 20 min, and cars – 2 min.
Length of vehicles – Taxi – 5 mt, coach – 12 mt, and car – 5 mt.
Departure peak = 5000 passengers.
Number of taxis = 750, coach= 17, and cars = 750.
Number of vehicles at peak = 38, 6 and 25 taxi, coach, and car, respectively.
The length of the kerb required is app 400 m in number of lanes.

Depending on the length of the building, we can decide the length of each lane in front of the PTB. For example, assuming the PTB length is 100 m, the number of lanes will be 4.

In any case, it is a practice to plan for three lanes for the bypass and a breakdown vehicle blocking the road.

If the vehicle split up and numbers are unavailable for a greenfield airport development, the thumb rule is 100 m per million passengers per annum.

The interface between the vehicular lane in front of the PTB and the PTB entrance is called the forecourt. See Figure 5.39 for an example of the layout. Each lane can be 3 m in width plus kerb of 3 m. Thus, the total width of the vehicular lanes in the figure will be approximately 30 m.

The minimum width of the forecourt is generally 15 m and to the entire length of the PTB.

See the image of the kerb side road of an airport in Figure 5.40.

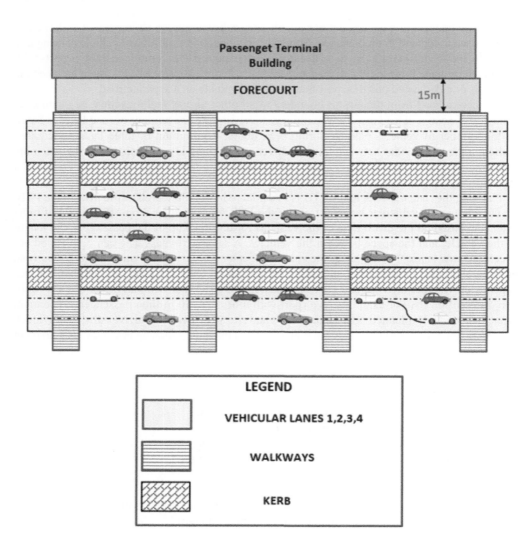

Figure 5.39 Kerbside of PTB with vehicular lanes and forecourt. Photograph by the author

Figure 5.40 Kerbside of PTB with vehicular lanes

Vehicle parking space

Depending on the number of car park slots required based on peak hour passenger numbers, meeters and greeters' numbers, and land availability, this could be on the surface or in a multi-level building.

One planning restriction to note is that for security reasons, only drop/pickup of passengers is allowed close to the PTB, and long-term vehicle parking is not allowed within a certain distance from the PTB frontage (commonly 75 m, unless otherwise, security ensured with technology and proper monitoring).

Car park/two-wheeler parking is also required to be planned for airport and stakeholders' staff vehicles. Car park space @ 1500 per 10 million passengers per annum is reasonable to assume for the preliminary estimate. Therefore, 25–30 sqm area per vehicle should be enough. Considering 30 sqm for 1500 cars, the land area required is 45,000 sqm. For 40 million passengers per annum, the land requirement works out to 180,000 sqm. It would be better to plan for a Multilevel Car Parking (MLCP) arrangement to optimize the land requirement and for passengers' convenience. However, a parking area at the ground level of the MLCP is required for coaches. The car park, whether a surface or multilevel building, is planned close to the PTB. The passengers will have covered access with MLCP connected to the PTB at the arrival and departure levels.

Planning for systems

The planning shall include buildings to accommodate electrical substation equipment to feed power to all the facilities at the airport. The equipment consists of HV panels, transformers, LV panels, and standby power equipment such as diesel generating sets. The substation is located at the load centre and close to PTB to reduce losses and capital costs. Large airports will have multiple substations closer to the loads.

Similarly, air-conditioning equipment (chillers and cooling towers, heating equipment) should be as close as possible to PTB.

Water receiving, storage, and distribution centre: Normally, three days of storage are planned. This facility shall also include water treatment plants before distribution through pumps. Wastewater generated at the airport will be treated in a sewerage treatment plant, and the treated water is usually used for flushing or landscaping. The location of these two plant rooms is usually planned away from populated areas of the airport, particularly the sewerage treatment plant.

These buildings are located, planned, and constructed for flexibility to expand as and when the airport expands with additional facilities, or the existing facilities are extended.

Baggage Handling System (BHS)

BHS is a very specialized system, and for medium and large airports, the system is integrated with the screening machines for screening the hold bags for security purposes to ensure no forbidden items are in the checked-in or hold bags. Therefore, the system is called an in-line screening system with the BHS.

The departure system consists of check-in conveyors, screening machines, and the makeup carousel. The area where makeup carousels are installed is called the baggage makeup area, which will be at the apron level. In this area, the bags are either sorted manually for each flight and loaded into containers or automatically sorted flight-wise and loaded into the containers. Generally, for an airport handling less than 20 million passengers per annum, the bags will be dropped at the makeup carousels from the check-in counters without any segregation regarding the flight/airline.

For large airports, bags will be dropped at a dedicated carousel for each flight/group of flights, which makes it easy to load the bags for respective flights. The segregation of bags is done by equipment called sorters. Such a system requires careful space planning, including the makeup area's height. The number and length of makeup carousels are determined based on the peak hour passenger number and the number of bags per passenger, which is usually assumed to be 1 for domestic and 1.5 to 2 for international passengers.

The arrival system is simple compared to the departure system. The hold bags from the aircraft will be brought to the PTB by vehicle and dropped into the baggage carousel. Each flight will be allocated a carousel, and all the flight's baggage shall be loaded into the system within a specified time (say 25 min for narrow-body and 35 min for wide-body aircraft). The carousel's length for planning is 75 m for narrow-body and 90 m for wide-body aircraft. The number of carousels is determined based on the number of flights in the peak hour with belt occupancy time indicated above. In addition, bags from international flights may go through screening machines installed for each carousel for screening the bags for customs purposes.

The list of systems that are planned for PTB are:
Mechanical, electrical, and plumbing systems.
Passenger boarding bridges.
Baggage and passengers screening system.
Escalators, elevators, and travellators.
Fire protection and firefighting systems.
Wayfinding signs.
ITC system

- Check-in system (Common User Passenger Processing System).
- Self-check-in Kiosks.
- Passenger Announcement (PA) system.
- CCTV system.

- Telephone system.
- EPOS (Electronic Point of Sales).
- Flight information display system.
- Access control system.
- Baggage reconciliation system.

Aircraft rescue fire fighting

The fire station building houses the fire trucks/vehicles, rescue equipment, storage of the extinguishing agents, staff training rooms, and a watch tower for visibility to the runway. Fire and rescue operations are essential and serve aviation safety; hence, the fire station must be placed in the appropriate location in the airfield.

The basis of the location of the fire stations is as follows:

1 The response time, as defined in SARPs, should be achievable (Chapter 4 mentions the response time as per SARPs). It is practicable to calculate the time the fire vehicles take to reach the runway ends from the identified fire station location.
2 The entry to the runway should be straight with minimum bends.
3 The location should not be in a location such that the vehicles will have to pass through the apron.
4 The number of fire stations may be more than one to meet the response time.
5 The building height should clear the transitional surface.

The location should be clear of the taxiway strip and runway strip. Refer to Figure 5.41, which shows three possible options for locating the fire station. Since fire station 3 is closer to the

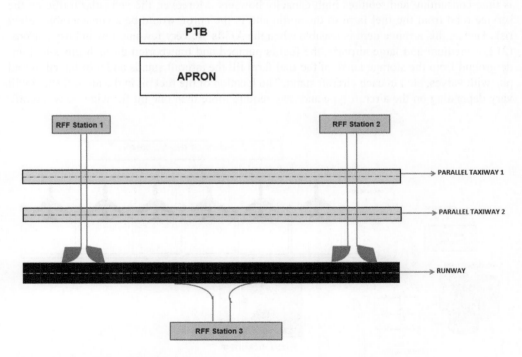

Figure 5.41 Locations of RFF stations – Options

runway and in the middle of the airfield, the response time may be better than the other two loca-tions, 1 and 2. Also, the height of the watch tower at location 3 could be minimum and will have better visibility of the runway from the watch tower. One drawback of location 3 is that the fire vehicles will cross the active runway to reach the aircraft stands or taxiways, which may not be ideal. Also, the secondary purpose of the fire vehicles is to attend to building emergencies, and location 3 is far off from **PTB and** crosses an active runway. If the building height is 10 m for location 3, it should be at least 70 m away from the runway strip (210 m from r/w centreline), assuming the ground elevation at that location is the same as that of the runway centreline.

For locations 1 and 2, the watch tower height could be 14 m which requires these to be 44 m away from the taxiway centreline (clear of the strip) and at least 98 m away from the runway strip (238 m from r/w C/L) to clear transitional slope.

All three options require an evaluation of the response time and, in some cases, may require more than one fire station.

The dimensions of the fire station are not critical for the master planning. However, 100 m × 20 m plot area can be marked for main fire station and if satellite fire station is required can mark a plot of 20 m × 20 m for the highest aerodrome category. Most important is the location of the fire station.

Aviation fuel storage facility

Aviation fuel supply is an essential facility for airport operations. Therefore, the infrastructure required for the system should be included in the planning stage. The land requirement for the ultimate capacity needed as per the traffic forecast is to be included in the master planning to avoid any space constraints in future. There are two ways to refuel the aircraft in the parking bays. (1) Transporting fuel from the storage location through bowsers and filling the aircraft is time-consuming and requires high-capacity bowsers. Moreover, the vehicular traffic on the service road from the fuel farm to the apron and in the apron would be a considerable safety risk. Hence, this arrangement is feasible when the ATMs are very few and few in busy periods. (2) For medium and large airports, the fuel is pumped and transported through pipes laid un-derground from the storage tanks of the fuel farm till the aircraft stands and terminated in fuel pits with valves, etc., in each aircraft stand. The location of the fuel pit in the aircraft stand will vary depending on the aircraft type and may require more than one pit for wide-body aircraft.

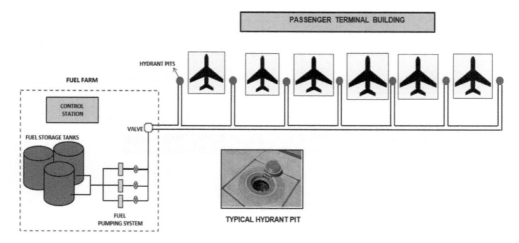

Figure 5.42 Layout of Fuel storage, hydrants, and refuelling

From this fuel pit, fuel is loaded into the aircraft through refueller vehicles much smaller than the bowsers. The fuel delivery through the hydrant system is with quantity, flow, and velocity to refuel the wide-body aircraft faster, thus achieving optimum aircraft turnaround time. Figure 5.42 shows the layout of the fuel storage, hydrants, and refuelling.

Figure 5.43 shows the fuel bowsers which is required if there are no hydrants at the airport.

Figure 5.44 shows the refuelling of an aircraft from the hydrant with refueller.

Figure 5.43 Fuel bowsers used for refuelling without hydrants. Photograph by the author

Figure 5.44 Refuelling an aircraft from hydrant

Source: Wikimedia commons

The size of the fuel farm storage facility depends on the aircraft fleet mix and refuelling requirement by the airlines per day and the number of days of storage considering the fuel sourcing from fuel suppliers. The number of days of fuel storage required depends on the number of suppliers, the location of the refineries, and the mode of fuel transportation from the supplier to the airport storage tank, i.e., through the pipe, fuel trucks, rail, or through seaport if it is an island airport. The certainty of fuel replenishment at the airport storage will decide the number of days of storage. However, planning is generally for seven-day storage.

The number of tanks and each tank's capacity is also based on the total storage capacity. However, it is a good practice to provide a minimum of three tanks, one for receiving, one for settling, and the third one for delivery through hydrants. The tank's height is usually less than 25 m, which should clear the transitional surface.

The facility is as close to the aircraft apron as practical, with the requirement of OLS examined above. For enhanced safety, the facility shall not be within the approach or take off climb surface even if they clear of these surfaces. Also, avoid the fuel storage facility adjacent to the above surfaces as an abundant precaution for safety. Usually, a safety distance of 100 m to any installation is maintained.

If the storage location is far from the aircraft stands or aircraft stands are in multiple places at the airport, far off from each other, it is possible to provide satellite storage tanks close to the aircraft stands. But in this case, there will be multiple pumps and controls, one at the main storage tank and one at the satellite tank.

The piping from fuel farm and hydrants in the aircraft stands are to be planned along with the initial planning as these are coordinated with other services, and redundant lines are to be designed in case shutdown of some pipe sections is required during operations. If the hydrants are not planned initially, it is difficult to introduce them later as the aircraft stands are rigid pavement. In addition, it is expensive to cut the pavement, lay the pipe and hydrant pits, and relay the concrete.

Fire stations should be able to reach the fuel storage location but not so close to each other.

Codes and regulations of mass fuel storage should be complied with, per local regulations. In addition, wind direction, the effect of fuel vapours travelling outside the airport, and the effect on communities shall also be evaluated.

An adequate number of storage locations are identified in the apron for parking the refuellers.

The approach from the city side to the fuel storage tanks is considered if the inflow is by fuel trucks, and the area for parking these vehicles is required in the planning. Approximately 3–4 hectares of land would be needed for a large airport to accommodate the fuel farm consisting of storage tanks, pumps, a control room, a powerhouse, offices, a firefighting system, a testing lab, etc.

The ideal location will be the interface of the airside and landside so that the parking of trucks and offloading of fuel, staff entry, etc., would be more accessible from the landside, and the airside, the operational personnel will have access, ensuring safety and security.

Isolated aircraft parking position

It is an aircraft parking area where an aircraft that is required to be isolated from the main apron stands for reasons such as bomb threat, hijacking or of, unlawful interference, or precautionary measure need to be isolated.

The siting criteria are as follows:

- At least 100 m from parking positions, buildings, and public areas.
- **Not** over underground utilities such as gas, aviation fuel, and electrical and communication cables.
- Parked Aircraft tail shall clear the OLS.

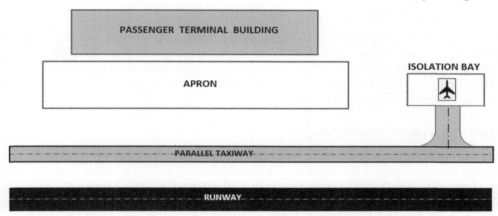

Figure 5.45 Location of isolation bay

The location shown in Figure 5.45 is normally chosen, so that it does not affect the normal operations including runway operations when an aircraft is parked. The orientation of aircraft parking requires close examination so that the aircraft tail clears the transitional surface, and the aircraft clears the taxiway strip.

Bulk Utilities – Power Houses, Water Supply, HAVC plants, Sewage Treatment Plants (STP), etc.

Most bulk utility facilities are located close to the load or at the load centre, except STPs are located away from the PTB and other airport activities areas and standby power generators away from the PTB to avoid noise and exhaust fumes. This location is also to be closely examined from a transitional surface as minimum chimney heights are mandated from environmental concerns. In large airports, it is usual to have one receiving station for power and water and, from these, distributed through multiple service buildings close to the various facilities. HAVC plant can also be centralized with conditioned water circulated through pipes, especially if the airport is large. Otherwise, plants located close to the loads are a typical design.

Service roads

Minimum width of apron service roads is 10 mt; other interconnecting roads to buildings can be 7 m. The road along the perimeter of the airport for inspection is normally 4 m.

Maintenance workshops for ground support equipment are to be located close to the apron without affecting expansion plans and connected to the apron with a road. Land requirement is not very high. Also, some major repairs can be carried out with workshops outside the airport. Large airports may require app 2–3 Hectares. Also, it depends on the operating philosophy whether major repairs are carried out at the workshop outside the airport.

In-flight catering facility is normally established by the specialist firms and the facility can be either airside or landside. The catering vehicle movement route is required to be identified to reach the apron and catered for with a road. Catering trucks coming into the airside from landside requires inspection by Aviation Security personnel before they enter the airport. Thus, it is preferable to keep it on airside, if on landside, a dedicated gate at the landside – airside interface is required. Requires app 10,000–20,000 sqmt for a large airport.

Security gates and fence

Security gates at appropriate locations are required at the landside–airside interface fence with a building to accommodate equipment for checking the personnel, their belongings, and the vehicle itself before entering the airside. Boom barriers and bollards are installed at these gates. Large airports will have two types of fence, one to protect the property boundary from encroachment and another for operational areas.

MRO of aeroplanes requires hangars.

The facility depends on the aircraft type (aeroplane reference code) to be serviced, and the number of aircraft parked simultaneously in the hangar. This facility could be on the interface between the landside and the airside. The business plan prepared for the airport will identify the viability of this facility, and mostly the airport earmarks an area for setting up this facility and implementing it by specialist firms in MRO.

Location consideration includes the noise generated due to the engine run-up and height at this location not to infringe on the OLS. The hangars, along with sufficient apron area for parking aircraft outside the hangar, storage of aircraft spares, special equipment, etc., must be planned. The city side requires space for offices and vehicle parking. Stormwater drains on the airside of the facility need an oil–water separator before the water is allowed to enter the main stormwater drain considering the environmental impact. An area app 200,000 sqm can be marked in the master plan at an appropriate place based on the criteria mentioned above and should be sufficient for two hangars for narrow-body aircraft and other facilities.

Offices for airport, airlines, Government authorities, vendors, etc.

Minimum office area requirement for operations is included in the PTB. Rest of the offices will be outside the PTB, on the cityside. The location chosen should not affect the airport expansion in future and should clear the OLS. For large airports approximately 20,000–30,000 sqmt can be earmarked in the master plan.

Cargo terminal and infrastructure requirement

A typical layout of the cargo facility is shown in Figure 5.46.

The area requirement of the cargo terminal depends on many factors like the dwell time of the cargo, cooling off time, international vs. domestic, and transfer cargo. Thus, airport planning at this level can consider 15–17 MT per sqm. For example, if the annual cargo quantity is 1,500,000 MT, the area required is app 100,000 sqm.

The number of aircraft stand depends on the peak ATM of freighter aircraft, and the turn-around time of the cargo aircraft will be 4–5 hours. It is essential to identify the number of aircraft of narrow-body and wide-body categories; accordingly, the stands are to be configured. Adequate areas for parking cargo handling equipment and ULDs are to be earmarked close to the apron. If the cargo terminal building is 100,000 sqm, as a thumb rule, 100,000 sqm can be allocated for an apron and parking of cargo handling equipment and ULDs.

Landside facilities include loading and unloading bays and long-term parking of trucks. In addition, offices for the regulatory authorities, freight forwarders, etc., are to be earmarked on the land side. For this, an area of approximately 80,000 sqm can be reserved with a depth of 150–200 m from the cargo terminal building for truck parking, offices, etc.

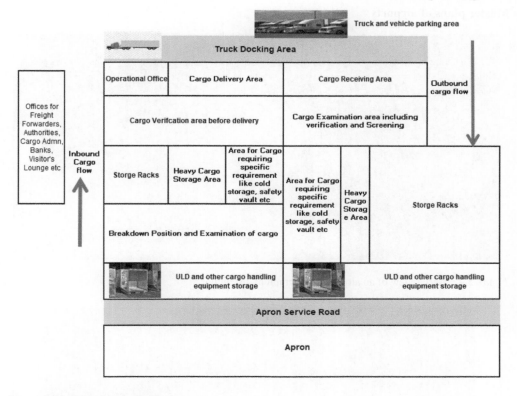

Figure 5.46 Typical cargo facility

The location of the cargo handling facility should be such that it is possible to expand the facility as and when required with the least operational hindrance, which means providing land/space for an extension on either side of the terminal, apron, and city side facilities.

If there is enough belly cargo from passenger aircraft, the cargo terminal should be close to the passenger terminal apron. Therefore, the plan should include adequate road width between the passenger apron and cargo terminal and easy access.

The height (considering ETV) and location of the cargo terminal and apron shall be clear from the OLS and not affect CNS equipment.

Landside road network should be planned with adequate care for the movement of heavy trucks and could be a dedicated road network at busy airports.

Commercial development outside the PTB

Any commercial development within the airport land will have to be examined to comply with the land use planning and permissible height restrictions as per OLS and CNS criteria.

Master plans of airports

Figure 5.47 Aerial view of an airport. Photograph by the author

Figure 5.48 An airport with staggered runway

Source: Wikimedia commons

An airport view showing staggered runway to avoid relocation of existing facilities is in Figure 5.48.

Airport diagram of Manila International Airport is shown in Figure 5.49.

A regional airport with a single runway and without parallel taxiway is shown in Figure 5.50.

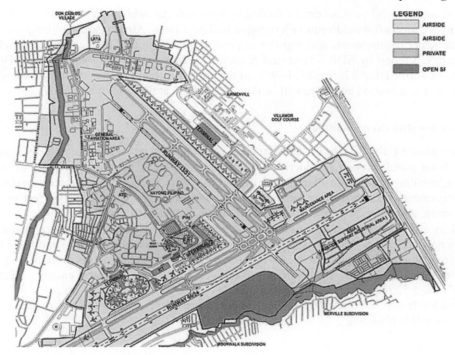

Figure 5.49 Airport diagram from the airport's website

Figure 5.50 A small regional airport with single runway and without parallel taxiway

Source: Google earth

Alternative aviation fuel

Master planning should cater for technology upgradation, especially replacing aviation turbine fuel with Sustainable Aviation Fuel (SAF), hydrogen, and electric.

SAF (for example, biofuel) can be mixed with jet fuel and hence does not need separate provisions. However, hydrogen in liquid form or fuel cells and electricity through batteries or fuel cells are in the initial stage of experiments. The planners should be aware of this development so that appropriate provisions can be made, for example, space required for these alternative fuels.

Ground Handling Equipment (GHE) powered by diesel/petrol is obsolete now. Either they are operated through CNG or electric power, which is required to be considered in the planning. Also, the use of hydrogen for GHE is getting attention.

Although ground vehicles can be fuelled by hydrogen gas, which can be piped directly into the airport, **aircraft would require hydrogen in liquid form**. Airports are exploring the costs, infrastructure requirements, and logistics of producing, storing, and delivering that liquid fuel to aircraft. A report by ADP is 'The studies conducted over the past year with Group ADP and Airbus confirmed that it is feasible in 90% of the group's airports'. 'The refuelling time will be equivalent to kerosene, and there will be no major change at the aircraft terminals'.

Non-renewable energy sources

Master planning should also include installing renewable energy sources, especially solar energy. Solar panel location considering OLS requirement, clear of runway/taxiway strips and RESA, avoiding glare to the pilots and air traffic controllers, access for fire vehicles, assessment of electromagnetic interference generated due to the solar equipment and its effect on CNS equipment, and others are some of the considerations in locating the panels.

Many airports have installed solar power generation systems, and there are airports that run 100% on solar energy. Most existing installations have solar panels on the ground tilted to receive maximum solar rays. In addition, some of the airport passenger terminal roofs have solar panels. Nowadays, double-sided vertical solar panels are used to maximize energy generation. See Figure 5.52 for ground-mounted solar panels.

Windmills may have interference to electronic navaids at the airport, hence, require careful analysis before planning.

Figure 5.51 Ground Mounted Solar Panels (https www.pxfuel.comenfree-photo-qmgch)

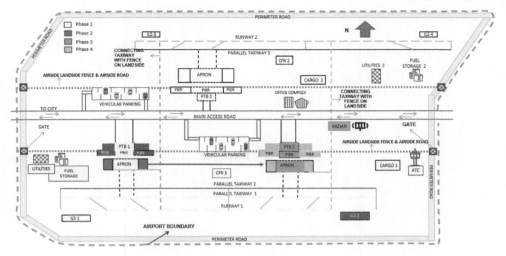

Figure 5.52 Phased development of an airport master plan

Figure 5.52 shows the phased development of an airport master plan.
The brief of the conceptual master plan is as follows:

1 Greenfield airport development for an ultimate annual capacity of 60–80 million passengers.
2 The runway and associated facilities on the south side of the airport, i.e., runway 1, etc. will be developed in phases and hence shown in detail.
3 The development of facilities to the north of the main access road is not shown in phases, except Runway 2 is planned for development in phase 4 of the project. Parallel taxiway 3 and all other facilities to the north of the main access road will be detailed out later phase wise, the master plan tentatively identifies the facilities and location.
4 The master plan includes the location of an office complex as an example. There are sufficient land parcels available on the landside. During the development period for the ultimate capacity, which may run 40–50 years, the timing and the development mode must be worked out.
5 The development, as outlined above, is planned in four phases, as indicated in Figure 5.53.
6 PTB 1 and 2 will be dimensioned for 20 million passengers annually. Apron stands of PTB 1 and 2 each will be planned to accommodate 50–60 aircraft and dimensioned for code C. During the detailed design, the exact split between MARS and code C can be worked out, presently all will be considered as code C. Can assume 75% contact stand and 25% remote stands. PTB footprint and the length of apron can be calculated with this information.
7 Table 5.3 indicates the facilities' distances to the nearest edge of the facility. Except for the airfield, pavement distances are from the centreline to the centreline, as indicated in the table. The distances from the runway centreline, lateral distance from the airfield pavements, and the permissible height of the buildings and other facilities can be worked out.

The facilities on the southern side of runway 2, i.e., PTB 3 and others, can be detailed out including the distances as an exercise by the readers.

Table 5.3 Illustration of distances between the facilities

Facility	Distance from taxiway 1 C/L	Distance from taxiway 2 C/L	CFR 1	Fuel storage	Radar	Utilities	Apron	Pier	Cargo	ATC
Runway 1 C/L	225 m									
Taxiway 1 C/L		130 m								
Taxiway 2 C/L			60 m	200 m		200 m				
Apron							100 m	30 m		
Apron depth	300 m									
PTB + pier depth/width	300 m									
PTB to main access road	100 m									
Main access road					50 m				100 m	50 m
Runway 1 C/L to main access road	**1185 m**									
Runway 1 C/L to airport boundary on south side	300 m									

Assume runway length as 3500 m for code 4E and Cat I approach lights for runway 1 at both approaches. It is assumed that runway 2 also will be of 3500 m length.

Conclusion

This chapter describes the master planning aspects by explaining the plan's purpose, benefits, and progressive development. More emphasis is given to airfield infrastructures in the planning because of regulatory requirements to enhance aviation safety performance. With this chapter, planners will know how to locate the runway and determine the orientation and length of the runway. With the description of the length and width of the land requirement, readers should be able to prepare a simple master plan with minimum facilities. Airfield components have been explained with sketches for easy understanding of the concepts. Adopting the required criteria is essential for locating other infrastructures like PTB, cargo, and fuel storage facilities. These are described with illustrations. Few master plan pictures will help the readers to understand the airport master plans.

References

ICAO. (2020). Aerodrome Design Manual Part 1 – Runways.
ICAO. (2022). ICAO Annex 14 – Ninth Edition: Vol. I.

Additional reading

Visit website of aeroplane manufacturers to get the technical data of aeroplanes for planning purposes.
Boeing: Airport Compatibility – Airplane Characteristics for Airport Planning
Aircraft Characteristics | Airbus
View the video of cross wind landing of a wide-body aircraft
https://www.linkedin.com/posts/fjrod_aviation-airplane-travel-activity-6964343412045029376-P6ny?utm_source=linkedin_share&utm_medium=ios_app
View the master plan of various airports and analyse the concept
Read the recent accident/incident reports of runway excursions and over run of aircrafts and note the investigation report recommendations on infrastructure improvements.

6 Visual aids, CNS system, and air traffic management

Introduction

Communication, Navigation, and Surveillance (CNS) system has three components, viz. communication equipment for ground–air and ground–ground communication, navigational equipment, which are non-visual aids for the aircraft providing distance information, approach angle, runway centreline, bearing, etc., and surveillance system identifying location and altitude of the aircraft for the air traffic controllers to monitor the airspace. Surveillance also includes identifying aircraft and vehicles' surface movement within the airfield.

Air traffic management is managing the aircraft movement from the aircraft stand at an airport through departure and monitoring and controlling airspace till the arrival of the aircraft at another airport, meaning in all phases of the flight.

Visual aids supplement the non-visual aids described above through marking, lighting, etc.

Airport planners should be aware of the fundamentals of the above critical functions and thus described here briefly and mostly related to the planning. However, the scope of the CNS system and visual aids are enormous, and an in-depth study for the preliminary planning is not required; hence, only the significant implications for the planning are included in this chapter.

CNS equipment, their siting criteria, and protection surfaces

All the CNS equipment will have two components antenna and equipment. The siting criteria include the location of the equipment shelter such that they are not on the runway/taxiway strips or RESA. If the antenna is to be in the runway strip, it should be frangible and shall meet the frangibility requirement. Another criterion is that the height shall comply with OLS requirements.

Communication system

Microwave Link: It is a radio facility that transfers voice and data to/from between two sites, mainly the radar intelligence, to an ATC Display site. There are no special requirements, except that line of sight between the two locations must be ascertained before finalizing the sites on a corridor of 30 m on either side of the direct line of azimuth and 10 m below the direct line of sight in the vertical plane.

Extended Range VHF is a two-way air–ground communication facility employing a VHF transmitter. The normal VHF range of 150–200 NM is extended to about 300 NM. The area may be free of obstructions.

Ultra-High Frequency (UHF) Link: No obstruction on a corridor of 30 m on either side of the direct line of the azimuth and 10 m below from the direct line of sight in the vertical plane

DOI: 10.4324/9781003319948-6

Instrument Landing System (ILS)

The Instrument Landing System (ILS) consists of two components – Glide Path (GP), which provides the vertical guidance, i.e., glide angle, and Localizer (LLZ), which will provide azimuth guidance, i.e., the centreline of the runway, while the aircraft is on the final approach. These GP and LLZ are installed near the runway.

GP provides the glide angle information to a landing aircraft with the help of an instrument in the cockpit which, when tuned to the glide path frequency, indicates whether the aircraft is flying up or down or along the correct glide angle. In addition, LLZ radiates very high-frequency signals which, when picked up by an aeroplane, guide it onto the runway's centreline in the horizontal plane.

GP is installed at about 300 m from the threshold towards the runway and offset by 120 m from the runway centreline. Thus, the antenna will be installed in the runway strip; hence, the frangibility requirement will apply. Whether the GP is to be located on the right or left of the runway depends on the airfield layout, mainly depending on the entry/exit taxiways.

LLZ is installed beyond the runway end at about 300 m.

One GP and one Localizer per approach runway are required. If it is decided to install ILS for both approaches, one set for each approach is required.

During the master planning, the distances of the GP and LLZ, as mentioned above, will be considered (subject to final confirmation from the manufacturers during implementation). Based on the locations, it is required to examine the sensitive and critical areas for these instruments, which are to be protected so that the performance of the equipment/instruments is not degraded due to the presence of objects – permanent or mobile – in these areas.

See Figure 6.1 for typical location of ILS.

The critical and sensitive areas for the ILS are defined as follows (ICAO – Annex 10):

ILS critical area is an area of defined dimensions about the localizer and glide path antennas where vehicles, including aircraft, are excluded during all ILS operations. The critical area is protected because the presence of vehicles and/or aircraft inside its boundaries will cause unacceptable disturbance to the ILS signal-in-space.

ILS sensitive area is an area extending beyond the critical area where the parking and/or movement of vehicles, including aircraft, is controlled to prevent the possibility of unacceptable interference to the ILS signal during ILS operations. The sensitive area is protected against

INSTRUMENT LANDING SYSTEM

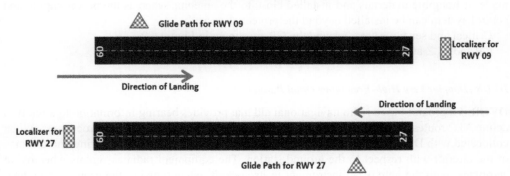

Figure 6.1 Typical location of ILS

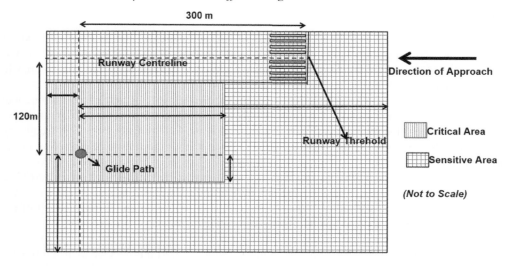

Figure 6.2 Critical and sensitive areas of GP. Reference – Annex 10/ICAO

interference caused by large moving objects outside the critical area but still normally within the airfield boundary.

To protect the critical area, vehicles are not allowed to enter the area and even taxing or parking of aircraft within this area during ILS operations. Hence, in the master planning the perimeter inspection roads or roads to these installations and the runway/road holding positions are to be planned according to this requirement. Critical area is very close to the GP and LLZ antenna.

Sensitive area is more spread than the critical area. The size of the sensitive area depends on several factors including the type of ILS antenna, the topography, and the size and orientation of man-made objects, including large aircraft and vehicles. If the sensitive areas extend beyond the boundaries of the airfield, it is necessary to secure the cooperation of the relevant authorities to carry out suitable control measures.

The dimensions of the sensitive areas will also vary depending on the Category of precision approach viz. I, II, or III operations. The stringent requirement is for Category III since only the least disturbance can be tolerated for Cat III.

Since the LLZ and GP antenna will be within RESA/runway strip, the equipment hut can be made of frangible materials and installed close to the antenna, whereas the power supply and control system can be installed beyond the protected areas.

Critical and sensitive areas around the GP are shown in Figure 6.2.

GP and LLZ at an airport are in Figures 6.3 and 6.4.

DVOR (Doppler Very High-Frequency Omni Range)

DVOR is a ground-based radio navigational aid that provides bearing information to aircraft to define ATC routes for en-route, terminal, and instrument approach/departure procedures. When collocated with DME (Distance Measuring Equipment) provides both the bearing and distance of the aircraft with respect to the ground station. The equipment radiates signals whereby an aeroplane, with the help of an instrument in its cockpit, when tuned to the ground equipment frequency, automatically gets its direction with respect to the facility and helps an aircraft to navigate on a predetermined course or home to an airport served by the facility.

Figure 6.3 Glidepath antenna and equipment hut. Photograph by Lakshminarayanan

Figure 6.4 Localizer antenna and equipment hut. Photograph by Lakshminarayanan

The siting criteria are that no objects shall exist within a 300 m radius of the equipment. Beyond 300 m, the structure, if any, shall subtend a vertical angle greater than 1.5 degrees. These criteria shall be used to locate the DVOR at the appropriate location, considering future expansion and additional infrastructures that are planned at the airport. In addition, during detailed design, the site and the grading requirement and impact due to development around the equipment must be verified in consultation with the manufacturers.

Figure 6.5 DVOR. Photograph by the author

Airport Surveillance Radar (ASR)

Airport Surveillance Radar (ASR) is a radar facility serving an airport to scan the air traffic within 50–60 nautical miles of the airport. ASR is a primary radar, and secondary surveillance radar is called MSSR. Primary radar provides the aeroplane's location, and secondary radar provides the altitude.

The siting criteria are up to a 500 m radius, no objects can exist which are higher than 3 m below the antenna pedestal, and beyond 500 m, the permissible slope is specified, and the height of the structure or object or building will be restricted below the slope.

Air Routes Surveillance Radar (ARSR)

Air Routes Surveillance Radar (ARSR) is high-power long-range radar covering 200 nautical miles approximately and it scans air traffic to a larger distance than ASR.

Siting criteria

No structure will be permitted on the land above the level of 5 m below the pedestal height up to 200 m from the radar antenna. Beyond 200 m, the permissible slope is specified, and the height of the structure, object, or building will be restricted below the slope.

Siting criteria for the following CNS systems, where applicable, also be considered as per the recommendations of the system manufacturers.

- Automatic Dependence Surveillance – Broadcast (DME/ADS-B).
- Airport Surface Detection Equipment (ASDE) or Surface Movement Radar (SMR).

Figure 6.6 ASR–MSSR. Photograph by Lakshminarayanan

- Advanced Surface Movement Guidance and Control Systems.
- Ground Based Augmentation System (GBAS) Reference Receiver.
- Ground Based Augmentation System VHF Data Broadcast (GBAS VDB) station.
- GBAS VDB monitoring station.
- Global Navigation Satellite System (GNSS) repeater restriction.

General notes

The requirement of CNS equipment depends on many factors which need to be discussed with the Air Traffic and Navigation Service (ANS) providers and, accordingly, the locations finalized in consultation with them. Once these lists of equipment and the site of these are finalized and marked in the master plan, the impact on these considering the airfield layout, buildings, and structures proposed are to be examined so that the performance of these critical systems is not affected. In addition, any future development not planned during master planning and required later is to be examined considering the locations of these equipment.

Figure 6.7 ARSR

Source: Photograph by Wikimedia Commons

There are specific restrictions about Electrical Power Transmission Lines at or near the airport which may impact the performance of the CNS equipment, which needs to be discussed with the ANS providers and the manufacturers and such restrictions shall also be considered in the planning.

Siting criteria for Air Traffic Control tower (ATC tower)

Figure 6.8 shows how the flight is monitored and guided by the Air Traffic Management team.

Air Traffic Controller directs aircraft movement on the ground and in the air within the airport zone. Information is issued to the pilot regarding airport conditions, airway traffic, visibility, speed and direction of ground winds, barometric pressure, and other relevant information for safe operation. The Controller from the control tower should have primarily adequate visibility to all manoeuvring areas and airspace (which falls within the Controller's responsibility) and a view of all runway ends and taxiways. Accordingly, the ATC tower is located at an airport and height is determined.

Before the flight departure, the pilot prepares a flight plan which indicates the aircraft destination, the air route to be followed, the desired altitude, and the estimated time for departure. If the flight plan is approved, any change is allowed with prior approval of the traffic control centre. When the aircraft is airborne, the movement along the air routes is regulated with adequate lateral and vertical separation between the aircraft to avoid collision through radar displays by the radar controller. These displays are installed in the technical building adjoining the ATC tower.

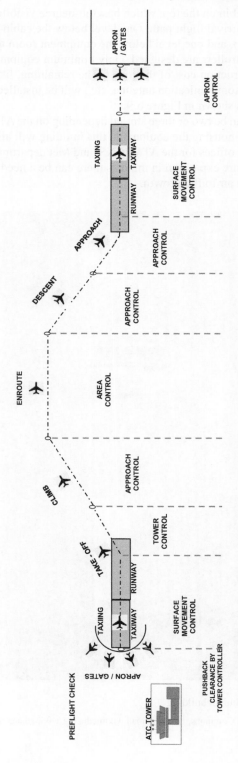

Figure 6.8 Flow diagram of air traffic management

ATC tower houses the cabin on the top, which has 360-degree visibility of the entire airfield and approach and take-off/arrival flight path. One level below the cabin is the apron control (if planned to be in ATC tower), and one level below the equipment room and below that services rooms, rest area for the controllers are designed. Only minimum equipment is positioned at the tower to optimize the construction cost of the tower. The remaining, like radar displays, communication equipment and communication antenna, etc., will be installed in a separate building but attached to the tower, as shown in Figure 6.9.

The technical building can be two or three storied depending on the ATS functions carried out at the airport. In addition to housing the equipment, this building will also have area control or approach control centre and offices for the ATM, CNS, and Met departments. This building will have to be planned with future expansion in mind as there can be a need to expand the services and systems in line with the air traffic growth.

Figure 6.9 ATC tower and technical building

Source: Photograph by Wikimedia Commons. https://upload.wikimedia.org/wikipedia/commons/5/5a/Air_traffic_control_tower_bangalore.jpg

Siting criteria for ATC tower

Siting criteria of an ATC tower is critical since it is the tallest building in an airport. The tallest ATC tower in the world is 136 mt.

Some of the aspects of the siting are as follows:

1 Adequate visibility of the aircraft operations – Air Traffic Controllers positioned at the ATC tower use air/ground communications and other ATC systems to provide air traffic services to the aircraft on the ground at the airport and those in the vicinity of the airport. For safe ground movement control of the aircraft and for viewing the take-off and landing of the aircraft, the ATC tower must be located near active runways to give controllers an unobstructed view of the aircraft.

2 The location shall serve all the operational areas, from initial to ultimate capacity. Thus, it will require an appropriate height for the visibility of the total operational area.

3 The air traffic controller in the ATC tower cabin should have an unobstructed view of all the taxiways and aprons (if the apron control is also situated in the tower). Practically if this is not possible with the consent of ANS provider and Certification Authority, at least it is planned such that the Air Traffic Controller will have the aircraft tail's visibility from the ATC tower cabin when the aircraft is on the taxiway to identify an aircraft movement. In the case of the apron, in large airports, the apron management and control are done remotely through number of high-resolution cameras installed in apron to cover aircraft movement.

4 As mentioned in this chapter, the location shall not interfere with the restricted areas of CNS equipment. One of the most prominent interference is with ASR equipment.

5 An appropriately located tower enables optimum height, thus avoiding additional costs since more height adds to the construction and maintenance cost.

In addition to the above requirement, particularly for the ATC tower location, the tower should not infringe on the OLS. In airports with a single runway, it is possible to locate in a way that the height is restricted and located to serve its purpose. However, in airports with multiple runways, the tower must cover all the runways, taxiways, and movement areas; hence, the height could be more than 45 m. In cases where the ATC tower protrudes the Inner Horizontal Surface (IHS), an Aeronautical Study is conducted to evaluate the probability (collision risk model) of an aircraft colliding with the tower. Such a study is a safety risk assessment study for the obstacle. Suppose the study finds the probability is extremely low, the location and height of the tower can be finalized and taken care of the obstacle while preparing the air traffic procedures.

On the other hand, suppose the study finds that the risk probability is high, an alternative location needs to be reworked with the height required for that location, or the air traffic procedure requires careful planning. Also, such obstacles are marked and lighted. Lighting could be day marking and night marking.

While planning small or medium airports, it is essential to closely review all the other surfaces, including the transitional surface, as the tower may infringe due to limited land availability.

Care shall be exercised in ensuring clearances from taxiways and aprons. In addition, the location shall be examined from the future development plans so that there is no clash with future development like an extension to PTB, Cargo, or other facilities.

Sufficient cark spaces need to be earmarked for staff and visitors.

The technical building attached to the ATC tower is not tall and can be easily located along with the ATC tower.

FAA (order number 6480-4B) provides more guidance on the ATC tower location requirement, some of which are briefly described below.

Object Discrimination means the controllers at the tower should be able to detect any object lying on the airfield pavement and recognize the object, from the safety point of view to avoid FOD (Foreign Object Damage) to the aircraft. The criteria are that the location should enable the Air Traffic Controller in the cabin able to notice the presence of an object on the airfield pavement surface, in a way that controller recognizes something is present but may not recognize or identify the object. The minimum probability criterion is 95.5%.

Line of Sight (LoS) Angle of Incidence shall be equal to or greater than 0.8 degree. See Figure 6.10 for (LoS) angle of incidence.

Two-point lateral discrimination

Figure 6.11 explains the lateral discrimination evaluation. The angle shall be greater than 0.13 degree.

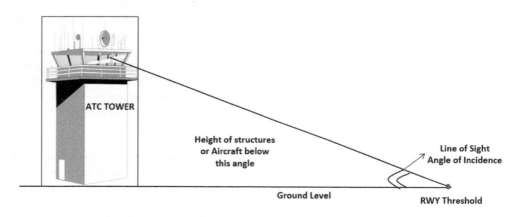

Figure 6.10 Line of sight from ATC tower. Reference Tower Siting Visibility Analysis – FAA

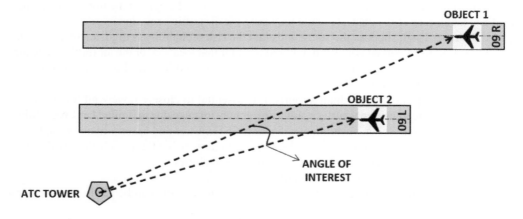

Figure 6.11 Lateral discrimination evaluation. Reference Tower Siting Visibility Analysis – FAA

ATC tower cabin orientation

As the Controllers view the airfield from the ATC tower cabin, the direction of the cabin be oriented such that it shall avoid all forms of glare, viz. sunlight, both direct and indirect and from glare due to manmade surfaces. The practice has shown that it is oriented such that the view faces north, east, west, or finally south in that order of preference.

Security aspect

It may be preferable to locate the ATC tower away from public areas, which may only sometimes be possible. An appropriate security system is planned and implemented during detailed design if the ATC tower is located on the landside.

Remote or Digital ATC towers – Restrictions in the tower's location and the vast land requirement research led to the remote tower. In this concept, an ATC tower can be anywhere by transmitting the live images of the aircraft movement and total airfield of an airport captured through several high-resolution cameras installed. Air Traffic Controllers can sit in the remote tower, watch the live images on displays, and guide the aircraft. If this can be achieved, the land occupied by the ATC tower can be released to other capacity-adding facilities or for commercial development, thus, revenue addition. Another advantage of the remote ATC tower is that more than one airport can be covered in one remote tower, thus maximizing workforce utilization. For example, one or more low-volume airports can be clubbed with a busy airport and a remote tower in a different location for ATC control. Refer to various articles on this topic.

One example of the system from a solution provider:

The On-Airport Equipment can be located at the local airport or at multiple remote airports. Its configuration varies as a function of the specific Digital Tower use case. It can include panoramic or IR or PTZ cameras providing coverage of the area of interest, as well as signal light guns and sound sensors to help capture the airport sound when needed. An environmentally protected camera house can be provided, as well as a shelter to house equipment that must be co-located with the cameras.

The Control Facility has a great degree of variability, depending on the specific use case. In the most common case, a Digital Tower Center (DTC), consisting of a number of Digital Tower Modules (DTMs), controls one or more airports, some simultaneously. The key component is the Visual Presentation (VP), which can show full 360 degrees views or distributed views. Several features further enhance the user's situational awareness, such as video and PTZ tracking, graphic overlays, and radar labels.

Satellite-Based Augmentation Systems (SBAS)

Satellite-Based Augmentation System (SBAS) reduces the dependency on ground-based infrastructure and leverages satellite technologies' precision and accuracy. Ground-based reference stations, satellite-based signals, and aircraft sensor systems comprise the SBAS architecture for aircraft navigation. The SBAS provides integrity and correction data that significantly improves the accuracy and reliability of the GPS position estimates and, most importantly, the availability. There are many SBAS service providers like U.S. Wide Area Augmentation System (WAAS), the European Geostationary Navigation Overlay Service (EGNOS), and the Japanese MTSAT Satellite Augmentation System (MSAS).

The Indian Space Research Organization (ISRO) and Airports Authority of India (AAI) have implemented the GPS Aided Geo Augmented Navigation called 'GAGAN' project as a SBAS for the Indian Airspace (About GAGAN | GAGAN (aai.aero)). GAGAN consists of a set of ground reference stations positioned across various locations in India called the Indian Reference Station (INRES), which gathers GPS satellite data. A master station, the Indian Master Control Centre (INMCC), collects data from reference stations, and creates GPS correction messages.

Aircraft are to be equipped for GAGAN operations. Airports must design the approach procedures for using the system. This technology is helpful for smaller airports with few daily operations and not equipped with navigational aids. For such airports, this system can enable operations with a visibility minimum of 800 m against 5000 m without the aid. Hence, using this technology will improve the certainty of operations at these airports with a reduction in cancellations, delays, etc., lesser fuel consumption, and improved safety. As of the Year 2022, 76 aircraft in India are fitted with compatible equipment for using GAGAN. As per AAI – 'The system is interoperable with other international SBAS systems'.

Meteorological equipment requirements for an airfield

Aircraft operation on an airfield is dependent on prevailing weather conditions. Therefore, ICAO prescribes the following Meteorological Elements are observed and reported.

- **Surface Wind** – The mean direction and the mean speed of the surface wind and significant variations of the wind direction and speed, reported in degrees true and metres per second (or knots), respectively.
- **Visibility** in metres or KM.
- **Runway Visual Range (RVR)** on all runways intended for Category I, II and III instrument approach and landing operations.
- **Present weather** occurring at the aerodrome and its vicinity.
- **The following present weather phenomena** shall be identified, as a minimum: precipitation and freezing precipitation (including intensity thereof), fog, freezing fog, and thunderstorms (including thunderstorms in the vicinity).
- **Cloud** amount, cloud type, and height of cloud base to describe the clouds of operational significance. When the sky is obscured, vertical visibility shall be observed and reported, where measured, in lieu of cloud amount, cloud type, and height of cloud base. The height of the cloud base and vertical visibility shall be reported in metres (or feet).
- Air temperature and the dew-point temperature.
- Atmospheric pressure.

The visual aids and the operating procedures usually are derived based on the weather conditions at an aerodrome. Weather information report also facilitates the aircrew in deciding the requirement for length of the runway requirement and operating at that particular aerodrome. Aerodrome operator declares the operating minima, and above the minima, only the operations can be performed at that airport. The operating minima comprise horizontal and vertical components and are expressed in terms of minimum visibility/RVR and minimum descent altitude/height or decision altitude/height. An airport's operating minima is also published in the Aeronautical Information Publication.

At an aerodrome, the following equipment is provided to collect and share the meteorological report.

1 Wind direction indicator – wind vane.
2 Wind speed measurement –Anemometer.
3 Temperature –air temperature, pressure, and humidity (Barometric Pressure Sensor, AT/Rh sensor).
4 RVR measurements – transmissometer.
5 Rainfall measurement – surface observatory – rain gauge.
6 Prediction of general visibility, weather conditions, and rain based on cloud movements – Radar.

While the information on wind direction, speed, temperature, rainfall, etc., are measured from one particular location of an aerodrome, the measurement concerning the RVR for deciding the category of operations is provided by the field equipment placed along the runway. These measurements are taken for:

i Touchdown zone of the runway intended for non-precision or Category I instrument runway.
ii Touchdown zone and the mid-point of the runway intended for Category II instrument runway.
iii Touchdown zone, the mid-point, and stop-end of the runway intended for Category III instrument runway.

The information on the RVR is also required for the appropriate intensity selection of the Aeronautical Ground Lighting System.

As a part of master planning, the requirement for the MET services is to be discussed with the concerned service providers. Provisions or infrastructure as required are to be incorporated, and details worked out later during implementation. Land requirement on the airfield is insignificant except for the location if it falls in the runway strip, and necessary mitigations must be incorporated. The service providers require space in the ATC tower and the equipment room.

Visual aids

Visual aids at the airport are:

- Markings.
- Indicators and signalling devices.
- Lights (Airfield Ground Lighting – AGL).
- Signs.
- Markers.
- Visual aids for denoting obstacles.
- Visual aids for denoting restricted use areas.
- Apron floodlights.
- Visual Docking and Guidance System (VDGS).

The visual aids in the airfield are for the pilot to identify the runway edge, runway end, runway threshold, runway centreline, touch down zone, taxiway edge, taxiway centreline, apron edge, aircraft stand centreline, runway holding position, intermediate holding position on taxiways, rapid exit taxiway indication, and so on. In addition, guidance during landing is provided with approach lights and Precision Approach Path Indicator (PAPI).

4 Cs are four elements of the character of AGL. These are colour, candelas, coverage, and configuration. For example, the colour of taxiway edge lights is blue, runway edge lights white, threshold green lights, and end lights red. In addition, each lighting system's fixture should meet the specific photometric requirement.

Colour and conspicuity are essential for the markings. For example, the colour of the runway marking is white, the colour of the taxiway marking is yellow, and apron safety lines are red. Marking conspicuity is achieved through bars of a particular width and specific distance between the lines, letters, and numbers of specific dimensions.

This chapter includes a description for AGL, and other visual aids figures are included to visualize how they look.

Pavement marking examples are in Figures 6.12–6.15.

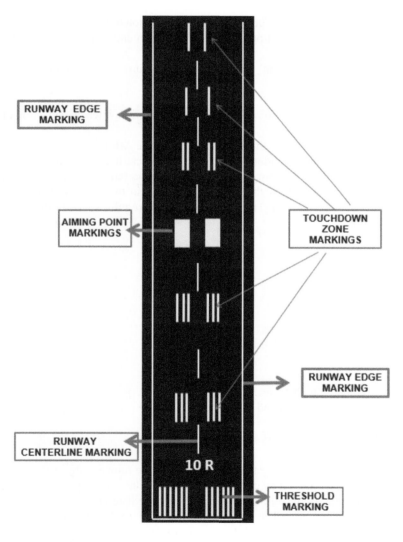

Figure 6.12 Runway pavement marking

Figure 6.13 Runway touch down zone and centreline marking. Photograph by Lakshminarayanan

Figure 6.14 Threshold marking. Photograph by Lakshminarayanan

Figure 6.15 Aiming point marking. Photograph by Lakshminarayanan

AGL and land requirement

AGL systems requirement and configuration are based on the type of runway operation, viz. non-precision, precision approach Cats I, II, and III. The configuration will be extensive for a higher precision approach.

All the AGL systems except some portion of approach lights will be along with the pavement. Therefore, while assessing the land requirement for airport planning, the only AGL system required to be considered is the approach lights as it extends beyond the runway pavement on either end/beginning of the runway. However, the master planning report should specify the systems planned at the airport and their configuration, typically incorporated in the master planning drawing.

Configuration of approach lighting system

There are three configurations of the system. The configuration is decided based on the type of runway operations. Thus, the weather minima for operations will be declared based on the configuration provided.

Simple approach lighting system

This configuration of approach lights is provided for non-instrument and non-precision approach runways. The system commences from the threshold. Figure 6.16 shows the configuration of the system. In this, it is assumed that the threshold and runway end are at the same location.

The land required for the approach lighting system is 480 m × 120 m. Read the description under Cat I approach lighting if 120 m width of land is not available.

If the threshold is displaced, the approach lights will start from the threshold and the first fixture will be at 60 m and the pattern remains the same as above. The lights which are within the runway pavement will be of inset/in-pavement type fixtures.

Category I approach lighting system as shown below.

This configuration is provided for precision approach category I runway operation.

This configuration shown in Figure 6.17 is called distance coded as the cross bars are at 150 m between them. This configuration has five cross bars and centreline lights extending up to 900 m from the threshold at 30 m intervals. The crossbar width (number of fixtures) varies, width

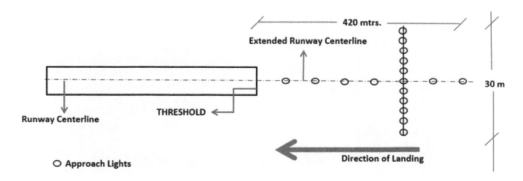

Figure 6.16 Simple approach lighting system. Reference – Annex 14/ICAO

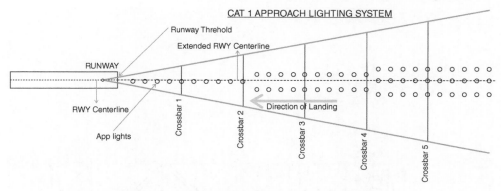

Figure 6.17 Cat I approach lighting system. Reference – Annex14 /ICAO

reducing towards the threshold. The approach funnel can be seen from the configuration, wider away from the threshold and pointing towards the touch-down zone. There is another configuration, with land length land requirement is the same as that of the distance coded.

The last crossbar is 52.5 m in width, and the length of the system is 900 m. It is preferable to protect 60 m on either side of the extended runway centreline and 60 m beyond the end of an approach lighting system. Thus, land with 1000 m length and 120 m width is required. If such a length of land is unavailable, plan for an abridged version of the system. But there could be some operational restrictions, like the visibility required will be more than the full-length configuration. However, all efforts should be made to get the whole pattern of approach lights. As seen from the figure, after the 750 m distance from the threshold (last crossbar from the threshold), the width of land required is only 4.5 m, but the approach light plane shall not get obstructed, with reduced width.

Similarly, if 120 m wide land is not available can work out some mitigation measures depending on the objects existing at the location. However, a minimum width of 60 m (30 m on either side of the extended runway centreline) should be available. Like a simple approach lighting system, it starts from the threshold; hence, inset fixtures would be required on the runway pavement for the displaced threshold. This configuration requires 120 nos. of fixtures in total. There is another configuration, but the length of land required is the same as that of the configuration described here.

Categories II and III approach lighting system

These are for precision approach Cats II and III runway operation. Cats II and III configuration consists of Cat I approach lighting system plus approach side row lights and touchdown zone lights. Touchdown zone lights are in the runway pavement with inset fixtures, hence do not need any additional land over Cat I system. Similarly, the approach side row lights extend up to 300 m and will be within the RESA and hence, no additional land is required (Provided RESA is of length 240 m from the strip).

If the threshold is displaced, the system will start from that location and hence requires inset fixtures within the runway pavement.

There are many variations of the system possible but for the purpose of land requirement and for incorporating in the master plan report, the above would be sufficient. The same can be reviewed during detailed design.

Figure 6.18 is an approach lighting system mounted on a frangible mast to maintain the light plane in varying ground profile.

Figure 6.18 Approach lighting system on masts. Photograph by AMA

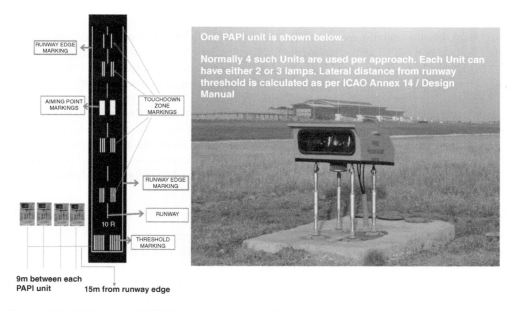

Figure 6.19 PAPI system. PAPI Unit photograph by AMA

PAPI system

The system is a visual aid for the aircraft landing and guides the pilot on whether the approach angle is correct or above or low with the combination of red and white lights of the four units shown in Figure 6.19.

Figure 6.20 shows the information to the pilot depending on the approach angle.

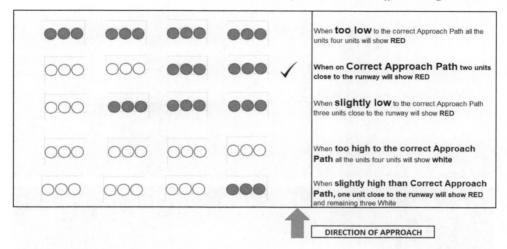

Figure 6.20 PAPI system colour code for approach slope. Reference – Annex14/ICAO

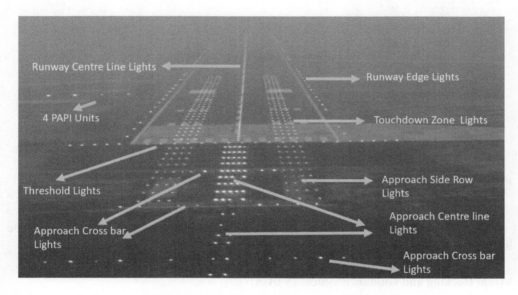

Figure 6.21 Cat III AGL system. Photograph by AMA and systems marked by the author

The units are installed within the runway strip, as shown, and it does not require any additional land. Being in the runway strip, the units will be with frangible supports. The approximate location of PAPI from the threshold is 300 m, to be adjusted for the level difference between the threshold and PAPI system locations. Also, the system requires coordination with the Glide Path of the ILS. Glidepath, as described previously, is an instrument non-visual aid for correct approach angle, whereas PAPI is a visual aid that provides the same information to the pilot through lighting; hence both should convey the same information to the pilot. Thus, it requires coordination in location, settings, and calibration.

Figure 6.21 shows Cats III AGL system at an airport indicating various systems.

Figure 6.22 Elevated and inset/in-pavement fixtures. Photographs by AMA

The elevated and inset/in-pavement fixtures are shown in Figure 6.22. Runway centreline lights are shown in Figure 6.23.

Visual Docking and Guidance System (VDGS)

VDGS guides the pilot while parking the aircraft in the apron stand with centreline guidance and the stop position. Correct stop position is vital for docking the passenger boarding bridges and refuelling through hydrants. Figure 6.24 shows how the VDGS guides the aircraft when it enters the aircraft stand. In the figure, left side unit shows the aircraft is to the left of the centreline of the stand and hence, required to move to the right. The unit on the extreme right shows that the aircraft is to the right of the centreline and hence, should move to the left. The middle unit shows that the aircraft is on the centreline of the aircraft stand. All the three units also show the distance to the stop position as 12 m.

The unit can be installed on a pole in front of the stand as shown in Figure 6.25.

Figure 6.23 Runway centreline lights. Photograph by the author

Aircraft 12 m away from Stop position and to the left of centre line

Aircraft 12 m away from Stop position and on the centre line

Aircraft 12 m away from Stop position and to the right of the centre line

Figure 6.24 VDGS guiding the aircraft. Photograph by AMA

Figure 6.25 VDGS unit mounted on pole. Photograph by AMA

Power supply requirement

The AGL system's power supply is provided with a backup system with a no-break source like UPS and a standby power source like Diesel Generators. The AGL system is system-wise connected in series and with interleaving, meaning alternate lamps are in one circuit so that in case of failure of one circuit does not leave the pilot without guidance, but the distance between two lights will be more than the standard spacing. AGL system requires constant current regulators and a control and monitoring system. The power station equipment and AGL equipment are all housed in a building close to each end of the runway. The building height and the location are planned to be away from RESA/Strip, and the height is within the OLS limits. The area of these substations is approximately 200–300 sqm.

Table 6.1 is an illustration of the AGL system with colour and direction. Unidirectional means only on one direction the light will be visible whereas if it is bidirectional the light will be visible on two sides of the fixtures at 180 degree and omnidirectional means the light will be seen 360 degrees.

Table 6.1 AGL system with colour and direction

System	Colour	Direction	Remarks
Runway edge lights	White	Bidirectional	
	Amber	Unidirectional	For last 600 m or one-third of runway, whichever is less
	Red	Unidirectional	From physical beginning to Displaced threshold
Circling guidance lights		Omni directional	Part of RWY Edge lights
Taxiway and apron edge lights	Blue	Omni directional	
Runway centreline lights	White	Bidirectional	
	Alternate red and white	Unidirectional	Last 900 m to 300 m
	Red	Unidirectional	Last 300 m
Touchdown zone lights	White	Unidirectional	
Taxiway centreline lights	Green	Bidirectional	
	Alternate green and yellow	Uni/ bidirectional	Alternate green and yellow from ILS/MLS sensitive/critical area (runway portion)
Stop bars	Red	Unidirectional	
Intermediate holding position lights	Yellow	Unidirectional	
Threshold and wing bar lights	Green	Unidirectional	
Runway end lights	Red	Unidirectional	
Approach lights	White	Unidirectional	
Approach supplementary lights	White	Unidirectional	Along with the centreline lights of approach (if threshold is not displaced)
	Red	Unidirectional	Additional row on either side of centreline
Sequential flashing light	White	Unidirectional	Flashing lights. Used with baratte type lighting
Aircraft stand manoeuvring guidance lights	Yellow	Bi/omni directional	
	Red	Unidirectional	For stop position
Aerodrome beacon	Alternate white and green		
Rapid exit taxiway indicator lights	Yellow	Unidirectional	
PAPI	Red/white	Unidirectional	
Runway guard lights	Yellow	Unidirectional	Flashing lights
Turn pad lights	Green	Unidirectional	
Mandatory signs	White letters on red background	Unidirectional	
Information signs	Black letters on yellow background	Unidirectional	For showing directions
	Yellow letters on black background	Unidirectional	For showing locations
Stopway lights	Red	Unidirectional	From runway end to stopway end
Threshold identification lights	White	Unidirectional	For displaced threshold
No entry bar lights	Red	Unidirectional	On the mouth of the taxiway

(*Continued*)

Table 6.1 (Continued)

System	Colour	Direction	Remarks
Road holding position lights	Red	Unidirectional	On the road leading to runway
Simple touchdown zone lighting	White	Unidirectional	
Runway status lights	Red	Unidirectional	Runway entrance lights and take OFF hold lights

Reference – Annex14/ICAO.

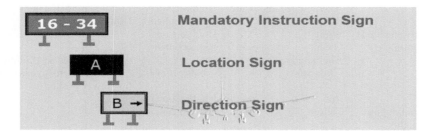

Figure 6.26 Airfield signs. Photograph by the author

Depending on the category of operations, the system requirement will be decided. For example, touchdown zone lights are required for airports with Precision Approach Categories II and III operation but not required for Category I operation. On the other hand, runway edge and PAPI systems are required for runway operations of the non-precision approach category onwards.

Signs installed on the airfield guides the pilot while taxing with taxiway designations, runway designations, runway holding position, etc. Various guidance provided by the signs are grouped together and shown in Figure 6.26.

The signs are illuminated. There are set of specifications for the size of the letter/number in the sign, the location, and the overall size of the sign.

Figure 6.27 Apron flood lights. Photograph by the author

Apron flood light

Apron flood is to illuminate the apron with an appropriate level for the pilot while manoeuvring the aircraft, the ground handling personnel, for example, while pushing back the aircraft, loading/unloading bags, refuelling, cleaning, etc. Illumination level, colour index is specified. The height of the mast is decided based on the principle that there would be no glare to the pilot.

Conclusion

This chapter provided the basics of the visual aids, CNS system, and Air Traffic Management from the airport planning aspect. The extent and type of the systems depend on various factors, like the category of runway operations and the volume of aircraft traffic. For example, an airport operating in Cat III operations with significant aircraft movement in an hour requires an advanced surveillance system like surface movement radar. Similarly, if the area control of the airspace is monitored at the airport, it requires more space in the technical building of the ATC tower. However, from the airport planning aspect, the location criteria of the systems are more critical, which this chapter covers. Additional land required is not significant for most systems except the approach lighting system. However, it is essential to locate these facilities so that the system's performance is maintained and allows seamless airport expansion. Additional reading materials will be an added knowledge to the readers.

References

Airport Traffic Control Tower Siting Process – Order 6480.4b. (2018).
Department of Civil Aviation, M. (2009). Communication, Navigation, and Surveillance Manual – Volume III.
ICAO. (2018a). Annex 10 Aeronautical Telecommunications – Volume 1.

ICAO. (2018). Meteorological Service for International Air Navigation – Annex 3.

ICAO. (2022). ICAO Annex 14 – Ninth Edition: Vol I.

Ministry of Civil Aviation, G. of I. (2020). Ministry of Civil Aviation (Height Restrictions for Safeguarding of Aircraft Operations).

Further reading

ATC System Y Tube Video. https://m.youtube.com/watch?v=LX3vir40iQQ&autoplay=1

Case Study of ATC Tower Location Siting Study for an Air Traffic Control Tower (ATCT) at Duluth International Airport.

Digital Towers – Services & Products – NATS.

IATA – User Requirements for Air Traffic Services (URATS) Communications, Navigation, and Surveillance (CNS) Technologies.

NPA 2022-02 (A) and NPA 2022-02 (B) – Remote aerodrome air traffic services | EASA (europa.eu).

Remote Tower Systems (RTS) | Federal Aviation Administration (faa.gov).

The Delhi Air Traffic Control Tower: Engineering, Architecture and Design with TMD for the Tallest ATCT in India. https://doi.org/10.2749/222137912805112680

7 Environmental impact and land use planning

Introduction

ICAO defines the environment as including the following:

a Air, land, and water.
b All layers of the atmosphere.
c All organic and inorganic matter and living organisms.
d The interacting natural systems referred to in a) to c).

Due to the interdependence of all these, any disruption to one could significantly impact the entire system. The airport operations, aircraft operations, aircraft maintenance, and construction activities at the airport all contribute to the impact. Thus, all the aviation stakeholders work together to minimize and regulate the source of the impact.

Land use planning, if implemented, will reduce the impact and contribute to aviation safety by minimizing the impact on lives due to incidents/accidents. Noise, deterioration of water quality, and air quality are the significant environmental effects mainly brought on by airport operations and aircraft operations. These environmental effects, land use planning, and zoning map to reduce the impact are covered herein.

Noise

Noise at airports is generated by planes taking off and landing while testing their engines at the airport, movement of ground handling vehicles, passenger movements, and use of vehicles by airport employees, freight trucks, backup power generators, and Heating, Ventilation, and Air Conditioning (HVAC) plants. Among all the noise sources, planes taking off and landing at the airport contributes to the maximum.

The main effect of airport operations is noise, which is mainly caused by aircraft operations. Even though planes are getting quieter, it is still a problem for people near the airport. Planes will keep making noise, so the only thing to do is figure out how to lessen its effects.

The Pittsburgh sleep quality index shows that 87% of the people surveyed in the area had trouble sleeping because of noise near an international airport in Columbia. The results also showed that 60% of the study area followed the rule during the day, but only 18% did so at night. Thus, the problem is making sure that the rules are followed.

Experiments on people suddenly exposed to very loud noise showed that their blood pressure and heart rate went up. This impact can cause hearing loss, high blood pressure, ischemic heart

DOI: 10.4324/9781003319948-7

disease, irritability, and trouble sleeping. According to the results of this study, the more people live near the airport, the more expensive it is to cut down on noise, and the more health problems there are for the public.

The magnitude of noise can be reduced by controlling the aircraft's noise generation with appropriate technology, a continuous process. In addition, the impact on the community can be reduced by locating them away from the source. It can be relocated if the community is already near the source and affected. If relocation is not possible or uneconomical, the mitigation is to provide noise barriers or soundproofing.

Land use planning around airports is the best way to avoid or reduce noise in areas that are sensitive to noise. The potential use in noise reduction lies in their ability to

- Indicate quiet areas that are to be protected against any new noise emission.
- Designate areas that are sensitive to noise based on strategic noise mapping.
- Identify where any new noise emission should be prevented.
- Assign land use to ensure there is enough space between the airport/approach/take-off path and noise-sensitive areas so that new noise does not get into those areas.
- Work out land use for vehicular traffic to minimize the generation of additional traffic within and outside the airport, especially cargo-carrying trucks, particularly in noise-sensitive areas.
- Locate commercial buildings to act as barriers to more sensitive residential buildings.

Water quality

Storms can collect pollutants from airfield pavements, road pavements, building rooftops, and other surfaces. Some construction works also contribute to this impact. These pollutants can then be washed into nearby bodies of water. Oils, greases, de-icing agents, extra jet fuel, nitrates, and metals like chromium, zinc, and copper can all be pollutants in runoff. Chromium, zinc, and copper concentrations that are too high in water bodies can affect aquatic organisms, especially fish, and potentially result in their demise. An excessive amount of nitrate in a body of water can lead to excessive algae development, which generates unstable levels of Dissolved Oxygen (DO), which stresses out fish and other aquatic animals and may even cause them to go extinct. The pH of the nearby waters can also be affected by airport runoff. The aquatic species that live there will perish when a body of water's pH is too high or too low. Fish deaths, algal blooms, and water contamination can all be caused by pollutants near airports.

Two airports were the subject of research to see whether runoff from the airport affects the quality of the water there. Twelve locations near these two airports had their water quality evaluated for pH, the presence of particular metals, and nitrate levels. According to the findings, zinc, copper, chromium, and nitrate concentrations rose closer to the airports and reduced as the distance from airports increased. However, over the course of the locations, the pH stayed consistent. Thus, airport pollution is likely the cause of some of the heavy metals and nitrates increased quantities.

Impact on water quality due to de-icing and anti-icing of aircraft

The de-icing and anti-icing of aircraft and airfield surfaces are required to ensure the safety of passengers. However, when performed without discharge controls, airport de-icing operations can result in environmental impacts. In addition to potential aquatic life and human health impacts from the toxicity of de-icing and anti-icing chemicals, the biodegradation of propylene or ethylene glycol (i.e., the base chemical of de-icing fluid) in surface waters (i.e., lakes, rivers) can significantly impact water quality, including significant reduction in DO levels. Reduced DO levels can ultimately lead to fish kills (Source EPA).

The impact on water quality due to airport operations can be minimized using lined stormwater drains for the areas where the surface water gets contaminated due to oil, grease, and cleaning agents and the de-icing/anti-icing of aircraft. In addition, the surface water is channelled into an oil–water separator before recharging the ground or storage in a pond. Therefore, during the master planning, either an oil–water separator for individual facilities or a centralized separator must be planned.

Air pollution

Green House Gas (GHG) emission is 2% of the total emission due to the aviation sector.

Emission sources at the airports can be divided into:

1 Due to aircraft operations called 'Landing Take-Off cycle' (LTO) contributing approximately 63%.
2 Electricity consumption for airport operations is approximately 12%.
3 Passenger airport access is approximately 11%.
4 Due to electricity consumption by tenants is 9%.
5 Auxiliary power units meant for aircraft contribute 3%.
6 Operation of ground handling equipment contributes approximately 0.20%, and others like engine testing, staff travel, etc., the remaining 1.8% of the emission.

A significant part of the emission that comes out of the aircraft operation is the LTO cycle. LTO cycles include all activities near the airport below a height of 3000 ft (914 m). Thus, it includes taxi-in and -out, take-off, climb out, and approach and landing. The impact of these can be managed operationally. Continuous Decent Operation (CDO; during approach and take-off) reduces fuel consumption and emission levels. This CDO methodology also reduces the noise as the aircraft stays at a higher altitude for a longer time and lesser time at a lower altitude as it continuously lands or takes off.

Another stage of the operation is aircraft taxiing from the stands to the runway for take-off and vice versa while landing. Few airports have tried using what is called 'TaxiBots', which enables the aircraft to move during taxiing without the aircraft engine ON. TaxiBot is attached to the aircraft, remotely operated by the pilot, and disconnected before take-off. Thus, the aircraft is on its power only from the runway holding position to take-off. Similarly, on arrival from the parallel taxi to the aircraft stand, TaxiBot is used.

Due to the increasing residential development surrounding airports and the continued growth of commercial air travel, air pollution surrounding airports has become a significant concern for local/regional governments. Local air quality concerns concentrate on effects created during the LTO cycle as these emissions are released below 3000 feet (914 m).

The emission source is Aviation Turbine Fuel (ATF). Alternative fuel sources are being pursued. Three prominent ones are Sustainable Aviation Fuel (SAF), hydrogen-powered, and electricity powered. SAF does not need any additional infrastructure at the airport, whereas the other two require some considerations.

Planning can contribute to minimizing the emission due to the LTO cycle by configuring the airfield pavements appropriately with an adequate number of entry/exit taxiways at suitable locations for the aircraft fleet mix. However, the operations and operational procedures play a significant role in minimizing this emission. Aircraft technology has changed a lot, and newer aircraft produce fewer emissions, but the traffic growth and consequent increase in aircraft movements have contributed to this problem. Emissions from airport operations are minimized through a selection of equipment with lesser emissions.

Regarding energy consumption for airport operations, the airports are targeting renewable source of energy. Thus, land use planning should include this aspect. The criterion for the location is described in the chapter on master planning.

Emissions due to vehicles and ground handling equipment are minimized with the use of battery-operated machines. Hydrogen as a fuel for these operations is also becoming popular, and airports are considering this. APUs are not operated nowadays when the aircraft is on an aircraft stand and are replaced with Ground Power Units (GPU), which are electrically driven instead of conventional diesel-operated machines. Land use planning should cater to the infrastructure required for more electrically operated vehicles, equipment, and hydrogen as fuel.

Cochin International Airport in India has become the world's first 100% solar-powered airport. The airport is run entirely on solar energy, making it the first airport in the world to do so.

Land use planning plays a very minimal role in air pollution by airport operations. However, land use planning on a broader aspect can minimize the impact due to air pollution as a part of urban planning by locating pollution-emitting activities like industries away from residential areas, educational institutes, hospitals, and other noise-sensitive facilities.

Land use planning within airport

As per ICAO, 'Land-use planning' is for compatible land uses considering airport development needs. Therefore, it more adequately describes achieving an optimum relationship between an airport and its environs.

As a business entity, the airport would exploit all revenue generation activities and would like to utilize the available land effectively. However, revenue enhancement due to aircraft operations (including pax) has some limitations as these are mostly regulated or market driven. Thus, airports look for aeronautical-related revenue sources like cargo and MRO. But more than these alone may be needed; hence, airports look for commercial revenue generation sources like office complexes, SEZs, hotels, convention centres, logistics centres, and educational institutes within the airport boundary. While locating these facilities, the principles mentioned below will be applicable, and in fact, these would be more stringent as these are to be situated in the airport.

Since airports are primarily for aircraft operations and passenger processing, the rest of the land parcels within the airport are to be used diligently, enhancing their utility simultaneously without compromising aviation safety.

Similarly, near the airport, even though outside the airport, some planning guidelines are required for orderly development without affecting aviation safety as well as minimizing the aircraft operations impact like noise on the occupants of the building/facilities outside the airport.

Land use implementation of the brownfield airport development with unplanned development around the airport must be managed through mitigation like ICAO's balanced approach.

Land use principles are as follows:

- Identification of a specific location for various facilities or infra or activities.
- Evaluation of the impact on environmental aspects – noise, water quality, and air pollution.
- Evaluation of the impact if the activities will increase the bird menace.
- Evaluation considering the obstacle limitation surfaces – location and height of the structures proposed.

- Activities match with the inhabitants, and activities are clubbed together. For example, industries are located close to each other in the same vicinity and away from residential units, hospitals, or schools.
- Identify permitted vs. not permitted activities in the defined area.
- Facilities and activities near the airport do not hinder or compromise aviation safety. For example, a slaughterhouse near the airport will attract birds, thus increasing bird menace and impacting aviation safety.
- Consider the planned expansion plans for the airport while land use plans are finalized, based on the ultimate master plan, especially the airside expansion plans like an additional runway.
- View from the air traffic control tower is not impacted (mainly for the proposed structures within the airport)
- Safety areas within the airfield are protected (for example, runway end safety area)
- Performance of communication and navigational equipment/systems not affected.
- Avoid wetlands, ponds, stormwater retention facilities, and other similar uses because they offer excellent avian wildlife habitat.
- Locate landfills away from the airport, which is another hazard due to its likelihood of increasing bird activity.
- Identify an appropriate location for the engine run up the bay.
- Appropriate location of sanitary landfill or wetland mitigation projects.
- Avoid highly populated facilities in the approach and take off climb surfaces for the following reasons.

1 To reduce the impact on the population in case of aircraft accidents. Aviation safety statistics show that most fatal accidents happen during the landing phase of the flight.
2 This restriction is also applicable to facilities that are noise sensitive. When the facility is closer to the runway end, the aircraft approach path is at a lesser height and hence, more noise from aircraft operations.
3 Avoid facilities where the lights or glare from the facilities can impact aircraft operations. Similarly, smoke-emanating facilities should be avoided, which can reduce the aircraft's visibility while landing or taking off.
4 Facilities that can impact navigational equipment through their electromagnetic emission should be located so that they do not create interference and thus affect their performance.

Land use planning and flood management

Land use planning is one of the fundamental options in flood management based on flood maps which are prepared as accurately as possible and work out flood mitigation measures. For example, before the airport was developed at 2100 hectares, the land would have absorbed the rainwater and protected the adjoining areas from the flood. But, after the airport is developed, at least 80% of the land would have been paved with concrete or asphalt pavement and buildings. There will be significantly less water infiltration to the ground. Most airports have Rainwater Harvesting structures on the airside and near all the facilities to partly recharge the soil. The water collected in the stormwater drains usually is channelled to a pond for storage and recharge the ground instead of letting the excess water outside the airport affect the inhabitants. In some airports, the pond is constructed with an oil–water separator. The oil–water separator removes the oil from the water before it is stored in the pond. Thus, it acts as an environmental control since if recharged with oil contents will affect the water groundwater quality.

At the same time, we are designing the system for controlling flood water. Usually, the rainfall data is based on a storm whose probability of occurrence is once in 50 years, called the return period of the storm. However, due to climate change, it is noticed that the intensity of rainfall is extremely high and lasts only for a few minutes or hours. Thus, the quantum of water will be huge, and the design may have to consider this.

Drains in the apron are usually provided with a standalone oil–water separator before the rainwater is let into the airport stormwater drainage system.

One of the primary approaches to managing floods is land use planning, which develops flood mitigation strategies using as precise flood maps as feasible.

ICAO guidelines

Airport planning and operations must work together to reduce the impacts. Airport planning must be recognized as an integral part of an area-wide comprehensive planning programme. The location, size, and configuration of the airport need to be coordinated with patterns of residential, industrial, commercial, agricultural, and other land uses of the area, taking into account the effects of the airport on people, flora, fauna, the atmosphere, water courses, air quality, soil pollution, rural areas (such as deserts), and other facets of the environment (ICAO).

Limiting or reducing the number of people affected by significant aircraft noise is, therefore, one of ICAO's main priorities and one of the Organization's key environmental goals.

ICAO's Balanced Approach consists of identifying the noise problem at a specific airport and analysing various measures available to reduce noise by exploring multiple measures classified into four principal elements.

Following are the Balanced approaches:

• Initiatives to reduce aircraft noise which is the source of the issue.
• Land use planning and management.
• Noise abatement operational procedures (noise preferential runways and routes and noise abatement procedures for take-off and landing).
• Operating restrictions (restrictions should be based on the aircraft's noise performance, curfews, night-time restrictions, noise quotas/budgets, etc.).

The goal is to address noise problems on an individual airport basis and identify the noise-related measures that achieve maximum environmental benefit cost-effectively using objective and measurable criteria.

Land-use planning and management is an effective means to ensure that the activities nearby airports are compatible with aviation. Its main goal is to minimize the population affected by aircraft noise by introducing land-use zoning around airports.

Compatible land-use planning and management is also a vital instrument in ensuring that the gains achieved by the reduced noise of the latest generation of aircraft are not offset by further residential development around airports.

ICAO's main policies on land use planning and management contained in Assembly Resolution A39-1, Appendix F urges States where the opportunity still exists to minimize aircraft noise problems through preventive measures to:

a Locate new airports at an appropriate place, such as away from noise-sensitive areas.
b Take the appropriate measures so that land-use planning is taken fully into account at the initial stage of any new airport or of development at an existing airport.

c Define zones around airports associated with different noise levels taking into account population levels and growth as well as forecasts of traffic growth and establish criteria for the appropriate use of such land, taking account of ICAO guidance.

d Enact legislation, establish guidance or other appropriate means to achieve compliance with those criteria for land use.

e Ensure that reader-friendly information on aircraft operations and their environmental effects is available to communities near airports.

To promote a uniform method of assessing noise around airports, ICAO recommends using the methodology contained in ICAO Doc 9911 – Recommended Method for Computing Noise Contours around Airports.

Airports can operate with limited environmental impact by incorporating environmental management plans and procedures with land-use planning. In the past, environmental management has concentrated on pollution abatement or control by finding ways to dispose of waste after it has been produced. More recently, organizations have been shifting towards pollution prevention, which focuses on reducing or eliminating the need for pollution control. Pollution prevention can be defined as 'the use of materials, processes or practices that reduce or eliminate the creation of pollutants and wastes at the source'. It includes practices that reduce the use of hazardous and non-hazardous materials, energy, water, or other resources. In addition, anticipatory action is used to pre-empt the need for control or remedy. ICAO guidance on this subject is contained in Annex 16, Volume I, Part IV and in the ICAO Doc 9184, Airport Planning Manual, Part 2 – Land Use and Environmental Control. In addition, to promote a uniform method of assessing noise around airports, ICAO recommends the use of the methodology contained in ICAO Doc 9911 – Recommended Method for Computing Noise Contours around Airports.

FAA guidelines

The development of land uses incompatible with airports and aircraft noise is a growing concern across the country. In addition to aircraft noise, other issues, such as safety and other environmental impacts on land use around airports, must be considered when addressing the overall issue of land use compatibility. Although several federal programs include noise standards or guidelines as part of their funding-eligibility and performance criteria, the primary responsibility for integrating airport considerations into the local land use planning process rests with local governments. The objectives of compatible land use planning are to encourage land uses that are generally considered to be incompatible with airports (such as residential, schools, and churches) to locate away from airports and to encourage land uses that are more compatible (such as industrial and commercial uses) to locate around airports.

While not the only compatibility issue, aircraft noise has been the primary driver of airport land use compatibility conflicts. Since the introduction of turbojet aircraft in the late 1950s, there has been a constant technical effort to reduce aircraft noise emissions. Although there has been a significant reduction in aircraft engine noise, little more can be expected in noise-reduction technology. Consequently, the focus must now be on airport-specific noise and land use compatibility planning. It also recognizes that state and local governments are responsible for land use planning, zoning, and regulation and presents options or tools that can assist in establishing and maintaining compatible land uses around airports.

The unwanted interaction between aircraft and wildlife is a situation that needs to be avoided. Bird strikes during flight and the interaction of terrestrial and avian species with aircraft on the ground are hazards to aviation. FAA Advisory Circular (AC) 150/5200-33, Hazardous Wildlife

Attractants on or Near Airports, guides locating specific land uses that have the potential to attract hazardous wildlife to or in the vicinity of public-use airports such as sanitary landfills and wetland mitigation areas. Specifically, the AC identifies land uses of concern in proximity to airports, including wetlands, ponds, stormwater retention facilities, and other similar uses, for they offer excellent habitats for avian wildlife. In addition, the location of landfills within the proximity of an airport is considered a hazard due to its likelihood of attracting flocks of birds. This guide recommends that no new sanitary landfill or wetland mitigation projects be sited within 10,000 feet of an active air carrier runway end or 5000 feet of a busy general aviation runway end.

CAA (UK)

There is no getting away from the fact that aviation can be noisy. When aircraft land and take off, depending on the aircraft and its altitude, they produce a considerable amount of noise as they fly overhead.

The highest levels of noise are experienced close to the busiest airports, with noise from Heathrow at a level classified as 'significantly annoying' and impacting more people than any other airport in Europe. The challenge for civil aviation is increasing capacity while reducing noise. The government and the aviation industry have worked to try and minimize the impact of noise by promoting the use of quieter aircraft, restricting the times airports can operate and the routes that can be used and, in some cases, capping the total number of flights that can depart from and arrive at an airport.

Guidelines in India (rules published under the environmental protection act)

Noise standards for the airports are published in Table 7.1.

Following are requirements for the airports being developed:

i   Noise modelling shall be conducted by the airport operators, and results should be submitted to the Government while seeking Environment Clearance for the airport.
ii Develop airport noise zone as specified and share the same with the Government for land use planning around the airport.
iii The concerned State or the Development Authorities should not allow any new residential, institutions and commercial facilities, and other noise-sensitive areas to fall in the airport noise zone area without any noise reduction measure

Table 7.1 Noise standards for the airports in India

Sl. No	Industry	Parameters	Standards	
		3	4	
1	2	Ambient air quality standards with respect to noise in airport noise zone		
		Type of airports	Limits in Db (A) Leq/8*	
			Day time	Night time
112	Airports	Busy airports	70	65
		All other airports excluding proposed airports	65	60

Reference – G.S.R. 568(E) of Government of India.

The rules also specify that Airport Noise Mapping for all airports should be carried out as per the requirements specified in the Director General Civil Aviation's requirements by the airport operators considering future aircraft movement and traffic projections of the airport as per the Master Plan of the Airport. This information is to be displayed at prominent places at Airports as well as on the website of the respective Airport Operator and State/Union Territory Development Authority.

Noise mitigation measures

Noise barriers

Around a busy airport in India, several residential colonies are situated; hence, to curb noise pollution, noise barriers have been installed on one side of the runway as a sound-reduction barrier. It is a 3.5-m-tall barrier over the boundary wall with noise insulation features. The sound reduction barriers are said to cut the noise levels by around 16–18 dBA.

Operational procedures

A runway rotation plan has been implemented at an airport for noise abatement to achieve a balanced distribution of noise exposure for the areas located below the flight paths of aircraft. As per the Runway Use Plan for Noise Abatement, two runways are used only for departure from 2301 hours to 0300 hours and from 0301 hours to 0600 hours on a rotation basis. The third runway is used for arrivals only.

Figure 7.1 shows an example of an airport measuring the noise at locations close to the airport.

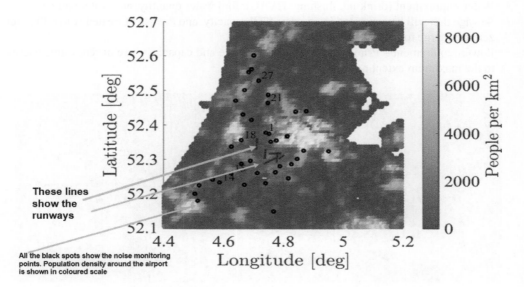

Figure 7.1 Noise measurement locations near the airport

Source: Comparative assessment of measured and modelled aircraft noise around Amsterdam Airport Schiphol by Dick G. Simons and others. https://doi.org/10.1016/j.trd.2022.103216

Land use plan and zoning map

When a greenfield airport is built, there may be few buildings, activities, or residential units, but as the airport develops, the surrounding area is wholly exploited to its greatest potential. For a greenfield airport, land use planning to guarantee compatibility with the airport is comparably easy. However, airport expansion is problematic if not planned as a master planning effort, and land use planning may not have been mandated. Because of this, a land use plan and zoning map are needed to account for any potential future airport growth that may occur over several years. If this were not planned for, development was allowed without control, and the facilities were later affected by the growth, the airport would be required to pay to move the affected facilities or take other steps to reduce the impact due to noise, like insulation of the buildings. However, despite all the measures in place, encroachment occurs when development violates authorized land use plans and height regulations, in which case the owners of such facilities bear the cost of relocation of such facilities.

An example of land use planning controls is shown in Figure 7.2; residential buildings **are not permitted** within the black boundary (65DNL), and between black and white, units are allowed but noise abatement measures are to be provided.

Noise mitigation through operational procedures, with various modes of approach and departure procedures, shows that for arrivals, Continuous Descend Arrival (CDO) has a lower noise level and stepped climb for departure as the engine noise is the primary component during departure.

Environmental assessment study and mitigations

This study consists of the following.

- Salient features of the project-building area, population.
- Water requirement (drinking, flushing, HVAC), foul water quantity, and water source.
- Sewage that will be generated in one day, STP capacity, and the use of treated water. Plan for zero discharge to the city sewage system.
- Power requirement – Primary and secondary source and capacity – use of renewable energy to the maximum extent possible.

Figure 7.2 Noise zoning map around an airport

Source: 'Aviation Noise Impact Management' by Laurent Leylekian and others. doi.org/10.1007/978-3-030-91194-2

- Vehicle parking requirement – split of vehicles – cars, two-wheelers, heavy vehicles – use of electrically operated vehicles and battery charging requirement.
- Quantity of solid waste expected in a day and collection and disposal methods.

To Assess

- Ambient air environment – existing through measurement at several points. PM2.5, PM10, SO2, NO2, CO. Likely impact due to the proposed project.
- Land environment – geology, hydrology, land use.
- Water – quality and quantity of surface and groundwater sources – measure existing water quality.
- Ecological – terrestrial, aquatic flora and fauna – assess the impact of flora and fauna and check its significance.
- Socio-Economic – demographic profile.
- Existing noise levels and likely impact due to the proposed project.
- Soil quality – to assess the construction methodology.
- The biological – presence or otherwise of rare or endangered species. Whether the site is a nesting or breeding ground.

During construction activities

Environmental impact and mitigation must be worked out during the construction of the airport and every time the airport is planned for capacity expansion with additional infrastructure or expansion of the existing facilities.

Air quality

Construction equipment and vehicles emit air pollutants such as NOX, SOX, and Particulate Matters (PM) that can harm health and the environment. Vehicles passing in dry and windy areas can generate dust and increase the ambient Total Suspended Solids (TSP). Demolition of existing facilities and paved areas can increase the ambient TSP due to the release of fine debris particles and the increase in exposed (un-vegetated) ground areas. As for land transportation emissions, the expected concentration of pollutants emitted, based on the projected increase in the number of vehicles, will generally contribute little to the overall ambient pollution concentrations.

To mitigate the impacts of air pollutants, vehicles, and equipment must first pass mandatory emissions testing based on local standards. In addition, during construction, areas considered vulnerable to dust generation will be sprayed with uncontaminated water periodically to suppress the proliferation of dust particles.

Noise impact

The most significant noise impact of construction activities in the airport is associated with the movements of heavy equipment and the transport of construction materials. Impacts of the construction noise, however, are anticipated to be low in magnitude, localized, and temporary.

Noise impacts will be mitigated by minimizing the construction activities between 10 PM and 5 AM and requiring construction equipment and trucks to be well maintained, including the appropriate use of mufflers. In addition, the noise generated from heavy equipment and high noise-producing operation will be restricted within the project boundary. During the expansion or renovation of the airport facilities, these will be designed so that intense noise-generating activities will be far from passenger movements.

Water quality

Wastewater generated can be treated in a sewage treatment plant depending on the quantum of wastewater and reuse of the treated water for other than drinking purposes.

Health and safety hazards

Unsafe activities and improper use of tools and equipment may result in accidents. People will also be exposed to high noise, vibrations, and air pollution while construction and renovation are ongoing.

To mitigate the impacts of these hazards, construction workers should be trained in Health and Safety applicable to their respective line of work. The necessary PPEs (Proper Protective Equipment) will be provided to the staff. To mitigate the impact on the health and safety of airport staff and passengers during the operational phase, the expansion or renovation works are planned and designed to minimize the impact of fire, earthquake, and extreme weather events. A proper evacuation plan during emergencies is necessary.

Drawbacks of land use planning

It restricts development and, thus, might affect the region's economic growth. Limiting the development may hamper economic growth and therefore hurt local economies in need, especially during times of economic recession.

Air pollution, noise, and catastrophic risk are some negative externalities resulting from airport operations. In contrast, job availability, well-developed infrastructure, and public transit are some of the positives due to airport operations. Despite the research showing a correlation between airports and urban growth, airport operations may negatively affect the surrounding area's quality of life. In terms of negative externalities, noise pollution is among the significant issue. When it comes to urban economics, proximity to an airport has a direct impact on real estate values. Airport noise has been shown to affect the value of homes in many nations considerably. There is often a conflict between the airport's capacity to operate sustainably economically (through long-term growth, secure employment, and the expansion of infrastructure) and sustainably environmentally (by limiting harmful externalities such as noise and pollution). Thus, airport expansion directly impacts local planning, typically resulting in restrictive zoning regulations that restrict development in the affected region to minimize the adverse effects of airport expansion.

Conclusion

Aviation growth with minimal additional environmental impact is an ideal way to develop the infrastructure. This can be achieved by adopting mitigation and minimizing measures during development planning firstly through land use planning. Environmental impact assessment due to the proposed development and the action plans to minimize the impact will enable the community to get convinced that these will not affect them most. As the aviation growth brings on economic growth and with huge benefits to the country a balanced approach is essential. Thus, this chapter highlighted the impacts as well as the mitigation measures. Development planning along with operational procedures is the best way to tackle the environmental impact.

References

Articles in Science Direct on Land Use Planning.

Batóg, J., Foryś, I., Gaca, R., Głuszak, M., & Konowalczuk, J. (2019). Investigating the Impact of Airport Noise and Land Use Restrictions on House Prices: Evidence from Selected Regional Airports in Poland. *Sustainability (Switzerland)*, 11(2). https://doi.org/10.3390/su11020412

da Silva, B. A. C., Santos, G. S., & Gomes, R. de A. (2020). Land Use Policy in the Vicinity of Airports: Analysis and Lessons Learned from the Brazilian Situation. *Land Use Policy*, 90(November 2019), 104314. https://doi.org/10.1016/j.landusepol.2019.104314

de Luque Villa, M., Mendez, A. C. A., Virguez, J. D., Rubio, M., & Triana, C. C. (2020). Evaluation of the Noise Impacts on Sleep Quality in Communities Near to the International Airport El Dorado in Colombia. *WIT Transactions on Ecology and the Environment*, 241, 397–405. https://doi.org/10.2495/SDP200321

Murphy, E., & King, E. A. (2014). Noise Mitigation Approaches. *Environmental Noise Pollution*, 203–245. https://doi.org/10.1016/B978-0-12-411595-8.00007-0

Radomska, M., Madzhd, S., Cherniak, L., & Mikhyeyev, O. (2020). Environmental Pollution in the Airport Impact Area–Case Study of the Boryspil International Airport. *Environmental Problems*, 5(2), 76–82. https://doi.org/10.23939/ep2020.02.076

Reduction of the Emission at Airport – EASA-Green Airport Infrastructure | EASA Eco (europa.eu).

Ribas Palom, A., Saurí Pujol, D., & Olcina Cantos, J. (2017). Sustainable Land Use Planning in Areas Exposed to Flooding: Some International Experiences. *Floods*, 2, 103–117. https://doi.org/10.1016/B978-1-78548-269-4.50008-1

Tezel, M. N., Sari, D., Erdol, M., Hamamci, S. F., & Ozkurt, N. (2019). Evaluation of Some Health Impact Indices in Two Airports' Domain. *Applied Acoustics*, 149, 99–107. https://doi.org/10.1016/J.APACOUST.2019.01.014

Walters, E., & Spuller, K. (2021). Effects of Airport Runoff Pollution on Water Quality in Bay Area Sites Near San Francisco and Oakland Airports. *Journal of Emerging Investigators*, 4(April), 8–11.

Additional reading

Continuous Descent Operations – A Low Hanging Fruit for Environmental Performance Improvements? EUROCONTROL Data Snapshot.

First Flight in History with 100% Sustainable Aviation Fuel on a Regional Commercial Aircraft. https://www.neste.com/releases-and-news/renewable-solutions/first-flight-history-100-sustainable-aviation-fuel-regional-commercial-aircraft

Hydrogen Infrastructure and Operations – Airports, Airlines and Airspace – Fly Zero, Aerospace Technology Institute.

More Than 260 Airports at Risk of Getting Submerged Due to Sea Level Rise, Coastal Flooding: Study by Jan Wesner Childs 23 January 2021.

Read an article about the new runway at Dublin International airport from initiation of the project and commissioning of the runway. Specifically, about the capacity addition and the environmental concerns raised and how these were minimised by the Authority. The link to the article – https://www.rte.ie/news/business/2022/0823/1318439-new-320m-runway-at-dublin-airport-opens-today/

Southampton International Airport Noise Action Plan 2018–2023.

8 Conceptual design of airport components

Introduction

Passenger Terminal Buildings (PTBs) are the first contact with passengers when they arrive at the airport. Its design could be quite simple and functional or very aesthetic and beautiful architecture with high ceilings and façade, etc. and meets the functional requirement. So, the design concept is very much airport specific to meet the city's tradition, culture, and passenger profile. The design alternatives are unlimited, and it evolves every time.

However, the airfield design is based on functional requirements and driven by regulatory guidelines for achieving aviation safety. Therefore, it is always better to evaluate the airfield layout with the view of operational efficiency and flexibility while complying with regulatory requirements as a minimum.

The following description is to cover these aspects.

Passenger Terminal Building (PTB)

The alternatives are described below. The levels discussed here are only for passenger movement. Commercial facilities and services could be at different levels.

Single-level operations

Single level suits for regional airports handling primarily turboprop type or smaller aircraft. There is no requirement for boarding bridges for turboprop-type aircraft. Depending on the need, the terminal building is expanded horizontally on either side or one side. Passengers walk from the terminal building to the flight to board and vice versa, except passengers requiring wheelchair assistance. Figure 8.1 shows a simple layout concept of single-level PTB with arrival and departure halls adjacent to each other. Movement of both the passengers and baggage will be at one level.

Two level operations

This design is for medium size airports. For example, departure passenger drop-off could be at the first-floor level, with all departure processes at this level. Arrival process will be at the ground level. The advantage of this concept is the passenger traffic of departure and arrival at the city side is segregated and thus has more capacity. Or the departing passengers arrive at the ground level, complete the check-in process at this level and then move to the first floor for the gate hold area. Passengers use the Passenger Boarding Bridges (PBBs) when the aircraft is on contact stand for boarding and deboarding at one level above the ground level. If the plane is on

DOI: 10.4324/9781003319948-8

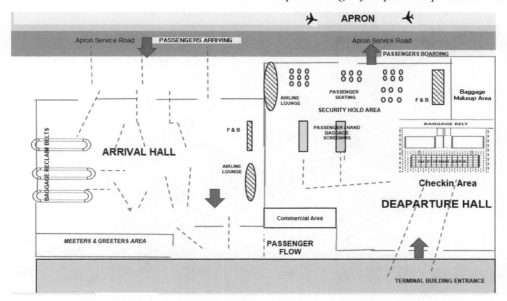

Figure 8.1 Layout of single-level PTB

a non-contact stand, the passengers move to the ground level to board the plane and similarly arrive at the ground level of the building.

All the arrival processes will be at the ground level, including baggage carousels.

The disadvantage of the two-level operation is that the arrival/departure corridor is common at the PBB level. Thus, departing and arriving passengers are not segregated and operationally challenging for airports with majorly origin-destination passengers. This concept may require a gate lounge concept, not a common gate hold area, with a dedicated security check for each gate lounge. An example of this design concept is Singapore Changi Airport. The advantage is lesser level changes for the passengers within the PTB.

Three-level operations

The three-level operational concept is popular for major airports where the arrival and departure passengers are segregated. An example of this design is Hong Kong Airport, Delhi IGI Airport Terminal 3, and many more.

In this arrangement, arriving passengers from the PBB level (one level above ground level) either go down to the ground level for arrival processes and exit the PTB or the transit passengers, after the security check, go up one level for the common security hold area and get down one level for boarding through PBB. Departing passengers originating from the city arrive at two levels above ground level for departure processes and reach the security hold area at the same level as transit passengers and board the aircraft at one level below. Check-in baggage from two levels above the ground level is required to be transported through the baggage handling system to the baggage makeup area at the ground level.

Conceptual plans of passenger flows

PTB with two levels of passenger flow is in Figures 8.2 and 8.3.

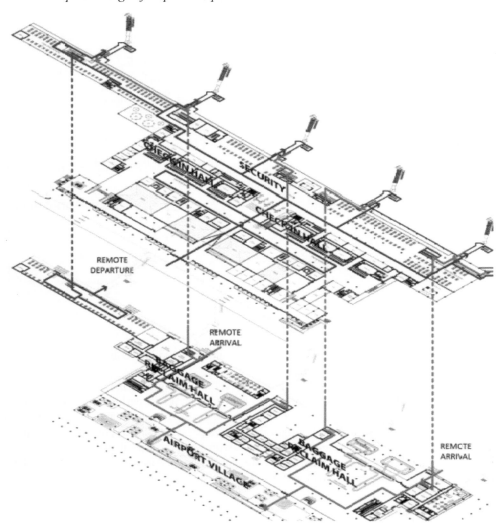

Figure 8.2 Passenger flows in two-level operations

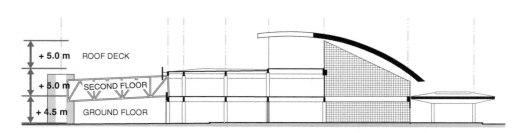

Figure 8.3 Sectional elevation of two-level terminals

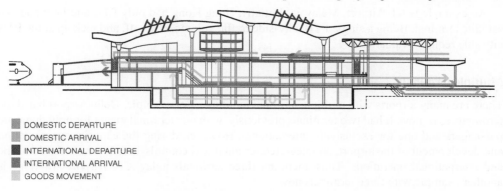

DOMESTIC DEPARTURE
DOMESTIC ARRIVAL
INTERNATIONAL DEPARTURE
INTERNATIONAL ARRIVAL
GOODS MOVEMENT

Figure 8.4 Passenger flows in three-level operations

PTB with three levels and passenger flow is in Figure 8.4.

Single PTB vs. multiple PTB

The concepts are as follows:

Single PTB with all processes.

The advantages of a single large terminal are the best utilization of the resources and equipment, easy navigation for the passengers, and easier transit passenger facilitation. Disadvantages are that too big a terminal may look crowded during peak hour traffic, system failure may affect the entire operation, and difficulties during emergency evacuation like fire will affect the airport as the whole operation. In addition, total passenger and baggage processing under one roof is a risk.

The passengers must walk a long distance between the processes from entry to the building and boarding gate and from the boarding gate to the PTB exit. Require travellators may also require Automatic People Movers (APM) if the walking distance is too much. Only a single terminal with less than some capacities is practical and challenging to manage a large capacity. City-side traffic should be carefully assessed and planned, specifically in front of the PTB for passenger drop off for departure and passenger pick up for arrivals.

Capacity augmentation with additional areas becomes complex with operational hindrances, some abortive works, and more integration issues. These could be minimized with meticulous plan initially but there could be some impacts. In addition, the architecture and interior for the extended portion would be the same as that of the existing building.

Single PTB with satellite terminal

In this concept, PTB handles the departure and arrival processes and a satellite terminal for boarding and arriving from the aircraft. APM or Bus Rapid Transport (BRT) connects PTB and satellite terminals for passenger movement. Bags are transported through high-speed conveyors connecting PTB and the satellite terminals. The satellite terminal concept, increases the airport's capacity as aircraft stands are added, and the gate/security hold area also increases, subject to the PTB capacity matches. Operationally easy as all the processes are carried out at the PTB. The only exception is the security check carried out as a dedicated gate lounge per boarding. The satellite terminal can also reduce the aircraft taxiing time as it could be close to the second runway.

An example is KL Airport, Malaysia. Initially, Hong Kong had only PTB and later added a satellite terminal. Being a single PTB, city-side traffic volume, drop off, and pick up at the PTB city side require evaluation.

Multiple terminals

There are many airports with multiple terminal buildings. For example, Delhi Airport has three terminals as of now. It had two terminals previously, with one terminal meant for only domestic passengers and one for exclusively international. However, during the capacity augmentation and development of the airport, an integrated terminal was commissioned to cater for domestic and international operations. Thus, there are three terminals today. CSI Airport, Mumbai, is another example with three terminals now.

Another example is Manila International Airport and Singapore Chang, which have four terminals, and there are many examples of airports having multiple terminals in the United States, Europe, and the United Kingdom.

The risk and disadvantages mentioned for a single terminal are avoided with multiple terminals. But the flexibility in operations, by utilizing the resources efficiently, may not happen. For example, some terminals may be busy with full utilization, and another terminal may have few passengers during some periods. Therefore, the operational cost could be more than a single terminal.

Interconnecting the terminals for passengers and baggage is a big task, especially if the airport is a hub airport with many transit passengers like Singapore Changi. Achieving the stipulated or minimum connecting time for the transit passengers is challenging and may affect the aircraft's turnaround time. In this aspect, the aircraft stand allocation is vital and complicated for efficient operation. Furthermore, passengers may need help navigating to the terminals as there are multiple terminals, and they need to ascertain the terminal to report for check-in.

If the terminals are on the same side of the runway and apron, they can be better managed for passengers and baggage transfer. But this may only sometimes be possible. If the terminals are otherwise located, the aircraft taxiing time may be reduced, but passenger and baggage movement get complicated with expensive APM and high-speed conveyors.

Expansion/renovation of the terminals can be planned by a terminal utilization plan during such periods.

Since multiple terminals will be developed progressively in ten years or more, there will be minimal operational hindrance. Different architecture and interiors can be planned for each terminal. The number of apron stands may be more for the same capacity when compared with a single terminal, depending on the location of the terminals.

Best option

Designers can create a matrix of all pros and cons of a single terminal expandable for capacity augmentation, a single PTB with satellite terminal(s), and multiple terminals with various options for the location with reference to runway and apron. This analysis must be airport specific depending on the land available, airfield layout, dimensions of the site, type of airport (O&D/hub), and period of capacity augmentation phase wise. This exercise must be undertaken during the master planning stage with a plan for the ultimate capacity of the airport. Some learnings from operating airports will add value to the concept.

Whether it is a single terminal or multiple terminals modular development plan and construction should be planned (more appropriate for a single terminal). This modularity should be specified in the master plan with conceptual design.

Read the article on the website of CAPA about 'Narita Airport considering plans to consolidate three terminals into one'.

PTB design of recent airports

Red Sea airport under construction in Saudi Arabia has been designed (Architect – Foster plus Partners) with five mini terminals, close to each other, to operate/close the terminals depending on the traffic to reduce operational cost.

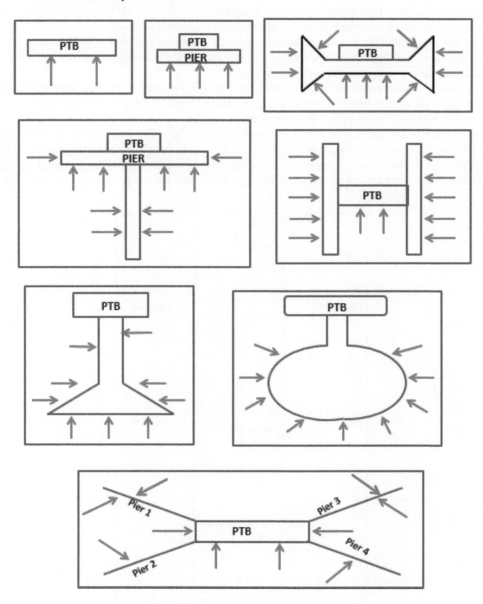

Figure 8.5 Conceptual sketches of piers

Noida International Airport, India (under development) is designed with departure and arrival passengers entry/exit at the ground level and two-level terminal operations.

New Goa Airport (India) is developed with two-level airport terminal with arrival and departure at the ground level.

Shape of the PTB and piers and satellite terminals

A few concepts are presented here. Figure 8.5 shows the PTB with various pier concepts. For example, the shape of the PTBs is shown as a rectangle, but these could be curved shapes. From the figures shown below, there is no end to the various conceptual development.

Shapes other than linear piers reduce the walking distances but require sufficient apron dimensions and working of various options and layouts to enable aircraft manoeuvring with adequate clearances without compromising safety.

Poland is developing a new airport, Centralny Port Komunikacyjny (CPK) Airport. The PTB has a very innovative shape Foster+Partners and Buro Happold consortium. The image can be viewed in M/S Hill International Website as well.

Figure 8.6 is the satellite terminal/concourse concept. The PTB, which is the main processor building and the satellite terminals/concourses, will have to be connected through APM. Walking distances between the passenger processes get reduced considering the large passenger numbers that will be handled. Also, conceptually it is to be decided the processes that will happen

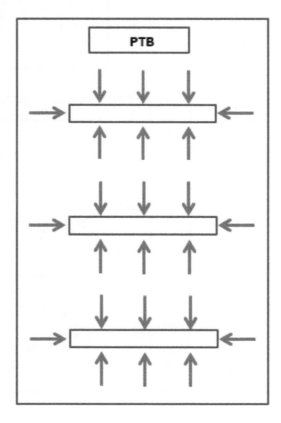

Figure 8.6 Conceptual layout of PTB and satellite building

at the PTB and satellite building (s). Wherever required, the regulatory authorities may have to accept the segregation of domestic and international passengers and their bags. Depending on the processes that will be handled between the PTB and satellite building, the transport of checked-in bags is also to be considered in the design concept.

Another unique concept for a regional airport

The concept in Figure 8.7 is with a separate building only for check-in and is connected to the main PTB through a covered walkway. This concept may be suitable in an existing airport when the PTB cannot be extended lengthwise, due to the unavailability of land, for additional capacity. Thus, the departure and arrival passengers and their vehicular movement are segregated to get more capacity.

Figure 8.7 Unique concept for segregating arriving and departing passengers

Figure 8.8 Check-in hall

Architectural views

High roof, natural sunlight ingress, and wide spacing of columns are the highlights of a PTB design concept nowadays. Wood as a construction material is being used by many airports for roof (Glulam type of material). Few architectural views are shown in Figures 8.8–8.10.

Figure 8.11 is the view of security hold area of Singapore Changi Terminal.

Figure 8.12 shows a bridge over the taxiway to connect a pier with PTB at Gatwick Airport.

Figure 8.9 Gate lounge

Figure 8.10 Kerb side of PTB

Figure 8.11 Changi Airport terminal

Figure 8.12 Bridge over a taxiway connecting terminal to a pier

Source: https://www.geograph.org.uk/photo/74055

Type of fence

There could be two categories of fence, one protecting the property boundary and another one for the protection of operational area.

There are two types of fences. One is seen through type as the name implies activities on both sides will be visible. Another type is the fence is a wall constructed with precast concrete slabs or using stone masonry.

Airfield components

Airfield pavement – runway, taxiway, and apron – structure is designed based on the fleet mix, number of annual aircraft movements, and the material used for the pavement. The design life usually is 20 years. Figure 8.14 shows the general layers of the pavement structure.

It is possible to determine the thickness of various pavement layers using airfield pavement design software. Figure 8.15 shows an example of software output providing the thickness of

Figure 8.13 See through Fence. Photograph by the author

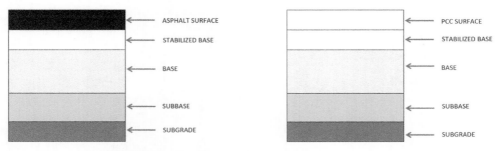

Figure 8.14 Pavement structure

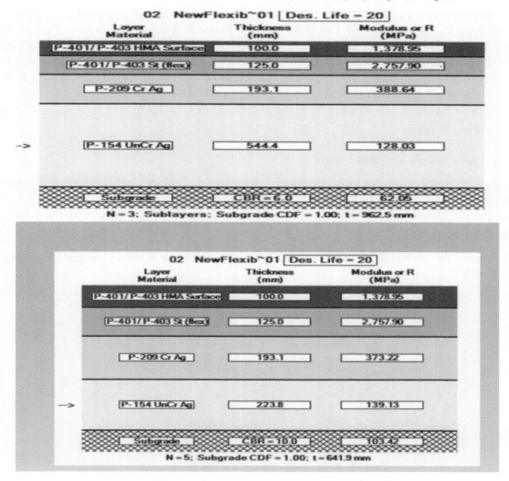

Figure 8.15 Pavement layer thickness for two subgrade strength

Table 8.1 Layer thickness of concrete pavement

Type	Thickness of the layer (mm)
Pavement Quality Concrete (PQC)	450
(Wet Mix Macadam) WMM	250
Subgrade	300

different pavement layers for an asphalt pavement for subgrade strength of CBR 6 and 10. The total thickness of the pavement for the two subgrades is 962.5 mm and 641.9 mm, respectively.

A typical cross-section of an apron pavement with concrete is in Table 8.1.

The airfield pavement could be either flexible, i.e., asphalt or concrete. Apron pavements and runway turn pads are typically concrete because of static load. The runway and taxiway could be either concrete or asphalt.

Both types of pavements have pros and cons; generally, concrete pavement is expensive compared to asphalt pavement. One major con of concrete pavement is that in case of cracks or pavement settlement, either due to deficiency in design or construction, repair or reconstruction of that portion will be time-consuming, which may affect the airport operation also. In comparison, it is possible to repair asphalt pavement very fast. But it requires a periodic overlay with fresh asphalt on the top layer, depending on the traffic and weather condition.

Stormwater drains

Open drain between airfield pavements

These are usually open drains, as the piped drains in the airfield are costly because of the considerable length of the drains in an airport (see Figure 8.16).

Drains in apron

In apron, the drains are slotted steel section and designed to withstand aircraft load (see Figure 8.17).

Figure 8.16 Open stormwater drain. Photograph by the author

Figure 8.17 Stormwater drain in apron

Source: A320-200 | HK Express | B-LPB | VHHH | Parked next to each o… | Flickr and Wikimedia Commons

Design options considering operational flexibility and efficiency

In the chapter on master planning, the separation distances between the airfield pavements were mentioned. These distances are the minimum to be maintained for operational safety. However, while designing the required distances, planners may consider the operational flexibility with aircraft flow simulated and check whether the separation distances need to be increased for this purpose. Below are the best practices and could be case studies for other airports.

Distance between the runway centreline and parallel taxiway

The minimum distance between the runway centreline and the parallel taxiway centreline may not always be sufficient for operational flexibility. **See Figure 8.18** to determine the distance between the runway and parallel taxiway for code 4E operations. The minimum separation distance between the runway and taxiway for code E is 172.5 m as per SARPs, Z in the figure below (Why 172.5 m? The aircraft is on the taxiway. Half of the wingspan of code E aircraft is 32.5 m. 140 m is the runway strip with no object).

In Figure 8.18, clearance from the taxiway to the object for code E is 43.5 m, dimension Y. The length of code E aircraft is 75.4 m, assuming 76 m for planning, X in figure. The minimum distance between the runway holding position for code E aircraft and the runway centreline is 90 m. If it is planned to pass through another code E aircraft on the taxiway, the distance Z should be 90 + 76 + 43.5 = 209.5 m, say 210 m. Thus, if it is planned to bye-pass the aircraft code E parked in the holding position, more than the minimum separation distance between the runway and taxiway will be required. Here, we assumed that the code 4E aircraft is bypassing a code 4E aircraft in the runway holding position.

Such a bypass is required for increased capacity at busy airports.

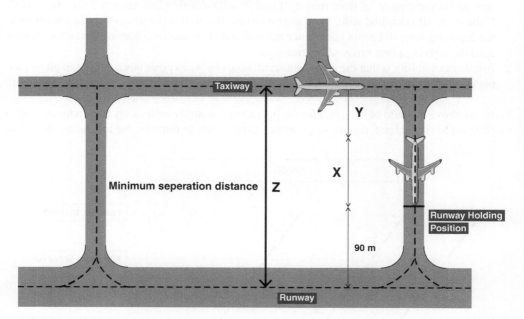

Figure 8.18 Calculation of distance between the runway and parallel taxiway. Reference – Annex14/ ICAO

(**Exercise** – Similarly, the distances for the code C runway/taxiway system can be calculated and checked whether the minimum distance between the runway and taxiway, as per SARPs, will be sufficient or not).

Another purpose is to increase the distance between the parallel taxiway and runway to more than the minimum, described in the chapter on capacity. If the parallel taxiway can be constructed to runway specifications, it can be used as a standby runway when the main runway is closed for operations. If it is located at or more than 210 m from the runway, there could be limited simultaneous operations subject to many safety precautions adopted. Technological advancement may help with this possibility. Adding airfield capacity with available resources is a continuing effort by all the airport planners and operators.

Operation of two runways separated at 210 m

As per ICAO SARPs, such runways can be operated in VFR (Visual Flight Rules). If the airport operates in IFR, the runways can be operated only as a single runway. The operation with two runways and the operational sequence can be understood from Figure 8.19 on VFR.

In Figure 8.19, the aircraft at location 'a' is the runway 1 vacation position, 'b' is the runway 2 holding position, and 'c' is the runway 2 vacation position.

Runway 1 is the main runway for IFR operations with ILS. Runway 2 is for VFR operations. When both the runways are used for operations in VFR, generally, runway 2 is used for departure and runway 1 for arrivals.

Analysis of the operations

1 In this mode of operation, the arriving aircraft must vacate the runway through the exit taxiway and beyond point 'a' from runway 1 and simultaneously clear runway 2, i.e., beyond C. If these are all complied with, there are no issues. But unless the aircraft crosses position C the departing aircraft cannot commence take-off roll. This means departing aircraft must wait until the arriving plane crosses two runways.
2 Another possibility is that the arriving aircraft holds between positions a and b and allows the plane's departure on runway 2. This requires more than 210 m distance for code E operation.

From the above, it could be seen that for the operation to comply with safety requirements and to increase ATM throughput, the arriving aircraft must vacate in time for the following aircraft to

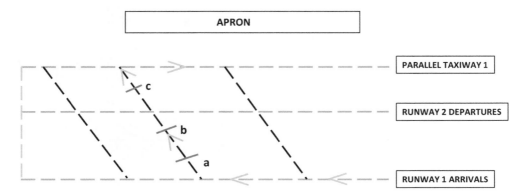

Figure 8.19 Aircraft operation with two runways closely spaced

arrive and allow departure in time through runway 2 by holding between position a and b which is not possible with 210 m separation distance. Therefore, the one option for this is to increase the separation distance between the runways, say, 300 m, which will allow the code E aircraft to hold between runways 1 and 2.

Separation distance – 300 m

With a 300 m separation distance between two closely spaced runways and as VFR operations, it is theoretically possible to hold the aircraft in the RET after vacating the arrival runway with clearance for the departure runway for runway holding position. However, the safety implication is that being a RET, the aircraft will be at high speed, and unless the aircraft stops at the holding position of the second runway, the departing aircraft cannot commence the take-off. So, the departing aircraft ensures that the arriving aircraft has stopped in the exit taxiway at the runway holding position b. With this distance, the effect of wake turbulence impact must be worked out. (Paris CDG airport studied the wake turbulence impact. The two closely spaced runways at this airport are with 384 m separation.)

In an existing airport, if the distance between two runways is less than 300 m, it is impossible to increase the distance. In this situation, three mitigations are possible.

3 The arriving aircraft taxiing to the end of runway 1 crosses the departure runway to reach the parallel taxiway and apron. The safety implication is that the aircraft crosses an active departure runway which is not ideal. The capacity addition is insignificant as the arriving aircraft vacates the runway late means the next arriving aircraft will get delayed. However, the departing plane can start the take-off roll when the arriving aircraft touches down on runway 1. The arrival aircraft's instruction is that it uses the exit taxiway at the end of the runway. In between exit, taxiways are not used by the aircraft. As the arriving plane takes a longer route to reach the apron, it wastes time and fuel. See Figure 8.20.

4 Construct a parallel taxiway to the other side of the arrival runway. In this configuration, after the aircraft lands on runway 1, it exits the runway and enters the 'new parallel taxiway'. This ensures that the next arriving aircraft is not delayed. Departing aircraft can commence take-off roll as soon as the arriving plane touches down, hence saving time. The concern now is that the aeroplane on the parallel taxiway must cross two active runways, which means delay of aircraft using runways 1 and 2 until the plane crosses both the runways or hold the arrival

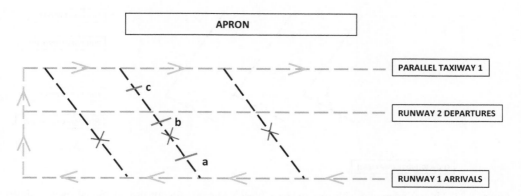

Figure 8.20 Aircraft operation with two runways closely spaced and aircraft using the last exit taxiway

aircraft on the 'new taxiway' until runways 1 and 2 are clear of any aircraft, meaning might spend more time awaiting runways 1 and 2 are clear. Long taxing by arriving aircraft means additional delays in reaching the aircraft stand, fuel consumption, and environmental impact. See Figure 8.21.

5. To overcome the complex operation of options 1 and 2, 'End Around Taxiway (EAT)' concept can be used, for which detailed specifications are provided in FAA's advisory circular. Figure 8.22 shows this concept. The parallel taxiway on the other side of the runway crosses the active runways beyond a distance 'X' such that the aircraft does not infringe on any of the OLS while crossing the active runways. Similarly, the distance Y is decided to avoid OLS. Planners should recollect the shape of the take-off climb surface and approach surface on the plan, which diverges from the runway's centreline. This means the departing aircraft can operate without any restrictions about arriving aircraft. Similarly, the arrivals can continue as the arriving aircraft vacates runway 1 quickly through the new parallel taxiway. See Figure 8.22.

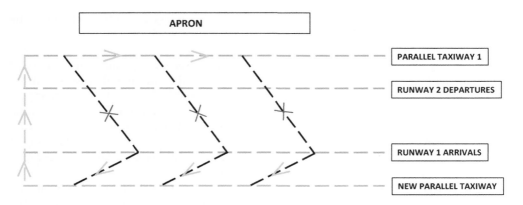

Figure 8.21 Aircraft operation with two runways closely spaced and aircraft use additional parallel taxiway (New)

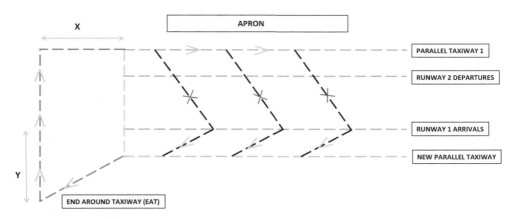

Figure 8.22 Aircraft operation with two runways closely spaced, aircraft use additional (new) parallel taxiway and EAT

OLS infringement is to be worked out for both take-off and approach surfaces. Also, the taxiway should be clear of RESA and not affect the performance of CNS equipment due to signal interference. The end around the taxiway is like a funnel extending outwards and a considerable distance from the runway end to ensure that the aircraft either departing or landing will not infringe the take-off climb surface and approach surface. The disadvantage of this option is long taxing by arriving aircraft means additional delays in reaching the aircraft stand. This might affect the turnaround time of the aircraft. More fuel consumption and additional environmental impact. More capital as well as operational cost. Require land to this extent within the airport boundary.

The distances X and Y are calculated like this. Assuming the taxiway is used by a code E aircraft. The height of the tail of code E aircraft is around 19 m. approach or take off climb surface, the permissible slope is 2%, meaning for every 50 m from the surface (60 m from the threshold). Therefore, for a 19 m obstruction to be cleared, the taxiway must cross the runways at 950 m from the runway strip. If the taxiway is planned only for code C aircraft, then the distance would be approximately 600 m. Since the permissible height is calculated with datum elevation, which is the threshold elevation or runway end elevation the taxiway's elevation at these locations is to be checked. For example, if the elevation is more than the datum elevation, the permissible height will be less than when the elevations are the same. In this case, the distance of 950/600 m calculated above must be increased. On the other hand, if the taxiway ground elevation is less than the datum elevation, the height permissible will be more, meaning the distance X will be lesser.

Figure 8.23 DFW Airport with two runways closely spaced, with additional parallel taxiway and EAT

Source: Marked in Google Earth map

How far the EAT must be away from the extended centreline of runway 'Y' is to be decided based on the divergence of the approach/take-off climb surface, which is 15% and 12.5%, respectively.

Considering the 950 m distance Y to be at least 285 m away from the runway extended centreline. Similarly, for a 600 m distance, it must be at 230 m distance. These are all considering the approach surface, which is more stringent than the take-off climb surface. At Dallas Fort Worth airport, EAT is approximately 800 m from the runway end (35 L and C), Distance between runways is around 380 m. See Figure 8.23.

For more details for EAT design, visit the following link of FAA.

https://www.faa.gov/v_ondemand/TDS8_Final_Large_FAA_1280x720.mp4

Case study

Visit the website of Gatwick Airport. Presently the airport has a single runway and a parallel taxiway constructed to runway specifications. The separation distance between the two is 198 m, and the airport plans to increase this to 210 m and then operate both runways on specific modes and conditions. The consultation process is going on for the approval of the proposal. For details on this proposal, refer to the airport's website.

Separation distance between two parallel taxiways

If bypass of an aircraft is required between two parallel taxiways, then the minimum separation distance as per SARPs between two parallel taxiways (76 m for code E)needs to be increased. See Figure 8.24.

The purpose of the above two examples is that SARPs specify minimum separation/clearances which may be required to be increased depending on the airfield layout and specific requirement. Such increased distances are to be incorporated in the master plan even if some of these are planned for introduction in the future, since if not considered initially, after the construction it is not possible to modify the layout in future to improve operational efficiency or flexibility or capacity.

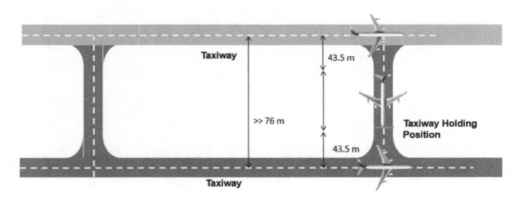

The above configuration is for Code E aircraft operation

Figure 8.24 Determining the separation distance between two parallel taxiways. Reference – Annex14/
ICAO

Length of runway

The calculation to determine the runway length is described in the chapter. It is also mentioned there that by determining the flying range from the airport, it is possible to optimize the length from the basis of MTOW of the aircraft.

Apron configuration

Flexibility to park either two code C or one code E aircrafts with proper orientation of the aircraft arrived at using simulation tool to ensure the practicability and without compromising the safety during manoeuvring of aircrafts. Figure 8.25 shows such an arrangement.

Parallel taxiways requirement and apron taxiways requirement are described in the chapter on master planning.

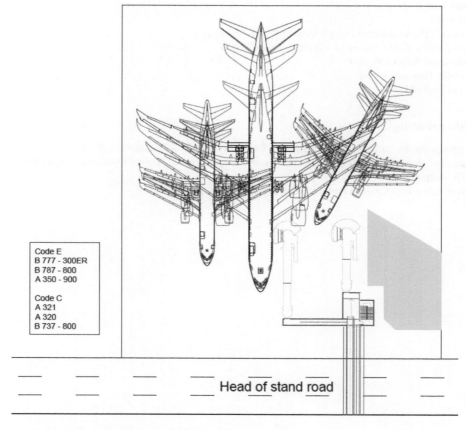

Code E
B 777 - 300ER
B 787 - 800
A 350 - 900

Code C
A 321
A 320
B 737 - 800

Head of stand road

Figure 8.25 Aircraft positioning in apron for maximum utilization

Conclusion

The brief description of design concepts shows that every airport development plan can bring different ideas, especially in PTB design. The number of PTBs in large airports requires analysing the single vs. multiple terminals' pros and cons. Wood as a construction material is becoming popular. Airfield design is standardized based on SARPs and capacity requirements. However, there is still scope for optimization of the pavement structure. The airfield layout requires a study to determine cost vs. benefit analysis for separation distances more than the minimum requirement between the runway and parallel taxiway and between parallel taxiways. Designing the parallel taxiway as a runway or closely spaced runways requires careful study, and cost vs. benefit analysis is needed to decide as it involves an additional parallel taxiway and end-around taxiway to reap the full benefit of such layout.

References

Airport World
e-AIP India
ICAO. (2020). Aerodrome Design Manual Part 1 – Runways.
ICAO. (2022). ICAO Annex 14 – Ninth Edition: Vol. I.
International Airport Review
Passenger Terminal World
Posts in Linked in

Further reading

Air Transportation Safety Issue Investigation Report A1700038 – 31st January 2019.
Progressive Implementation of Wake-Independent Departure and Arrival Operations (WIDAO) at Paris CDG Airport.
Runway Incursions between Parallel Runways at Toronto Airport.

9 Pre-feasibility study

Introduction

As mentioned in the previous chapters, airfield configuration in phased development takes precedence over other airport components. There is no one solution for the airfield layout, and many iterations may be needed depending on the site characteristics, like topography. Similarly, there could be many options that are all required to be evaluated as brainstorming for optimization of the scope of work, thus the quantities of high-value items of work at the same time compliance to SARPs. Passenger Terminal Building (PTB) design specifications, especially the finishes, roof, and façade, play a significant portion in the cost of the building. It is not easy and very accurate to benchmark construction costs with other project works and operational revenues and, thus, requires a cautious approach.

Since the project includes development and operations for, say, 30 years or so, the financial viability is to be assessed during the project life using appropriate methodology. Phased development by incurring expenditure at the right time, not too early in the project timelines, improves the project viability. In addition to capex, planners should also be aware of the revenues and costs during operations.

Capital cost of major airport works

Airfield pavements

Runway and taxiway pavements.

The cost per sqm varies depending on whether the pavement is rigid or flexible, i.e., concrete or asphalt material. A typical flexible pavement cross-section is shown in Table 9.1.

Table 9.1 A typical flexible pavement cross-section

Type of layer	Thickness (mm)
Dense Asphalt Concrete (DAC)	75
Semi-Dense Asphalt Concrete (SDAC)	75
Wet Mix Macadam	300
Granular Subbase	600
Subgrade	500
Total Depth	1550

DOI: 10.4324/9781003319948-9

The unit rate of the pavement thus depends on the thickness of various layers arrived at from the pavement design. The layer thickness will vary between the runway, taxiway, and roads. With the design output of the layer thickness and the pavement area, it is possible to calculate Cum of each layer material.

The cost per unit of work varies from region to region, even within a country and widely across different countries, in terms of material cost and labour cost. The source of materials, availability of materials locally, and other ongoing major projects in the city/region also affect the cost of work. Similarly, skill sets availability locally or not also affects the cost.

The cost also differs depending on the clear weather days for working. The number of working days may get hampered due to frequent rains or due to fog/snow, thus affecting the productive working days/hours. A higher cost is observed in an operational airport compared to a greenfield site due to restricted work hours because of the airport in operation.

The airfield pavement design is different compared to road pavement, but the materials used are the same. Thus, unit rates of these materials in the region/location can be used to assess the cost. Therefore, the rate per sqm of airfield pavements based on the thickness of the pavement structure's various layers and the cost of laying will be a better estimate of the work.

Earthwork

Its quantum depends on the specific airport site, as previously mentioned. The unit cost per cubic meter of cut and fill depends on the soil type. For example, rocky soil will be more expensive to cut compared to ordinary soil. The fill unit cost also depends on whether the fill material is from the cut or is to be brought to the site from other areas. Cut materials are also to be broken to an acceptable size for compacting, and the material is tested for its suitability as fill material.

Thus, the unit rate of the earthwork is very much site-specific and has to be ascertained locally.

Passenger terminal building

The airport terminals are unique in terms of size, finishes (material of floor, walls, ceiling), system/technology adopted, the number of levels, etc. The type of baggage handling system and screening systems, number of VHTs, i.e., escalators, elevators and travellators, and the number of passenger boarding bridges may vary between the airport terminals. So, comparing and benchmarking the cost of PTB is more challenging than airfield works. Comparing two airports of the same size is more appropriate than the number of passengers being handled, with adjustments for known variation while comparing.

The below-mentioned process provides a better way to arrive at the cost reasonably but requires some effort and collection of data from the local market.

Comparing components of the buildings in that region, like airport terminal buildings, in terms of look, importance, and usage gives a better picture and would provide a reasonable estimate.

Indicative proportion of costs between the components/works in a PTB is shown in Table 9.2.

Table 9.2 shows that the civil works cost 45% of the total cost of the building and around 10% for finishes works. Hence, estimating these costs with bottom-up costing of the items is appropriate.

Table 9.2 Indicative proportion of costs between the components/works in a PTB

Item of work	% Of total cost	
PTB – 50,000 sqm		This project scope is to
Civil works – Foundation	10	construct a PTB for an area
Civil works – Roof	25	of app 50,000 sqm. Indirect
Civil works – façade	10	costs over and above the
Finishes – Flooring, false ceiling	10	direct cost @ 25%
Mechanical, electrical, plumbing, and fire protection	16	
PBB, screening equipment, VHT	17	
ITC	10	
Furniture, signage, misc	2	

Thus, the cost analysis components could be as follows:

- Cost of foundation with type.
- Cost of structure.
- Cost of roof and facade.
- Cost of finishes (for example, carpet, marble, or tiles).
- Cost of electrical, HVAC, fire protection, fire fighting.
- Preliminary assessment of VHT quantities and cost of these (cost can be obtained from the manufacturers).
- Information Technology and Communication (ITC) – scope and technology are to be understood when comparing.
- The number of contact stands and thus the number of PBBs. The unit cost of PBB can be obtained from the manufacturers.
- Estimate the quantities of various baggage and passenger screening equipment (check-in bags, cabin bags, explosive trace detectors, DFMD, HHMD, and body scanners). Manufacturers can provide the cost of these items.
- Airfield ground lighting system – manufacturers can provide the cost of these items.
- Equipment and vehicles like rubber removal machines, friction testers, pavement sweepers, grass-cutting machines, operational vehicles, fire trucks, and rescue equipment – With assessed quantities, can get the cost from the manufacturers.

Bulk utilities airport-wide campus system (benchmark with projects of similar capacities in the region).

- Electrical system including distribution and a standby power source.
- Water supply system, including pumps, storage tanks, and treatment plant.
- Sewage collection and treatment plant.

The above approach to determine the cost of PTB provides the cost with reasonable accuracy.
  Cost of city side and airside roads, car parks, and other buildings.
  Buildings other than PTB are of standard finishes. The cost of an ATC tower is required to be assessed based on the cost of high-rise buildings in the region. The cost of roads and buildings other than the ATC tower could be based on per sqm of the area of similar works of the ongoing projects in the region.
  Illustration of proportion of cost of various works in Table 9.3.

Table 9.3 Proportion of cost of works as an example of four projects

Item of work	% Of total cost	
Project 1		This project scope includes 3000 m runway, parallel taxiway and 130,000 sqm apron. The earthwork is huge around 17 million Cum of cut and fill. The cost does not include indirect costs, which was 38% of the project cost
Earth work	60	
Airfield pavements	15	
Drains and culverts	7	
Operational buildings	2	
Utilities	5	
Fence, car park, and misc.	6	
Roads	5	
Project 2		This project scope includes 3000 m runway, parallel taxiway and 60,000 sqm apron and 40,000 sqm PTB. The cost does not include indirect costs, which was 35% of the project cost
Earth work	15	
Airfield pavements		
Drains and culverts	35	
Operational buildings	10	
Utilities	5	
PTB, ATC tower	25	
Roads	10	
Project 3		This project scope includes 3000 m runway, parallel taxiway and 60,000 sqm apron and 40,000 sqm PTB. The cost does not include indirect costs, which was 35% of the project cost
Earth work	15	
Airfield pavements	35	
Drains and culverts		
Operational buildings	10	
Utilities	5	
PTB, ATC tower	25	
Roads	10	
Project 4		This project is a brownfield airport development. Scope includes the second runway, parallel taxiway and 200,000 sqm apron and 200,000 sqm PTB The cost does not include indirect costs, which was 35% of the project cost
PTB	31	
Airfield pavements and AGL		
Drains and culverts	31	
Operational buildings	8	
Utilities	10	
Support facilities	17	
Roads	3	

Optimization of works and thus their cost

The following paragraphs identify the items of work for review.

1 Master grading of the site

After identifying the location and orientation of the runway, the first and foremost in the planning is to fix the finished levels of the ground at the locations of various airport components. This exercise is necessary and time-consuming, especially if the existing ground profile has significant differences. For example, airports have been planned and developed at sites that require cutting a hill and filling the valley within the airport site. In such complex areas, the cut and fill quantities are to be optimized by calculating the quantities of cut and fills by many iterations of shifting the locations of various airport components and varying the slope of the runway, taxiways, connecting taxiways, aprons, and the finished levels of the PTB. Through this exercise, the quantities of various iterations will be known, and the minimum cut and fill option will be chosen.

In large airports, the PTB will have a basement for accommodating baggage make-up and break-up areas, which require large areas if the system automatically sorts outgoing passenger bags. In addition, since within the airfield, the maximum and minimum slope of the pavements, both longitudinal and transverse, are specified in SARPs, the runway/taxiway strips also have permissible slopes.

The location and size of the drains and slope to collect and store or drain outside the airport is another component to be considered in the preliminary design. The drain levels are to be tied with the runway and taxiway strip. The drain sizing is critical to ensure no flooding in the facilities, including airfield pavement. In addition, open drains are cheaper than closed drains, except in the apron, the drain is to be covered with steel grating designed to withstand aircraft load.

The maximum permissible slope is specified in SARPs for the apron. The apron's downward slope should be away from the terminal to protect PTB. In addition, the plan shall include an oil–water separator to remove the oil content in the water accumulated in the drain before it is let out to the main drain.

So, more emphasis is given to the industry's 'master grading' of the land, including future development within the airport land. For example, future runway levels and connecting taxiway levels between the present and future runways. Such master grading of the ground at various locations is also essential for OLS evaluation as the datum elevation and height permissible over the revised ground level will be applicable.

2 Length and orientation of runway

As the runway length, the flight range and take-off weight are all interrelated; it is required to decide the same. Length for the longest range with the most demanding aircraft means longer runway length and more cost, which is needed to be analysed realistically if such flying range is assessed in the traffic forecast with destination airports. If not, may consider the range per the traffic forecast and optimize the runway length with revised calculations.

Another option is to examine whether it is possible to extend the runway in the later phase of development. If so, what are the abortive works that will be carried out now, their cost, and the practicability of doing so when the airport is in operation? However, there are examples of airports in developing countries where the runway length has been extended during operations when there is a demand for an increase necessitated by the introduction of wide-body aircraft and an increased range of operations. For this analysis, the planning document should describe the runway length for various aircraft and the range considered based on traffic forecast and likely range and its impact on the runway length.

Orientation of the runway can be reviewed by slight shifting from the ideal direction without compromising crosswind component requirements due to obstacles outside the airport and for the reduction in earthwork.

Separation distances and others

The previous chapter described the minimum separation distance between the runway and parallel taxiway, as specified in SARPs, which may be required to increase operational flexibility. Such an increase over the minimum separation distance also requires a cost-benefit analysis. However, once this is planned and implemented, it is challenging and has substantial cost implications for changing later. Similarly, a cost-benefit analysis is to be carried out if the parallel taxiway is to be designed for runway specifications to use this as a standby runway. Again, this option involves additional costs.

In summary of the above, the options to be examined are:

- Finished levels of the site for various components, more for airfield pavements.
- The airfield pavements' slope requires optimum cut and fill, simultaneously complying with SARPs.
- Drain location and sizing.
- The optimum slope of runway and taxiway strips, complying with SARPs.
- Consider the ultimate master plan for master grading.
- Phased development of the airfield is to be worked out with consideration of minimal/no abortive works, lesser operational hindrance, and no business opportunity loss by not implementing the facilities required by the airlines.
- If any obstacles within the airport are required to be removed and obstacles identified outside the airport, an analysis of their impact and mitigation are identified.
- Orientation of the runway.
- Operational flexibility in the design concept and their cost-benefit analysis.

Finally, the feasibility study on the technical aspect should identify the various phases of development of the airfield from the initial phase to the ultimate phase, along with identified facilities and the traffic against each phase. Deviations from ICAO SARPs, if any, are to be included in the study.

3 Passenger Terminal Building (PTB)

The pre-feasibility study should examine the following:

1 Consider the ultimate capacity required and the floor area required for the capacity. Ultimate capacity is primarily based on airfield capacity.
2 Single terminal vs. multiple terminals for large airports.
3 Number of levels of the PTB with passenger flow in plan and sectional elevation. Possibility to swing between domestic and international sections of an integrated terminal, where the peak passenger flows do not coincide. This will reduce the area of PTB.
4 Finished floor levels of the PTB at various levels and thus, the height at each level.
5 Number of contact stands and remote stands.
6 Number of narrow-body aircraft stands, wide-body aircraft stands, and for turbo prop aircrafts.
7 Number of MARs stands.
8 Number of vehicular lanes in terminal kerb, both arrival and departure.
9 If the PTB area is based on thumb rule of annual passenger capacity, quickly assess the processing areas based on peak hour capacity and include service areas and commercial areas as described previously. This is to ensure that the estimated area is within reasonable accuracy, neither overestimated nor underestimated.

4 Utilities

Preliminary assessment of utilities requirement with capacities, distribution schematic, voltage level of distribution, standby power capacity requirement and source, and renewable energy sources. The details should be broadly enough to assess the capital cost and be able to optimize the cost.

5 Vehicle parking

Review the requirements, type, dwell time, etc. as discussed previously. Assess the pros and cons of surface parking vs. multilevel car park facility.

6 Cargo facility

Can review the sizing of the cargo terminal and other related facilities. The most important one is mode of development and operation of the facility. The options are (i) lease the land and the cargo operator invests on the facility including buildings, equipment, apron, etc. and operates the facility for the lease period. Or (ii) The airport operator invests in the facility including buildings, equipment, etc. and the cargo operator operates the facility for a defined period in the agreement. Or (iii) The airport operator invests in the facility and operates. Options (i) and (ii) will enable the airport operator to realize revenue from the cargo operations by way of revenue share from the cargo operator. Option (i) may also entail land lease fee to the airport operator.

7 Operational buildings are listed below.

1 Utilities – power and water.
2 Sewage water treatment.
3 AGL substations.
4 CFR stations.
5 Ground handling equipment maintenance workshop.
6 Airline engineering workshop.
7 Airport maintenance workshop.
8 Airline stores.

The area requirement can be reviewed for optimization. Out of the above-mentioned buildings, can review items 5–8. These can be developed by the airlines or ground handling agencies. If this option is accepted by the airlines or ground handling company the airport operator need not invest the capex.

Commercial development

The model could be to lease the land to the developer, and they incur the capital and operational expenditure and collect revenues from the tenants. In addition to the land lease fee, there could be some mechanisms for sharing the revenues with the airport.

Indirect costs

Over and above the cost of construction of facilities and systems, the following costs are to be included.

- Project management fee.
- Design fee.
- Statutory fees.
- Site establishment costs like site offices, IT systems, and software.
- Staff and administration cost for the airport company if the project management is done by an external agency.
- Cost for operational readiness like staff recruitment, training, and readiness trials.

All the above will be 25%–35% of the project cost, depending on the mode of development and the location. Over and above, an additional % for contingencies are typically added to the cost. This may vary between 5% and 10% for variation in quantities and missing scope of work.

Construction cost assessment

Below are the two examples from which the unit rates worked out for the project in consideration can be compared as a part of prefeasibility assessment.

ADRM/IATA

The ADRM has a chapter titled 'Financial Assessment' wherein it provides the unit rate of various construction works of airports on a low and high-range basis. These unit costs are in the UK £. For example

The runway overall rate per sqm is 216 UK £ in the lower range and 348 UK £ in the higher end of the range.

Terminal building/pier for the regional airport- overall rate per sqm is 2106 UK £ at the lower range and 3796 UK £ at the higher range.

Inclusions and exclusions are mentioned against each item. Finally, in general notes, it mentions the indirect cost applicability.

To consider the cost of labour and material in different cities, the brief includes a chart showing the location factors for various cities, which should be considered with the unit rate mentioned above as the unit rates are for London, based on 100. The location factor is also a range. For example, the factor for Mumbai is between 30% and 55% of the unit rate mentioned above. For Hong Kong, the factor is approximately 70% and 110%, and for Singapore between 50% and 81%.

ADRM mentions, 'The data provided enables the user to inform project inception stage appraisals and to challenge design and associated estimates against an indicative range of figures'. However, the brief also mentions that the costs cannot be considered as tendered prices or contract sums.

M/S Turner and Townsend's report

The firm provides data and information about the construction industry worldwide and its other core expertise. A document titled 'International Construction Market Survey' is a yearly publication that includes construction costs region-wise and for a few cities in that region. The recent report for the Year 2022 includes high-rise office buildings, hotels, and hospitals, to note a few sectors. The unit rate per sqm for the construction of such a facility is mentioned in the report. For example, the unit rate per sqm of a high-rise office building in Hongkong is 32,000 CNY, for Mumbai, it is 58,000 INR, and for Singapore, it is 3600 SGD. The rate is also mentioned in USD after conversion from the local currency. In addition, the report includes the unit rate of labour cost and material cost for the cities included in the report.

Air Navigation Services (ANSs)

The scope of the airport owner/operator and the ANSP is to be defined as who incurs the capital, operational expenditure, and revenue. If these are with the ANSP, the airport planning should include providing utilities to these installations, and ANSP is responsible for all capital and operational expenditure.

Thus, during this pre-feasibility study, the ownership of the Air Navigation Services (ANSs) is essential and identifies the system and equipment required phase-wise until the ultimate airport capacity. As the traffic grows, the system and equipment must be upgraded. Therefore, it requires a Memorandum of Understanding (MoU) with the ANSP for the scope inclusion and exclusion of the airport owner/operator and ANSP's consent to augment their equipment and system if required for an increase in capacity and possibly a Service Level Agreement with them.

Advanced technologies in the pipeline should also be considered.

Airport revenues

Airport revenues are from providing aeronautical services, CNS/ATM services (ANS), and commercial activities within the terminal building like retail, lounges, F&B, and offices and commercial activities outside the terminal building but within the airport boundary like Hotels, Office complex, Convention centres, and SEZs. Revenues from commercial activities are in the form of revenue share from the commercial revenue. Thus, the revenues are classified as aeronautical, non-aeronautical, and commercial.

Aeronautical charges are regulated either by Regulators or, in the absence of the Regulators, by the Government. For example, in India, AERA (Airport Economic Regulatory Authority) regulates Aeronautical charges for Major airports. For other airports, the charges are regulated by the Government.

To estimate the aeronautical revenues, the service included under this category is to be specified. Aeronautical services are defined with specific services by the regulatory authority or the Government, which must be understood.

The most included services are (for example, in India):

1 For navigation, surveillance, and supportive communication for air traffic management.
2 For the landing, housing, or parking of an aircraft or any other ground facility offered in connection with aircraft operations at an airport.
3 For ground safety services at an airport.
4 For ground handling services relating to aircraft, passengers, and cargo at an airport.
5 For the cargo facility at an airport.
6 For supplying fuel to the aircraft at an airport.
7 Others, as decided by the Government.

The fees charged by the airport for these services are described below.

Passenger Service Charge (PSC) or fee This is collected from the passengers for using the terminal building and other passenger processing facilities. The PSC is paid only by the departing passengers. This fee is charged per passenger.

Aircraft landing/take-off charges

This is payable by the airlines for using the airfield infrastructures. A landing or take-off will be considered as one movement for the charge. The charges are based on the aircraft's Maximum Take-Off Weight (MTOW).

Airfield lighting charges

This is payable by the airlines for airfield ground lighting – approach, runway, taxiway lighting, etc., provided this is not part of landing/take-off charges.

Aircraft parking charges

This is payable by the airlines for the use of the apron. Charges per aircraft are based on the MTOW of the aircraft and the number of hours of parking for the use of the apron for parking the aircraft.

Cargo charges

Cargo charges and any other charges or fees collected concerning cargo for using the airport's freight-processing facilities and areas. If the airport operates the cargo facility, cargo handling charges will be applicable. If the cargo operation is outsourced to a third party, there will be a fee levied by the airport operator to the cargo operator based on per MT of cargo handled.

Ground handling charges

If the airport operator provides ground handling services, the airport will charge the airlines for the services offered based on the agreement between the airlines and the airport. If the airlines' carryout self-handling or through ground handling companies, the airlines pay a fee to the airport.

Noise-related charges

Airports may incur expenses for noise abatement measures to minimize the noise impact, even though the present generation aircraft are quieter than the earlier ones. ICAO recommends that costs incurred in implementing such measures may, at the discretion of States, be attributed to airports and recovered from the users. States can decide on the method of cost recovery and charging to be used considering local circumstances if noise-related charges are to be levied.

Emissions-related aircraft charges

ICAO's recommendation is as follows:

This charge by the airlines to the airport is to address Local Air Quality (LAQ) problems at or around airports. Costs incurred in mitigating or preventing the problem may, at the discretion of States, be attributed to airports and recovered from the users.

Fuel concession fees

Refuelling of aircraft at the airport is carried out by specialized companies handling aviation fuel. The infrastructure required for refuelling includes the following.

- Bulk storage of the fuel.
- If the fuel hydrant system is not installed, the required number of refuelling bowser.
- If a hydrant system is installed at the apron stands, fuel storage tanks with pumping system, fuel hydrant pits and valves at the apron and the required number of refuellers.

Usually, the airport operator charges the refuelling agency the 'throughput' charges per KL of fuel used for refuelling the aircraft.

Distinction between aeronautical and non-aeronautical revenues

All the above charges are considered Aeronautical Revenues for the airport. However, there could be some differences between countries in classifying the services and thus revenues between aeronautical and non-aeronautical, which should be kept in mind.

ANS charges

ANS includes one or more of the following services to airspace users.

Air Traffic Management (ATM).
Communications, Navigation, and Surveillance (CNS) systems.
Meteorological service for air navigation (MET).
Search and Rescue (SAR).
Aeronautical Information Services (AIS).

ANSs are provided in three main phases of flight: movements at and around the aerodrome (aerodrome control), approach and departure of flights including initial climb and descent (approach control), and en-route and thus the charges for these three phases are specified. The approach and take-off operations are considered as a single service under this.

The basic principles established by ICAO in the area of charges for airports and ANS are expressed in Article 15 of the *Convention on International Civil Aviation* (Doc 7300), usually referred to as the Chicago Convention. In addition, ICAO Doc 9562 – Airports Economic Manual and ICAO Doc 9082 ICAO Policies on Charges for airports and ANSs provide adequate guidance on the charges for these services.

Revenues from non-aeronautical services

Non-aeronautical services include a wide range of retail shops, F&Bs, airline lounges, hotels, convention centres, SEZs and other service activities, offices and other buildings occupied by airlines, and government authorities.

Revenues from non-aeronautical activities may be rent per sqm of the built-up area occupied by the tenants, like offices within the terminal building. Another method is monthly rental plus revenue share from the business activities like retail shops and F&B. If the land is allotted to the entity, they pay a lease rental for the land. The facility is developed and operated by them for a period defined in the lease agreement, like hotels, convention centres, etc. There could be revenue share from the facility as well.

Commercially oriented non-aeronautical activities cover a wide range. However, the most common services provided at the airport are described below.

Within the passenger terminal building

• Restaurants, bars, coffee shops, automatic dispensers for water/soft drinks, etc.
• Shops for example souvenirs, handicrafts, and medical shops.

- Banks/foreign exchange.
- Kiosks for taxi booking.
- Kiosks for car rentals.
- Advertisement signs.
- Duty-free shops:

    - Liquor and tobacco.
    - Perfume and toiletries.
    - Watches.
    - Optical and electronic equipment.

- Hairdressing/barber shop.
- Freight consolidators/forwarders or agents.
- Souvenir shops.
- Airline lounges.
- Hotels.
- Hotel reservation kiosks.
- Porter services.
- Tourist information kiosks.
- Nap and shower facilities.

Outside the terminal building (within airport boundary) classified as commercial revenue

- Hangars.
- Warehouses.
- Vehicle parking.
- Airport/city public transport services.
- Refueling stations for vehicles – petrol/CNG/diesel outlets.
- Automobile service stations.
- Hotels, convention centres.
- Special economic zones.
- F&B outlets.
- Advertisement signs.

The charges are market driven and not regulated but subject to compliance with local laws.

Miscellaneous revenues – These are all non-operating revenues but earned by the company, for example by providing consultancy services to other airports.

Operating costs

Following are the line items of the costs at an airport for the operation, maintenance, and management:

- **Manpower Expenses** – Staff salary and other welfare measures like uniform, training, traveling expenses, and others.
- **Operating expenses**

    - Repair and maintenance of buildings, IT system, all other system and equipment, landscaping, airfield pavements and AGL, utilities system and equipment, and spare parts cost.

- Airport operation costs include outsourced manpower costs of terminal operations, airside operations including safety, landside operations, and ARFF operations.
- Utilities (electricity, water consumption) charges.
- House keeping costs (cleaning and janitorial).
- Security cost (landside and other than aviation security).
- Fuel cost.
- Vehicle maintenance.
- Others.

- **Administration expenses** – Insurance, advertisement, business promotion/event management, rent, taxes (other than corporate tax), office expenses – printing & stationery, communication, community development, conveyance, and others.
- **Consultancy expenses and professional fee (if any)**

The expenses mentioned above can be for aeronautical, non-aeronautical, and ANSs; hence, each line item is to be apportioned to the three classifications of services.

The following describes the operating cost of some selected airports. The financial numbers are from the published annual financial statement of the respective airport. The cost indicated excludes depreciation and amortization.

For the pre-feasibility study, the idea is to know the operating cost per passenger. Then, in the next level of the project evaluation, more details of the design and systems/equipment will be available, and the cost can be further scrutinized.

Examples of operating costs

Gatwick Airport

The financial statements show the following line items of the operating cost:

1 Staff cost.
2 Retail expenditure.
3 Car parking expenditure.
4 Maintenance and IT expenditure.
5 Utility costs.
6 Rent and rates.
7 Other operating expenses.

Operating costs	Year ended 31 March 2019 £m	Year ended 31 March 2018 £m
Staff costs	203.6	201.9
Retail expenditure	3.4	2.5
Car parking expenditure	19.1	19.5
Maintenance and IT expenditure	45.2	40.6
Utility costs	23.1	21.1
Rent and rates	32.8	30.3
Other operating expenses	42.2	37.1
Total operating costs	369.4	353.0

The proportion of the costs under various line items are shown in Figure 9.1.

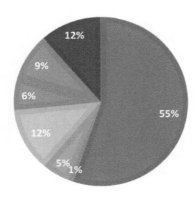

Figure 9.1 Proportion of costs for Gatwick Airport

In this case, the staff cost is the highest proportion. The overall cost per passenger for the year 2017–2018 is 7.72 UK £, and for the year 2018–2019, it is 7.96 UK £.

Operating costs of three airports in India

Table 9.4 shows the operating cost per passenger of the chosen airports, as an example.

Table 9.4 Operating cost per passengers at three airports in India

Airport	Apr 2016–March 2017	Apr 2017–March 2018	Apr 2018–March 2019
Delhi	146	142	141
Bengaluru	167	156	140
Hyderabad	131	134	139

The cost indicated is in Indian rupees

The operation and maintenance expenses are provided in the financial statements of the airports with breakdown of the following items:

1 Staff expenses consist of salaries, wages, bonus, and other welfare like gratuity, training, retirement fund, and PF.
2 Operation and maintenance expenses consist of repair and maintenance of buildings, plant and machinery, IT services and cost of outsourced manpower, spares cost, and housekeeping cost.
3 Electricity and other utility charges.
4 Administration expenses.

Figure 9.2 shows the proportion of these line items. From this, it could be seen that staff and their welfare expenses are the highest line item, followed by operation and maintenance, utility charges, and administration costs.

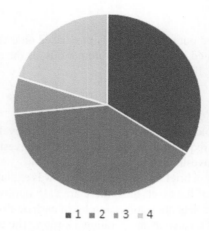

■1 ■2 ■3 ■4

Figure 9.2 Proportion of operating cost line items

The financial numbers are taken from the financial statements of the airports. However, there could be some differences in the items included or excluded which may not make a significant difference.

Benchmarking the costs between airports

The proportion of the line items also may vary marginally between the airports within the country and when comparing across the countries. Also, if there is a significant difference between the airports even within the same country, it is required to identify why there is such a significant difference. For example, an airport that is saturated in capacity may have a lesser cost per passenger than an airport that has actual demand less than its capacity.

Operating costs per passenger

Operating costs for the pre-feasibility study can be assumed based on the cost at similar regional airports. Therefore, for the feasibility study and financial analysis, one can consider operating costs @ 160 INR per passenger for airports in India. In the case of the UK, for example, based on the actual cost per passenger at one airport, we can assume that 10 UK £ per passenger. Also, in this example, we considered the costs for three years and less in the case of Gatwick Airport. It would be better if we consider at least the costs of the past five years and take a number from that.

For further reading, refer to the 'CAP 1060 Airport Operating Expenditure Benchmarking Report 2012' document to understand the principles.

Conversion of revenue/cost from local currency to USD

Converting one country's currency to another based on the exchange rate and comparison based on these numbers do not provide an accurate comparison. For this reason, benchmarking airports within the country with ratios like cost per passenger may be more appropriate than comparing airports across the countries.

Corrections for inflation

The revenue and cost worked out either bottom-up or based on estimates, as mentioned above, are to be applied with assumed inflation for future periods, as the assessment is for the project life cycle of longer duration, like 25–30 years.

Financial analysis

Whether it is a new greenfield airport project or a significant development work in an existing airport, financial analysis is required to be carried out for the investment being made, source of funds, and return from the investment.

Previously in this chapter, a brief on cost and revenue was explained. Those costs are for the operation and maintenance of the asset; thus, these are cash outflows. Similarly, on capex, the interest and repayment of the debt are some examples of cash outflows. The operating costs will increase when a new asset is created in an operational airport. The cash inflows are the revenues that should enable the investment to recoup in several years. Thus, in the financial analysis, cash outflows and cash inflows are to be listed and see whether the investment is worth making or what level of investment to be made or rework the source of funds so that the cost of capital is reduced.

The investment decision is made either by calculating Net Present Value (NPV) or through the Internal Rate of Return (IRR). But in practice, both the NPV and IRR are estimated to take a decision.

Let us see the examination of the investment with revenues as an example. In this example, the first four years are the capital invested in developing a greenfield airport; thus, there is no O&M cost in the initial three years. Similarly, revenue starts only from the fourth year when the asset is put into operation. See Table 9.5.

Table 9.5 Cash flows

Cash out flows

	Year 1	2	3	4	5	6	7	8	9	10
In US$ for capital cost (in million)	10	20	50	20						
Operation and maintenance (in million)	0	0	0	2	10	12	15	18	20	25
Replacement capex (in million)									10	15
Total cash out flow	10	20	50	22	10	12	15	18	30	40

Cash inflows (revenues)

	Year 1	2	3	4	5	6	7	8	9	10
In million				20	25	35	45	50	55	60

Net cashflows

	Year 1	2	3	4	5	6	7	8	9	10
In million	−10	−20	−50	−2	15	23	30	32	25	20

Table 9.6 Revised cash flows

Total cash out flow	10	**10**	30	22	10	12	**25**	18	**40**	**50**
Total net cash flow	−10	**−10**	−30	−2	**15**	23	20	32	**15**	**10**

In the NPV method, the Present Value (PV) of the net cash flow in future years is calculated by applying the discount rate, as the value of the cash flows in future years will be less than when compared with the value today, considering inflation, called as 'Time value of money'. The discount rate is to be assumed and estimated based on the available information but not less than the bank lending rate. The higher the discount rate, the less the PV of future cash inflows. NPV is the sum of the PV of all the cash inflows subtracted from the PV of the total cash outflows. NPV should be positive as a minimum for a project to be considered for further evaluation. The project with a positive NPV will only be considered, and projects with negative NPVs are not considered with the estimated cash flows. The key point to note here is the discount rate being applied.

In the above example, the total cash outflow is 227 million, whereas the PV of this will be less than 227 million. The total cash inflow without applying the time value of money is 290 million. However, the PV of the cash inflow will be less than 290 million. The discount rate to arrive at the PV can be applied individually on cash outflows and inflows year-wise. Another method is to find out the net cash flow and apply the discount factor. This method is used here; the net cash flow is shown in Table 9.5, year-wise. The cost of capital is assumed to be 15%. With a 15% discount rate applied to the net cash flow, the NPV of the net cash flow is **minus** 6.65, and since it is negative, this is not acceptable. The options are either

1 postpone some of the cash outflows to later years or
2 reduce the discount rate considered or
3 increase the revenue projections, either the absolute numbers of all the years or pre-pone the revenues.

Considering option (i), the revised cash outflows and corresponding net cashflows are shown in Table 9.6, highlighted are the changes in outflows and resultant net cashflows.

The NPV of the **revised net cashflows** at 15% discount (same as previously applied) is now **positive** at 4.99 million.

If the cost of capital can be reduced, then option (ii) can be applied. Considering a discount rate of 12% with previous cash flows, the NPV is **positive** at 0.38 million.

Such iteration is carried out with realistic and practicable changes to the cash inflows and outflows and examines the financial viability of the investment. NPV evaluation is very sensitive to the discount rate assumed and the timing of the cash flows. One way of evaluating the project is to consider the discount rate at least equal to the cost of capital so that the least is there is no loss. However, any investment must bring profit to the investor for their effort in the project.

Internal Rate of Return (IRR)

This method will calculate the discount rate that will make the NPV zero. That internal rate or required rate of return must be more than the cost of capital.

In the above example, with the rate of return as 12.15%, the NPV is zero. On the other hand, if the Required Rate of Return (RRR) is more than 12.15% (which will make the NPV negative), this project is not acceptable with the current cash flows, and hence, a reworking of the cash flows, as discussed above, is required.

The RRR will have to be more than the cost of capital. Thus, the cost of capital itself can be optimized by the sources of funds. Hence, the term Weighted Average Cost of Capital (WACC). WACC represents a firm's average after-tax cost of capital from all sources, including equity, bonds, and other forms of debt. WACC is the average rate a company expects to pay to finance the project and is used as the discount rate for future cash flows. Hence, if the cost of the capital is reduced, the investor also will reduce their RRR. So, either it is required to rework out the cost of capital with various sources of funds or rework out the cash flows or both.

NPV and IRR are very easy to calculate in MS Excel, which has functions for these two workings.

The above is the simple but fundamental way to understand the method to check the financial viability of the investment. Working out the line items of all cash inflows and outflows is essential. Key issues are how accurately the total capital cost is estimated and how the capital cost is spread over the investment and the phasing period. How accurately the project completion period is assessed so that the asset is put into operation at the earliest so that the revenue starts flowing. Investing in high costs early in the project will decrease the financial viability. On the revenue side, listing all revenue sources, the quantum of the revenues with realistic assumptions, and early availing of all revenue sources after the asset is put into operation means better project viability. And finally, assessing the sources of funds, cost of capital with better precision will provide the proper guidance about the project viability.

Some equations for cash flow working

Free Cash Flow to Equity (FCFE) = Cash from operating activities – Capital Expenditure+ Net Debt repaid
FCFF – free cash flow to the firm
FCF = NET OPERATING PROFIT AFTER TAXES- INVESTMENT DURING THE PERIOD

The cash flows shown are for example and simplified way for understanding the financial evaluation fundamentally. The cash flows consist of the following.

1 Operating cash flow (inflows).
   EBITDA (Earnings Before Interest Taxes Depreciation and Amortization) minus Tax minus interest expenses.
2 Cash flow from investment Outflows).
   Capex + Cost of financing + recurring capex + debt
3 Cash flow from financing (inflows).
   Debt + Equity
   FCFE = 1 – 2 + 3
   FCFE is calculated for years 1 to N (life of the project) and this is the PV of the project. NPV is calculated by applying the discount rate mentioned above.

Prefeasibility report

The report contains the following:

- Introduction of the project and background information with a brief description of the project, need for the project, and employment generation due to the project.
- Project description with a location on a map, site layout, project boundary, details of alternate sites considered and the reasons/basis for the selection of the proposed site, project

proponent, availability of utilities (water, power, and communication network), quantity of wastes expected to be generated, interlink and interdependent projects if any.
- Site details with connectivity, the topography of the land, existing land use patterns like agriculture or other use, land ownership, nearest waterbodies, soil classification, habitats at the site, number of trees to be cut and mitigation measures, and nearest existing airport. Description of proposed land use planning of the project site.
- Proposed infrastructure – phase-wise development and ultimate.

  - Number and area of terminal buildings and all other airport operation-related buildings with passenger and air traffic movement per day and annually.
  - Airfield layout with runways, taxiways, apron, etc.
  - Proposed Green belt development like landscaping.
  - Commercial development plan.
  - Residential units.
  - Estimated population per day at the airport during operation.
  - Connectivity to the city centre.
  - Utility management – power, water, and sewerage – with capacities.
  - Stormwater drainage plan.
  - Solid waste management plan.
  - Preliminary environmental impact and management plan.
  - Preliminary drawings depicting the proposed infrastructures.

- Rehabilitation and resettlement plan, if required, with numbers, type of existing infrastructure/facilities, and estimated time for the completion of this activity.
- Project schedule and cost estimate, including financial analysis and viability calculations.
- Financial and social benefits due to the proposed project.

Conclusion

Examining the pre-feasibility of the airport development based on the master plan prepared with identified items of works with alternatives/options is a part of the project report. This assures that the preliminary design complies with SARPs and considers various options with cost and benefit. Assessing the possible revenues and operating expenditures is also a part of the project assessment, not restricted to capital expenditure. The project viability is examined with capital expenditure, operating expense, and revenues. The costs and revenues assessment are challenging and not readily available. Thus, knowing the scope of work, the cost of materials, labour, and other construction-related costs in that region/location is essential. The operating cost per passenger in that region for similar airport capacity and revenues derived for aeronautical and non-aeronautical by experience and business opportunities exploration. Consider benchmarking costs or revenues with caution.

References

Airport Development Reference Manual – IATA.
Airports Economic Manual Doc 9562 – ICAO.
Financial Statements of Airports.
International Construction Market Survey 2022 – Turner and Townsend.
Policies on Charges for Airports and Air Navigation Services Doc 9082 – ICAO.

Question bank

1 What is an 'Annex' to Chicago Convention? How many Annex are published and name the most relevant Annex for airport planning.
2 Write five significant factors to be considered for the site selection of a greenfield airport.
3 Length of land required for an airport is based on (a) _____ (b) _____
4 What is CSPR? Write a brief note on this.
5 Aeroplane dimensions are the basis for the airfield dimensions. Which dimension is the basis for the width of the taxiway pavements?
6 How is the fleet mix contributing to the airport's capacity?
7 ICAO has many publications. Mention three publications related to airport planning.
8 Brief on the category of operations and airport planning.
9 Compare the forecasting modelling using time series analysis and regression/causal analysis.
10 What are the data sources for traffic analysis? Using one source, identify passenger traffic statistics of the last five years of any one airport.
11 Write the usage of the traffic forecast based on the forecast time horizons.
12 Write an additional factor that needs to be considered for brownfield airport development.
13 Write short notes on increasing the airport capacity without additional major infrastructure.
14 List four major parameters that determine the airfield capacity.
15 What is an aeroplane reference code?
16 What is the difference between ICAO and Civil Aviation Authorities?
17 What are the functions of ICAO?
18 What are the differences between qualitative forecasting and quantitative forecasting?
19 What are the types of taxiways?
20 Level of Service for roads' and capacity. Write a short note.
21 Differences between Standards and Recommended Practices (ICAO SARPs)
22 Write a brief note on the aerodrome category for Crash Fire and Rescue (CFR) services.
23 What is the importance of datum elevation and ground elevation at the object's location for analysing the OLS?
24 Describe the purpose of the zoning map and draw at least two Obstacle Limitation surfaces around an airport.
25 Write the various parallel runway configurations and a short note on the dependent instrument approach.
26 What is the runway holding position?
27 Draw the take-off climb surface in the plan and elevation with dimensions.
28 How is non-compliance to SARPs dealt with?
29 List all the obstacle limitation surfaces for precision approach runway.
30 What are the key takeaways from the chapter on ICAO SARPs?

31 What is aeroplane reference field length?
32 Write the factors that must be considered for a specific airport site's required runway length calculation.
33 What are the three criteria to be examined for determining the permissible heights of structures/buildings/objects in and around an airport?
34 What are the parameters that determine the apron dimensions? What is MARS in an apron configuration?
35 Write short notes on the Level of Service (LOS) ADRM (IATA) concept for PTB.
36 How can the master planning exercise add value to operational flexibility and capacity enhancement?
37 Brief on cargo infrastructure planning concepts and planning considerations.
38 Write the criteria for locating the CFR station and isolation bay at an airport.
39 Describe declared distances of a runway and the effect of stop way and clear way if provided.
40 What are runway shoulder, runway strip, and RESA and what is the purpose of these
41 What are the components of ILS, and how do they aid the aircraft?
42 Write a brief on marking as a visual aid at an airport.
43 Write at least five airfield ground lighting systems.
44 What are the 4 Cs of the airfield ground lighting system?
45 What extent of land is ideally required per Annex 14 for Simple Approach Lighting and Cat I approach lighting systems?
46 Three criteria to be considered for aviation fuel storage facility at an airport are_____.
47 Describe the equipment that is to be considered in the planning for the Meteorological system.
48 Write about object discrimination requirements and Line of Sight evaluation for the height and location of Air Traffic Control Towers.
49 Why are the PAPI and ILS to be co-located and calibrated together?
50 What are runway threshold and displaced threshold? Why is the displacement of the threshold required?
51 What is the 'balanced approach' by ICAO?
52 What are the environmental impacts of an airport operation that must be considered in the planning and their mitigation measures?
53 Describe land use planning in and around the airport and the negative impacts of such planning.
54 Mention the ICAO documents describing the policy on principles of airport charges.
55 rite a short note on the zoning map around the airport for noise mitigation.
56 What are the advantages and disadvantages of one large passenger terminal and multiple passenger terminals for an airport with an annual capacity of 60 mppa?
57 Explain the design concepts for the separation distance between runways and between the runway and parallel taxiways.
58 Briefly describe the environmental management plan during the construction works at the airport.
59 Describe the separation distance required for an apron taxiway system with 3 and 2 taxiways. Write the operational philosophy for both configurations.
60 Describe NPV and IRR methods for financial analysis.
61 Classify the operating cost and revenues with examples.
62 What should the pre-feasibility report contain for the decision-makers to review the project proposal?
63 Why benchmarking of costs or revenues between airports should be adopted with caution.

64 Airport diagrams can be viewed from the airport websites or the e-AIP. With airport diagrams, draw the PTB pier concepts of at least five airports in different regions.

65 Explain how the phased development of the facilities improve financial viability and the precaution to be taken for such phased development in the planning.

66 Airport diagrams can be viewed from the airport websites or the e-AIP. With an airport diagram, analyse five airports' runway/taxiway layouts and write a short note about the layouts.

Index

Note: **Bold** page numbers refer to tables and *italic* page numbers refer to figures.

For Product Safety Concerns and Information please contact our
EU representative GPSR@taylorandfrancis.com Taylor & Francis
Verlag GmbH, Kaufingerstraße 24, 80331 München, Germany